The Scholar's Art

THE SCHOLAR'S ART

Literary Studies in a Managed World

Jerome McGann

The University of Chicago Press · Chicago & London

Jerome McGann is the John Stewart Bryan Professor at the University of Virginia. Among his many publications, most recently, are *Byron and Romanticism* (2002) and *Radiant Textuality* (2001), which won the Lowell Prize of the Modern Language Association.

The University of Chicago Press, Chicago 60637
The University of Chicago Press, Ltd., London
© 2006 by The University of Chicago
All rights reserved. Published 2006
Printed in the United States of America

15 14 13 12 11 10 09 08 07 06   1 2 3 4 5

ISBN: 0-226-50084-5 (cloth)
ISBN: 0-226-50085-3 (paper)

Chapter 4 was previously published as "My Kinsman Walter Scott" in *Scotland and the Borders of Romanticism,* ed. Leith Davis, Ian Duncan, and Janet Sorenson, 2004. Reprinted with the permission of Cambridge University Press.

Portions of chapter 10 were previously published as "Impossible Fiction; or, The Importance of Being John Cowper Powys" in the *Times Literary Supplement,* December 1, 1995.

Chapter 11 was previously published as "Beauty, the Irreal, and the Willing Assumption of Disbelief" in *Critical Inquiry* 30 (summer 2004): 717–738.

Library of Congress Cataloging-in-Publication Data

McGann, Jerome J.
 The scholar's art : literary studies in a managed world / Jerome McGann.
  p. cm.
 Includes bibliographical references (p.   ) and index.
 ISBN 0-226-50084-5 (cloth : alk. paper) — ISBN 0-226-50085-3 (pbk. : alk. paper)
  1. English literature—History and criticism. 2. American literature—History and criticism. 3. Literature—History and criticism—Theory, etc. 4. Literary historians—English-speaking countries. 5. Criticism—English-speaking countries. I. Title.

PR99 .M26 2006
820.9—dc22   2005024582

⊗ The paper used in this publication meets the minimum requirements of the American National Standard for Information Sciences—Permanence of Paper for Printed Library Materials, ANSI Z39.48-1992.

For Geoffrey, Christopher, Jennifer

Available Muse

O Heart's Muse, palace lover
When January winds hover
Over saddest darkness of snowy night
Will you have embers to make blue feet white?

Will you bring to life marbled shoulders
With evening rays piercing shutters?
Knowing money's spent and throat's dry
Will you harvest gold from azure sky?

Every night you've got to earn your bread
Like a boy in a choir giving head
Blowing smoke to a God nearly dead

And your laugh
Soaking in tears unseen
Makes joy for a vulgar spleen

> —Charles Bernstein, translated from Baudelaire, "La Muse Vénale"

: : :

He left me: I called after him aloud;
He heeded not; but, with his twofold charge
Still in his grasp, before me, full in view,
Went hurrying o'er the illimitable waste,
With the fleet waters of a drowning world
In chase of him; whereat I waked in terror,
And saw the sea before me, and the book,
In which I had been reading, at my side.

> —William Wordsworth, *The Prelude*

CONTENTS

PREFACE

Scholarship is a service vocation. Not only are Sappho and Shakespeare primary, irreducible concerns for the scholar, so is any least part of our cultural inheritance that might call for attention. And to the scholarly mind, every smallest datum of that inheritance has a right to make its call. When the call is heard, the scholar is obligated to answer it accurately, meticulously, candidly, thoroughly.

As with the poets, artists, and philosophers the scholar regularly serves, therefore, censorship—political or moral correctness—is intolerable to the scholar. All act under the ancient motto passed down to us from Terence, Cicero, and our Western tradition of learning: "Homo sum; humani nihil a me alienum puto" (I am a human being, and I judge nothing human to be anathema to me).

In our brutal and sanctimonious age, where so many are schooled in violence, where propaganda and the management of thought are public policy, and where culture wars mirror a broad social and political condition, the scholar's art may be usefully recalled.

May be recalled by scholars themselves, as well as by a public at large. It is a worthy mission to seek the preservation of our cultural memory—all of it, the great as well as the small, the high-minded and the pornographic, the official and the underground, Books of Virtue as well as Bibles of Hell. We save all these things as perfectly as we can because we never know when they will be needful, or how. Like the earth we misuse and neglect, these things are precious in themselves.

It is also a worthy mission to study critical thinking, perhaps especially in times like these. Human beings, like their diverse cultures, are not just interesting in their differences, they move and touch us through those differences. The scholar's commitment to truth and method, to set aside bias and prejudgment for critical care and honest report, can make a world of difference to that world of differences. Do we enlist theories and their abstractions to expose those differences? How could we not? But the scholar must also be agnostic to the theories we fashion and, paradoxically, put our faith in. Certainly this is the case with the humanities scholar whose gods are, like the God of Thomas Hardy, precious for their very limitations and fallibilities. Theories serve only so long as they serve—like the scholar who uses them.

This book pledges allegiance to those ideas and attitudes, which found our humane inheritance. Here they license a particular argument about works of imagination and their place in society, and about the scholar's art in preserving and elucidating those works.

I tie the argument most, though not exclusively, to works of poetry because of the bad eminence poetry has gained in the last half-century. "Poetry" has become a byword for incomprehensible language.

It is our fault, scholars and educators, that poetry has acquired this reputation. We have hyped its depth, profundity, importance. Two hundred, one hundred—even fifty—years ago people read and heard it very differently. A simple poet spoke modestly of the poet as "a man speaking to men." A livelier, less sincere, and far more self-critical poet mocked himself as "the grand Napoleon of the realms of rhyme." And for that exemplary self-effacing poet of modernism, poets were simply the emperors of ice cream.

We have some important unlearning to do.

We get into trouble, we get others into trouble, when we set either the criterion of "meaning" or the criterion of "beauty" as the measure of value for imaginative works. Like theory, criteria are ponderous things, deadly to the imagination. Yet these criteria pervade the discourse of culture, both inside and outside the academy.

On the contrary, poetry and art function at more fundamental, even primitive, levels. Beauty and meaning, what the ancients called pleasure and instruction, are secondary constructions laid upon poetry by scholars who try to explain how poems work, how they arrest, astonish, reveal. How they force us to see what we see differently. Scholars try to explain these experiences to others, which is well and good so long as we do not, as Blake said, mistake the scholar's candle for poetry's sun.

II

An early reader of this book remarked a certain indeterminacy in the way I use the first person plural. That's true. The book is a kind of dramatic monologue. The first person, that's myself, is addressing directly—conversing with—an implied audience of other scholars and educators. There you have the first "we." The subjects addressed in the book—poetry, fiction, ideology—are what we talk about all the time.

"You"? There we have the second "we," which comprises a wider circle of people who also have an interest in the cultural values that are at the center of our lives: all of our lives. I think the conversations we scholars have with each other need to be overheard. I have written the book for that overhearing. In doing so, I sometimes find myself thinking about what others might think about the way we scholars talk together. When that happens, I find myself involved with a larger first-person plural.

Scholars' conversations can become hermetic to a degree, and I am certain that a nonscholarly reader will find parts of this book uninviting, difficult, pedantic even. I have tried to minimize "the jargon of the schools" and its often difficult syntax. Nonetheless, this is not written for passive consumers of *Survivor*, *Grand Theft Auto*, or *Left Behind*, but for people who engage with such things for their complexities and conflictions. Those works need critical reflection as much as *Paradise Lost* continues to need it. Popular and contemporary works are important and interesting exactly because they dominate so much of our immediate cultural life. Thinking about them in a scholarly way, however, means that we include them in a larger conversation—a conversation that embraces the people Wordsworth called, in his sweetly archaic way, "the noble living and the noble dead." We don't talk like that any more nor should we. Noble and ignoble, present and past, the remembered and the forgotten: because scholars find all cultural work interesting to think and talk about, the scholar's art becomes, in a certain sense, impossible. To insist on pursuing that kind of scholarly conversation is therefore ludicrous. And so we insist.

III

Remember: the scholar's vocation is to preserve and pass on our cultural inheritance. Scholars do it by studying that inheritance and talking—usually among themselves—about what they find. Schools select parts of it for everyone to read and think about. These conversations are important because they help us remember how we came to be who we are.

The conversation has been going on for millennia. Vast and complex as it is, scholars are expected to devote themselves to it, like the spider artist of Alexander Pope. But then too, like Tennyson's Lady of Shalott, the scholar's tasks often end by creating strange webs, unseen or incomprehensible. In doing that, scholars find themselves becoming custodians in a Library of Babel. Conversations then get carried out in specialized if crucial languages, like bibliography and hermeneutics, forbidding creatures who live, it seems, to spawn their beasty offspring.

This book reconstructs a fragment of that conversation. The subjects undertaken, beasts and all, were available to a public discourse not so long ago. That they have since become recondite is part of the cultural emergency here being addressed.

The book's implicit arguments are two: first, that the scholar's conversation about who we are needs to be heard and engaged—more than superficially by the nonscholar, less than intramurally by the specialist; second, that the conversation needs to break free of the constraints that administer the conversation. Scholarship is about what we forget or refuse to remember, and in carrying out that mission it often finds itself, as it does today, at odds with instituted and censorious authorities. Because scholarship functions within its own institutional framework, it is always censoring itself, even—as today—under an Enlightenment heritage wearing a coat of many colors.

Our culture wars have been marshaled by these opposing administrative authorities, which are committed to prescribing cultural norms. But all norms are the residue of a higher order of investigative procedure. The logician C. S. Peirce called it "abduction," artists have called it "imagination." Alfred Jarry said it was "the science of exceptions."

This book talks about how that science can be practiced. Its view is circumscribed largely to the last two hundred years, but as the introduction argues, it sees that period—our immediate historical horizon—in a larger frame of reference. The book then breaks into three parts. The first ("Not My Literary History!") asks what we would gain by reimagining the way scholars have codified the literary and cultural history of the past two hundred years. The second ("Philological Investigations") gives a series of case studies that illustrate how scholarly method can help to bring about such reimaginings. The last section is in two related parts ("Interpretation in a New Key" and "Humanism for the Twenty-First Century"). The first discusses how some recent technological developments are being harnessed to the reimagination of our cultural memory. The second then closes the book with two exemplary acts of critical reflection: one on the interpretive tradition—let us call it Coleridge's—that has dominated Anglo-American scholarship for the past two hundred years; the other on a singular character, John Cowper Powys, whose work our scholarship, to its cost, has been strengthless to imagine.

INTRODUCTION

Loose Canons

How serious do we mean to be about poetry? I mean serious the way Oscar Wilde and Wallace Stevens were serious, Emily Dickinson or Susan Howe. Serious where we set aside altogether those moral tags and promoter's labels: "great," "timeless," "enduring," "visionary." Artistically and critically speaking, we mustn't take any of that seriously. It's just advertising for the auctions of the mind. Dante Gabriel Rossetti seems to me an important cultural figure because, having taken the idea of artistic greatness seriously, he made the nightmarish result the foundation of his work. As a poet and an artist his cultivations are often very unpleasing to read or look at — which is precisely why we should.

One of Rossetti's heroes, William Blake, understood these matters very well. Scarcely known during his lifetime, he often felt the pain of that neglect. And we admire his perseverance in adversity; it is uplifting for us to do so, to have such moral models of behavior. But we might also remember that they are models of moral behavior and so have little to do with art or imagination as such. Emily Dickinson has been another uplifting model, or at least she can seem quite uplifting until someone like Camille Paglia comes along to remind us of her savageries. And then there are so many like Ezra Pound, the architect of modernism for the English-speaking world. A commanding presence — but not very attractive, is he? And Wordsworth, Laura Riding, whoever? Perhaps, as Auden said, we should pardon them for writing well.

So we do; and so we take an artist's personal moral derelictions according to Byron's proverb for his Corsair: "He left a Corsair's name to other times, / Linked with one virtue, and a thousand crimes" (*The Corsair* 3.695–96). The

1

Corsair's "one virtue" was "love," but here I use Byron's text allegorically. I take the Corsair's saving virtue as a figure of poetry. For that we set aside all personal "crimes." The writing says to us "sursum corda," and we are uplifted.

But what if the writing does not uplift?

There is a high-minded Angel in Blake's *Marriage of Heaven and Hell* who pities the moral danger Blake's wickedness is preparing for him. But Blake will have none of it. So he takes the Angel and drives him down into the Bible itself for a fetid vision of the Bible's world of moral righteousness. "And lo! it was a deep pit," Blake says — echoing the Bible itself! — full of chained monkeys and baboons where "the weak were caught by the strong and with a grinning aspect, first coupled with them and then devoured . . . and here and there I saw one savourily picking the flesh off his own tail" (plate 20). This isn't pleasant. The passage has taken us through some perverse doorway of a perverse imagination to the heart of the Good Book and its commentators, including its latest commentator, William Blake. Here "the stench" of the book and its imaginings are equalized in a moment of vision that is mildly repellent to everyone: to the Angel, to the Blake of this text, to us as readers. "Terribly annoyed" by "the stench" of it all, Blake and the Angel get out and take us with them.

The moral reading of this passage uplifts our view of it. We are asked to take it as a satire on the hypocrisies concealed in all moral codes, especially the Western Bible. This is a good reading, in several senses. It is also a moral reading. But it is a reading that skirts the unsavory aspects of the passage — an evasion the Angel and Blake do not choose. An artist of the grotesque, Blake is frequently repellent. Consider his famous proverb, "Prudence is a rich ugly old maid courted by incapacity" (plate 7), which today will seem more than just mildly repulsive.

We skirt much of Swift the way we skirt Blake, and all the best of Rochester, who rarely does not write well. But a reader like (say) Thackeray did not skirt Swift's obscenities. He thought much of Swift should be forbidden reading — and he thought so not because he judged Swift a bad writer but exactly because he admired him.

I am being polite. The difficulties of Blake's text are easily negotiated. Blake has become a classic, taught in all the schools. He has been editorially sifted and prepared for us — not to say weighed out and left wanting in that very process. So we read him with pleasure. We read Swift with pleasure — although reading him can often seem, as it seemed to Thackeray, like watching the fall of an empire.

Or we don't, we rather read "critically" and expose (for example) Blake's persistent misogyny. This is Blake as we wouldn't have him writing — if we are anticanonist — or as we wouldn't have him read — if we are canonist. In the schools, everybody wants approved texts. It's just that different people have different ideas about where to put their good housekeeping seals.

I am creating problems, as I mean to. Consider a text like the following from a climactic moment in Blake's epic *Milton* (plate 25/27). It describes what Blake calls "the winepress of Los," Los being the fourth of the four Zoas, otherwise known as "the human imagination." Blake first explains, somewhat ominously, that

> This winepress is called War on earth; it is the printing-press
> Of Los, and here he lays his words in order above the mortal brain,
> As cogs are formed in a wheel to turn the cogs of the adverse wheel.

He then goes on to describe this winepress in operation:

> Timbrels & violins sport round the winepresses; the little seed,
> The sportive root, the earth-worm, the gold beetle, the wise emmet
> Dance round the winepresses.

The description of nature continues for almost twenty more lines, which gradually emphasize the erotic energy driving nature's turning transformations. The sexual theme then breaks into the open at the overwhelming conclusion of the passage:

> But in the winepresses the human grapes sing not nor dance:
> They howl & writhe in shoals of torment, in fierce flames consuming,
> In chains of iron & in dungeons circled with ceaseless fires,
> In pits & dens & shades of death, in shapes of torment & woe
> In plates & screws & racks & saws & cogs & fires & cisterns,
> The cruel joy of Luvah's daughters, lacerating with knives
> And whips their victims, & the deadly sports of Luvah's sons.
> They dance around the dying, & they drink the howl and groan;
> They catch the shrieks in cups of gold, they hand them to one another.
> These are the sports of love, & these the sweet delights of amorous play
> Tears of the grape, the death-sweat of the cluster, the last sigh
> Of the mild youth who listens to the luring songs of Luvah.

What is the pleasure of this text? Whatever it is, pain functions as one of its chief elements. The passage isn't unpleasant exactly, like the *Marriage* text, but it is unsettling. Blake represents a vision of the last judgment, a story of God's benevolence toward the fallen human world. It is equally a story of the beauties of nature and of the physical ecstasies of human love. In the end it is just another marriage of heaven and hell— a vision wondrous, astonishing — and terrible. Or, in interpreting the "meaning" of such a text, have we lost the ability to feel its awful and amazing view? Have we become readers no longer to be moved or even shocked, who neither weep nor cry out at our poetry, who cannot prove upon our pulses what the texts bring us into? That is not the way Thackeray read Swift. He was appalled, reading Swift. And so he should have been.

Blake is obscure in ways that Swift and Rochester are not. So, seeing, many do not see his strange and disturbing visions; and when Blake scholars and in-terpreters try to elucidate his texts, their commentaries filter as much as they reveal.

Here are two passages from fairly recent texts that have yet to be entirely managed by academic commentary. Jean Genet and Kathy Acker both write a kind of Newgate fiction. Strictly speaking, the term is scholarly jargon for certain early-nineteenth-century novels treating criminal society, like *Oliver Twist*. Dickens's novel has been standard high school reading for decades, but Genet and Acker are unlikely to be chosen as school authors. For good and understandable reasons, most educators — at all levels — avoid writing that involves pornography.

In point of fact my classes, including my first-year undergraduate classes, regularly study both Acker and Genet. Through them we are called to engage some interesting, difficult, and — especially for our time — relevant ques-tions, moral and aesthetic. But I am not trying to persuade anyone to put them in the curriculum. Genet is of course an acknowledged twentieth-century master, and Acker is one of our most highly regarded contemporary artists. Both are thus canonical, but they are clearly loose — loose canons, as Blake was, once upon a time.

I bring them in here because a comparison of their styles helps to explain how different the im- or non- or a-moralism of artists' practices can be. Acker, for example, offers an especially interesting case. People sometimes compare her to Genet or William Burroughs, but her most direct literary progenitor is neither of these writers — it is clearly Charles Dickens. Much of her writing involves a deliberate rewriting of standard school texts, like *Great Expectations, The Scarlet Letter, The Adventures of Huckleberry Finn*. Aggressively feminist, her writing descends from the same kind of social consciousness she likes to parody: "Dead, your Majesty. Dead, my lords and gentlemen. Dead, Right Reverends and Wrong Reverends of every order. Dead . . . and dying thus around us every day."

Contemporary social and political questions are paramount concerns. So one of art's most common goals, the construction of beautiful forms, appears in Acker's writing only in (morally) negative terms. As the heroine of her novel *Empire of the Senseless* says, "beauty is a representation of what's past, over with, dead." Indeed, "beauty" in Acker's imagination is the false and seductive appearance that our world's characteristic savageries assume. Love is therefore revolting (in at least two senses) in Acker's work: it is repulsive and it is in revolt. Love's characteristic form appears as violation, torture, rape; women are dirty words ("cunts"), men are the benighted fools of a social system they stupidly think operates for their benefit and under their control; and so on.

Acker is an artist, however, not a politician or political activist. An artist of words. This means that she works through the aesthetics of language, and of language as we have it today. Her language swings, wildly and often hilariously, between the dialect of the contemporary streetworld to the most abstract academic talk. These define the limits of her chief preoccupation, what she calls "dead language," which is similar to the language of those creatures George Romero has famously named "the living dead." Dead language is language bearing false appearances of life and feeling. Obscenity is crucial for Acker partly because it is a sign that language has preserved a minimal (which in Acker rhymes with "criminal") life, and hence that some hope remains for the reconstruction of language and a human world. Acker drops into the gangrene jargon of the intellectual activist for much the same reason.

If we are not moved by Acker's language, by its obscenity and its academicism alike, if it does not horrify and disgust at both those extremes, then our reading — from her texts' point of view — will already have passed over into the night of the living dead. So the first level of her style is directed at the reader's primary doors of perception, that is to say, at fundamental cultural and ideological taboos. These appear most dramatically as forbidden words and an uninflected treatment of loathly subjects. Let's look at a typical passage.

> I was in the bathroom fucking some boy. Daddy came home. I heard the front door close. I threw on my clothes and ran up to daddy. "Hi! Hi!" I kissed him. There's only one picture I have of me as a kid. I'm three years old. My arms close around my father's thighs. "Shall I get you some Jack Daniels?" . . .
>
> I handed it to daddy. He was holding up a boy's tie which he'd found in the bathtub. He didn't believe my lies. He sat down on his bed where he always sat. My daddy was almost crying. . . .
>
> "Abhor, I know what you've been doing." Lies never work except as lies. Like language and love. My mother taught me this. Like love.

"These men don't respect you, Abhor." How could I explain that I cared neither if they respected me nor who they were. "Abhor," daddy explained, "I'm the only man who'll ever take care of you properly." His hands were reaching for my breasts while tears were coming out of his eyes. . . .

"I'm going to phone mommy." Over the phone I told her that her husband was trying to do something to me. I didn't use the word "fuck." She said, "Let me speak to him."

I don't remember if his hand left my nipple. I don't know what they said to each other. After he put the phone receiver down on the table, he put his cock up me. There was no more blood than in a period.

Part of me wanted him and part of me wanted to kill him.

So I stayed in their apartment and that night I dreamed that the blood lying over the ocean in front of my eyes was light. The light by which I could see. The fishing boats sink or stink.

The German Romantics had to destroy the same bastions as we do. Logocentrism and idealism, theology, all supports of the repressive society. Property's pillars. Reason which always homogenizes and reduces, represses and unifies phenomena or actuality into what can be perceived and so controlled. . . . It is here that literature strikes, at this base, where the concepts and actings of order impose themselves. Literature is that which denounces and slashes apart the repressing machine at the level of the signified. (*Empire of the Senseless* 11–12)

Acker typically works at three discourse levels simultaneously: soap opera talk (or middle-class cliché); street obscenity and vulgarity; and the language of the academic intellectual. All three come into this passage, and they are held together by Acker's characteristic deadpan.

The text outrages at all its registers, not just in its use of dirty words or choice of horrid subject. In terms of Acker's notorious textual obscenities, this is one of her milder texts. But the passage shocks nonetheless, for while it seems to be telling the truth — while it repeatedly does tell the truth, and speaks with alarming candor — its truth-telling appears meaningless, blind, as ludicrous and obscene as its discussion of the social function of "literature," which is also, of course, a discussion of itself. Worst of all, Acker's style seems not to care. For her, style always works as a "seeming," an appearance.

But such horrors operate only at the first level of her style. The next level is more subtle and ultimately more devastating. Here style subsumes its own primary level into the writing as a whole. Acker does not reserve shocking words and topics for special scenes or dramatic textual moments, she makes them a steady presence of vocabulary and storyline.

Such a style, it is said, destroys its own shock effect. So Burroughs or Acker or even Henry Miller, say, will be judged finally "boring." Perhaps the most famous literary example of this kind of judgment was Wordsworth's, when he condemned various sensational styles of the 1790s. But an artist like Acker is not finally interested so much in shocking her readers as in revealing her imagination of the sources of social corruption. This is not the revelation of those (transcendental) "sources," but of a particular way of imagining. The absurd discussion of the "German Romantics" and the heroism of literature is a radically leveling move. A poisoned ecology infects this cultural scene at all its levels. Obscenity measures the social order from top to bottom. The wickedness of her writing — and it is wicked by all conventional standards — lies exactly in her assumption that readers will seek ways to avoid contact with what are, after all, widespread and everyday realities. In this respect she writes out of a satanic tradition best known through the work of Byron and Baudelaire, who assumed a hypocritical readership dulled either by philistinism or spiritual pride.

So, in *Empire of the Senseless,* Acker's ultimate state of loathing is literally embodied in her main character (appropriately named) Abhor — an allegorically constructed young black woman who exists in a state of such inured and perpetual pain that her chief feeling is a raging indifference. She represents what Marx's revolutionary theorizing could not imagine, a figure of the lumpenproletariat who yet bears social consciousness and consequence. In Acker's hands, Abhor's obscene language becomes not shocking, least of all rich and splendid. Rather it appears dull, mortified, colorless. It represents Abhor, the index of her social character. Brought forward in this way, under the sign of art (deliberate reflection), that which was dead suddenly comes to life, comes alive as and in its deadness. But not as a "slice of life," a glimpse into an inconsequent underworld of evil. Abhor's deadness, in Acker's work, reflects the reader — us. And the more we refuse the identification, the more the work makes it stick. That is the point of the discussion of German Romanticism and a New Left view of art's redemptive functions.

The world according to Genet is very different from Acker's Mephisto Waltz. All that matters in Genet's world is the beauty Acker refuses. He is, famously, the consummate prose stylist. Filth, dirty words, degradation: in Genet these are what Blake called the windows of eternity. They transport Genet to a Baudelairean heaven, "anywhere out of this world." Acker's comedy is tough, hardboiled; Genet's is angelic, celebratory. The plot climax of *Our Lady of the Flowers* turns on a moment of linguistic crudity and moral indifference that can recall Acker's deadpan manner. The scene is a courtroom where Our Lady is being tried for the murder of an old man. "What do you have to say in your defense?" the judge asks the young murderer. Our Lady's liberal lawyer hopes to explain to the court what a terrible upbringing Our Lady has had, and how society's evils have simply made a return visit in the person of this child-murderer. He pleads eloquently for understanding, for mercy.

When the judge puts his question to the boy, Our Lady runs through various answers he might make. As he does so we see that, true to his nature, Our Lady's criteria for speaking truthfully are purely aesthetic.

> The phrase "I didn't do it on purpose" took shape on his lips. Had he said it, nobody would have been surprised. Everyone expected the worst. All the answers that occurred to him came forward in slang, and a feeling for the proprieties suggested to him that he speak French, but everyone knows that in trying moments it is the mother tongue that prevails. He had to be natural. To be natural, at that moment, was to be theatrical, but his maladroitness saved him from ridicule and lopped off his head. He was truly great. He said: "The old boy was washed up. He couldn't even get a hard-on."
>
> The last word did not pass his jaunty little lips. Nevertheless, the twelve old men, all together, very quickly put their hands over their ears to prevent the entry of the word that was as big as an organ, which, finding no other orifice, entered all stiff and hot into their gaping mouths. (288)

Appalled that the boy is sealing his doom with such an answer, Our Lady's lawyer makes frantic efforts to excuse him in the eyes of the jury. But the text is laughing at the lawyer's pathetic imagination, its true sympathy being with the outraged jurors, the vaudevillian backups for the old man murdered by Our Lady. The oral-sex image, a classic instance of slapstick comedy, introduces pure poetical justice into this fantastic courtroom. Poetic justice comes to reign over the realms of criminal justice: Our Lady turns into Christ, and Genet appears as a fathering god, bringing him back to life: "Forty days later, on a spring evening, the machine was set up in the prison yard. At dawn it was ready to cut. Our Lady of the Flowers had his head cut off by a real knife. And nothing happened. What would be the point? There is no need for the veil of the temple to be ripped from top to bottom because a god gives up the ghost. All that this can prove is the bad quality of the cloth and its deterioration" (291–92).

I am telling a story with these stories, and it has a moral. It is simple: that academic conventions too often want to handle such texts with protective clothing. Like AIDS victims, certain texts, we think, ought to be put away, "disappeared." This is what the jurors at Our Lady's trial think. Others sometimes argue they should be kept around for moral instruction or other worthy purposes. This is the way Our Lady's defense lawyer thinks. So we say that certain works do or do not have "redeeming social value," as if redeeming value were the point of art. It is the point of art only to judges, jurors, lawyers, and moralists, not to the artists themselves, as Our Lady — a figure of poetry and art — so clearly shows. From Our Lady's point of view, his artistic acts stand entirely apart from moral, intellectual, and cultural concerns. These concerns are not declared unimportant, they are just handled differently. Art asserts the prerogatives and authority of feeling as such, the wisdom of the body which in the case of poetry is the body as language. The writing of Acker and Genet is meant to affect us.

When people nowadays speak about art as an "aesthetic" event, the word "aesthetic" often signifies something rarified, even spiritual. But this understanding travesties the word, and ultimately the art it designates. "Aesthetic" means "in the senses, of the body." If an aesthetic experience touches spiritual orders, that is because the body is instinct with spirit, in precisely the sense Rossetti had in mind when he wrote to and of his lover: "Thy soul I know not from thy body, nor / Thee from myself, neither our love from God."

In a (Christian) doctrinal perspective such a thought has sometimes been harshly judged: condescended to as confused, condemned as wicked and voluptuous, denounced as blasphemous. And all those judgments seem to me true. Rossetti's thought is immoral — not because of its paganism, but because it tries to make a marriage of heaven and hell, of spiritual and fleshly orders, of transcendental Christian ideas and interpersonal erotic experience. So the passage is unsettling, and it shocked many of its original audience. Later more sophisticated readers, like T. S. Eliot, defended themselves (and others) against this text with their cool and orthodox condescension. Like Rossetti, Eliot knew and admired Dante, but Eliot could not bear the reality of Rossetti's renegade transmutation of the great Florentine. So Eliot let his moral conscience come between himself and Rossetti's poetry. Rossetti was thereby removed from the canon of "the tradition," so-called. As a poet, Rossetti did not think the way Eliot approved — did not think like Donne, or Dante, or even Tennyson or Baudelaire. And of course Eliot was correct.

In thus avoiding an experience with Rossetti on his own poetic terms, Eliot read him like too many schoolteachers, too many professors, too many of us. Confronted by Rossetti's peculiarly tormented verse, Eliot forgets to read as a poet, with his doors of perception cleansed. He reads as a philosopher, a moralist, a student of culture and perhaps cultural studies.

Blake, as so often, provides a useful corrective. His comments on Henry Boyd's *Translation of the Inferno of Dante* . . . (1785) state the artist's position with alarming directness: "The grandest Poetry is Immoral . . . Cunning & Morality are not Poetry but Philosophy." Note that equation, "Cunning & Morality." To Blake, Boyd is an ideologue and hence doesn't have the faintest idea about what Dante's work means. Boyd thinks the *Inferno* a great work because it defines and inculcates "the difference between right and wrong." But Blake's idea is different. Blake's idea is that art is candid rather than cunning, open instead of morally restricted. Even when, as in Dante's case, the artist is completely invested in moral judgments, the candor of art's body works against the cunning of its mind. That is exactly Blake's "argument" in his epic translation of another great moralist of the imagination, Milton.

From a perspective like Blake's, our canon wars represent a struggle for control of the cultural apparatus. Which ideological line — pluralist or essentialist — will dominate the state's educational bureaucracy? I do not mean to suggest that such a question is unimportant — far from it. But as a battle for educational power, the canon wars have sometimes shown how sublimely disinterested priests of culture can be toward art and poetry as such. And yet all would agree, surely, that another function of our priesthood is the defense of the poetic heritage: not simply by preserving the works themselves, but by maintaining the integrity of imagination and its (apparently) immoral missions.

In this view of the matter — I admit its perversity, though not its untruth — the poets' greatest scholarly friend is probably the pedant, and their greatest enemy the interpreter. The wickedness of the interpreters, so far as poetry goes, can be easily shown. Interpreters lust for the fleshpots of meaning, it is their characteristic, their besetting sin. The traditional form of that sin can be found — was found by Blake — in Boyd's way with Dante — as if Dante's work had a core of moral meaning that interpretation should seek to uncover and define, for our edification. The twentieth century developed a modern version of the same sin when it began to place interpretation before imagination, the clever and self-conscious reader before the artist, "blind, blind as a bat," as Pound said. The pedant, on the other hand, is a craven creature — dusty and indoors, stooped with collations and other tedious tasks of his mean office. Yet his assumed inconsequence and drudgery may prove a great virtue when it comes to maintaining the integrity of the works we inherit. Or so we can imagine. Effaced before the original, the pedant dies so that something else — something judged better — might live. It is a modest, an ancient, a "priestlike task." Such a concern for textual integrity might well be taken for a symbol of the artist's more famous commitment to imagination. Neither pedant nor artist are licensed to their work by codes of morality. They serve other gods altogether, artisanal and crafty gods. Both are literalists of their respective imaginations.

Blake's idea that "the greatest poetry is immoral" corresponds exactly to Plato's idea. But of course the two judge the value of such work very differently. When Blake calls Plato a "heathen" he is thinking of Plato's ethics, which are for Blake worldly and unchristian. He aligns himself with Jesus and Saint Paul, and especially the latter, when he argues (in the *Epistle to the Hebrews*) that sin comes from the imposition of moral laws like the Ten Commandments. According to Paul, that law — the whole system of moral prohibitions — is abrogated by the new law of love instituted with the coming of Jesus.

Now whatever we think of Blake's ethics here, or his reading of Paul (or Plato for that matter), his aesthetics could not be more traditional. He looks at art and poetry from the point of view of the practicing artist, whose principal obligations are to craftsmanship and the muse — the two being, it seems to me, alternate perceptions of a single calling: to craftsmanship, or one's material and practical duties; to the muse, or one's source of inspiration, which does not flow from quotidian orders — from cultural studies of the Right or the Left — but from "the god": that White Goddess (or White Devil) of traditional (male) myth.

Asking that students read poetry "in the same spirit that the author writ," instead of in a spirit we would like the poet to have written (whatever our moral perspective might be), can produce an educational experience not otherwise available. It helps, for example, to put us on a way of sympathetic double-reading — for we always read under the auspices of at least one tasking spirit, our own. What I mean is best illustrated by an example. (Where art and poetry are concerned, the optimal procedure is always by experience and examples. When we "teach" poetry, probably the most useful service we can render our students is to help them learn to articulate the words, to play the instrument of language with as much skill as care can bring; simply, to make them recite).

In book 21 of Homer's *Iliad*, Achilles has returned to the war. Homer sets him beside "the fair-running river of whirling Xanthos," where Achilles lays waste the hosts of Troy. Suddenly out of the river comes a naked young man, a Trojan warrior who has thrown aside his armor and weapons, "being weary and sweating with the escape from the river." Achilles recognizes Lykaon, whom he encountered in battle once before, captured, and then set free after the youth was ransomed by his father. Lykaon once again asks Achilles to take him prisoner, promising a handsome reward in return. But Achilles, bloody-minded in his love of Patroklos, refuses. "Why all this whining?" Achilles asks the pleading Lykaon:

> "Patroklos also is dead, who was better by far than you are.
> Do you not see what a man I am, how huge, how splendid
> and born of a great father, and the mother who bore me immortal?
> Yet even I have also my death and my strong destiny,
> and there shall be a dawn or an afternoon or a noontime
> when some man in the fighting will take the life from me also."
>
> (107–12)

Achilles then coldly dispatches Lykaon, and the text narrates the brutal event with the same astonishing objectivity we see in this passage and for which Homer is so celebrated. We see it again in the text that immediately follows, where Achilles vaunts over Lykaon's dead body. Taking the corpse by the foot, Achilles

> slung him into the river
> to drift, and spoke winged words of vaunting derision over him:
> "Lie there now among the fish, who will lick the blood away
> from your wound, and care nothing for you, nor will your mother
> lay you on the death-bed and mourne over you, but Skamandros
> will carry you spinning down to the wide bend of the salt water.
> And a fish will break a ripple shuddering dark on the water
> as he rises to feed on the shining fat of Lykaon.
> Die on, all; till we come to the city of sacred Ilion,
> you in flight and I killing you from behind; and there will not
> be any rescue for you from your silvery-whirled strong-running
> river, for all the numbers of bulls you dedicate to it
> and drown single-foot horses alive in its eddies. And yet
> even so, die all an evil death, till all of you
> pay for the death of Patroklos and the slaughter of the Achaians
> whom you killed beside the running ships, when I was not with them."
>
> (120–35)

The passage takes one's breath away, even in this modern English translation. It is pure Homer — indeed, it could be an emblem of Homer's style, so indifferently and passionately alive at once to so much horror and so much beauty. The text's doors of perception, as Blake might have said, seem entirely flung open. Nor is it that moral issues do not enter such a text. On the contrary, the passage flaunts its moral attitudes as nakedly as its physical perceptions. The lines force our modern sentimental consciousness to confront directly an alien heroic ideology, to judge it and be judged by it in turn. "Die on, all": no one today could make such a prayer and not be thought a monster; and yet here we see, quite clearly, a monstrous thought imagined heroically and sublimely.

Poetry, it has been said (by Shelley), turns all things to loveliness. But that just isn't the case, as this text — like the earlier texts from Acker and Genet — shows so plainly. The morals of even the canon are loose, loose as the Bible, like the gods of the ancient (or the modern) world. Even canonical works won't simply give us what we or others judge to be good or for our good. As their morals are loose, so are their commitments to loveliness and the beautiful. When Swinburne translated Villon's great "Ballade de Villon et de la Grosse Margot," his English words all but glossed the original as a kind of Nietzschean testament "Beyond Good and Beauty":

> What though the beauty I love and serve be cheap,
> Ought you to take me for a beast or fool?
> All things a man could wish are in her keep;
> For her I turn swashbuckler in love's school.
> When folk drop in, I take my pot and stool
> And fall to drinking with no more ado.
> I fetch them bread, fruit, cheese, and water, too;
> I say all's right so long as I'm well paid;
> "Look in again when your flesh troubles you,
> Inside this brothel where we drive our trade."

This way of thinking is not only commonplace in poetry, it is poetry's central fire. Villon, Swinburne's emblematic poet, drives his trade in the brothel of language. Yeats, more polite, called it the foul rag and bone shop of the heart. Literalists like Villon prefer more direct forms of speech. Forms like those celebrated — not, mind you, created — in Robert Burns's songs, and especially in the magnificent verse medley "Love and Liberty — A Cantata" (commonly called "The Jolly Beggars"), which is also set in a brothel.

These examples do not convince you, perhaps. For Villon and Swinburne and Burns write with such verve and high spirits that we may think to add another criterion of aesthetic judgment: energy. Poetry may carry us away, take off the tops of our heads, as Emily Dickinson thought it should. And so it may. But then it may be poetry and do the opposite — it may shrink us up and leave nothing but a foul taste behind. As a matter of fact, some of

T. S. Eliot's best work is exactly of this order — for instance, "Sweeney among the Nightingales."

> Apeneck Sweeney spreads his knees
> Letting his arms hang down to laugh,
> The zebra stripes along his jaw
> Swelling to maculate giraffe.
>
> The circles of the stormy moon
> Slide westward toward the River Plate,
> Death and the Raven drift above
> And Sweeney guards the horned gate.
>
> Gloomy Orion and the Dog
> Are veiled; and hushed the shrunken seas;
> The person in the Spanish cape
> Tries to sit on Sweeney's knees
>
> Slips and pulls the table cloth
> Overturns a coffee-cup,
> Reorganised upon the floor
> She yawns and draws a stocking up;
>
> The silent man in mocha brown
> Sprawls at the window-sill and gapes;
> The waiter brings in oranges
> Bananas figs and hothouse grapes;
>
> The silent vertebrate in brown
> Contracts and concentrates, withdraws;
> Rachel nee Rabinovitch
> Tears at the grapes with murderous paws.

And so forth. To the end the poem is horrid, relentlessly mean — unhealthy! Who wouldn't rather visit Burns's raucous den? It is Eliot's fastidiousness, his civilized trappings, that transform his ballad to a bolge. So far as brutishness goes, this poem comes forth as its only begetter. Its fear and loathing of the working class, of the Irish, of Jews, of women, of the body: all these are represented in the most undisguised fashion. But the capstone comes when the text — the poem itself — is seen to be what it is, its own best example of the indecencies its imagination has summoned.

The host with someone indistinct
Converses at the door apart,
The nightingales are singing near
The Convent of the Sacred Heart,

And sang within the bloody wood
When Agamemnon cried aloud,
And let their liquid siftings fall
To stain the stiff dishonoured shroud.

"The most important person in this poem," as Eliot said of Tiresias in *The Waste Land*, "uniting all the rest," is here "someone indistinct." Wearing the disguises of six poetic surrogates, he is yet unmistakable in this text. His name is T. S. Eliot.

Yet what a remarkable poem — indeed, how remarkable exactly because it has sunk so completely into its own disgusting imagination!

Of language by imagination we may well say, "I never met a word I didn't like" — or loathe. "Serpentine," "garage door," "phlegm": all have, like the beast Ahab, their humanities. Their eyes are watching God, even when they watch from that cesspool titled "Sweeney among the Nightingales." Faggot, sidekick, drone; stuck-up, nigger, dickhead, spoon. Meeting them in the everyday — when they are out running errands for us — their divinities get obscured. But as poetry returns us to the word-as-such, language becomes talismanic, its world comes thick with many kinds of devil and angel. They are common, even indecent: cunts and pricks; they are impossibly highfalutin: antinomian, diacritical, hermeneusis; many are nerds: the precession of the equinoxes, logarithm, megabyte. We may even hear the voice of the turtle in the land of those dismal persons from Porlock: headhunter, leverage, empowerment.

A poet himself, Plato couldn't in the end get out of nature, or out of the bodily forms of his life, his language. So perhaps his call to exile the poets was only a joking word, a call to exile a call to exile, as Gertrude Stein might have said. But there is no end of how to say it in poetry. I think of Stein's roses, and then of Keats's more figural poets, who "breeding flowers will never breed the same." Stein's project is in breeding flowers that always breed the same: "Rose is a rose is a rose is a rose." So "is" arises, for Stein, like Stevens's "Let be be finale of seem." Let be be; or, in Laura Riding's words, "Love as Love, Death as Death." (So much for the world of the figural.)

In poetry, the only emperor is the emperor of ice cream — a remark open to various interpretations, not all of them gratifying. I mean, if interpretation is what you want.

PART ONE

"Not *My* Literary History!"

CHAPTER 1

High Instincts and Real Presences:
Two Romantic Responses to the Death of Beauty

> Beauty is momentary in the mind—
> The fitful tracing of a portal;
> But in the flesh it is immortal.
>
> —Wallace Stevens, "Peter Quince at the Clavier"

Few passages in twentieth-century poetry are better known than this. It re-formulates the idea and ideal of Beauty in mortal rather than ideal terms. In this view, as Stevens also famously wrote, "Death is the mother of beauty" because from death is born "the heavenly fellowship / Of men that perish and of summer morn" ("Sunday Morning").

But are we confident of our confidence in these poetical formulations? Or let me ask the question another way: does Stevens's mortalist perspective on Beauty involve anything more than a stylistic flourish? *Is* Beauty immortal in the flesh? Do we agree with that, do we agree that Stevens actually means us to assent to that statement? To the *idea* being pronounced, presumably, *by* the statement? I ask these questions in order to clarify the full depth of the para-dox involved here, which asks our assent to the statement that Beauty is im-mortal in the flesh. In that event our mortal, enfleshed minds would have not an immersion in some immortal Being of Beauty but only Beauty's fitful and momentary trace. For that is how our mortal minds work, according to this presentation on the matter.

I

The standard approach to these issues and problems in Stevens is through a certain way of reading Wordsworth, as the normative commentaries by

Harold Bloom and Helen Vendler show. In this line of interpretation, whose primary source is Coleridge, the mind's fitful view of Beauty is taken as an emblem of what it means to be a perishing person. Beauty is what Yeats called "the land of the heart's desire" because and as it escapes our ceaseless efforts to possess it. Beauty is immortal, then, not from its transcendental reality *as such* but from our mortal experience of its perpetual flight.

We know that way of thinking about Beauty is as foundational as Pythagoras, Plato, and Plotinus. We also know what new depths and difficulties Beauty gained with the coming of Enlightenment. Scholars have traced "the decay of beauty as an ideal and as a technical enterprise in the last two centuries" (Turner 17) to the historical moment when Beauty passed between the Scylla of empirical and sensationalist philosophy and the Carybdis of the aesthetics of sensibility. Those reciprocating powers placed the ancient ideal of Beauty in — quite literally — mortal peril.

The problem is fully articulated in Kant and the subsequent tradition of idealistic philosophy, which struggles to preserve a transcendental ground for human judgments in the face of the radical process of secularization set in motion by Locke. In this tradition, beauty and sublimity are both conceived as a priori categories. We respond to the sublime and the beautiful through the erotic dialectic of distance and desire. Most important here is the emergence of sublimity as the determining category of both morality and aesthetics, displacing the ancient *to kalon*. That shift licensed art and poetry to experiment with novel, and distinctly disharmonic, forms of order — a signal feature of all romantic practices. Mountain glory is a function of mountain gloom, as Wordsworth makes abundantly clear in those key sections of *The Prelude*, books 6 and 14.

The problem of Beauty during the past two centuries followed on that initial Kantian displacement. So far as art and poetry are concerned, the move would relegate comedy and satire to a secondary order of practice until the cultural emergence of sensibilities we now associate with postmodernity. A famous passage in Kant's *Critique of Judgment* forecasts this cultural shift. Distinguishing between the beautiful and the sublime, Kant says that the former "represents freedom rather as in *play* than as exercising a law-ordained *function.*" Sublimity, by contrast, is for Kant a figure for that function, "which is the genuine characteristic of human morality, where reason has to impose its dominion upon sensibility" (1.120). When freedom appears better imagined as play than as ordained law, the dark spell cast on Beauty will begin to be lifted.

Of course Beauty does not disappear from the practice of art in "the last two centuries." Indeed, we can see from our current perspective that the exile of Venus would eventually supply her with the privilege of historical backwardness. That fact becomes clear, I think, through an examination of certain key moments in our anglophone culture when the crisis of the ideal of Beauty was most saliently engaged. My aim here is to indicate how certain roads were taken and others refused, and what differences followed from those choices. Ultimately I shall also be arguing that we might usefully retrace this history — rethink it — in order to see why the malaise of Beauty was but a nightmare "owing to [our angelic] metaphysics," as Blake's Devil told his benighted Angel.

Recall when the two plunged into "eternity" together in plates 17–20 of the *Marriage of Heaven and Hell*. An "immense" Gothic city unfolds itself through angel eyes, an "infinite Abyss" of "fiery tracks," "terrific shapes" and "monstrous" forms "advanc[ing] . . . with all the fury of a spiritual existence." When the angel flees from his own scary vision, the devil "remain'd alone, & then this appearance was no more, but I found myself sitting on a pleasant bank beside a river by moon light hearing a harper who sung to the harp." This famous poetical event has rarely (if ever) been seen for what, in at least one important sense, it clearly is: a conflict between an imagination of reality as Sublime and an imagination of it as Beautiful. Blake is of course knowingly "of the devil's party" in this conflict — that is to say, on the side of Beauty rather than Sublimity.

Because so much of Blake's work is bent on exposing the evil of a world consumed by what he called "the torments of love and jealousy," we forget — commentators forget — that he is a poet committed to Beauty, and that his Sublime is a nightmare function. He puts his position with great simplicity in the incomparable "Auguries of Innocence" sequence:

> God appears and God is light
> To those poor souls who dwell in Night,
> But does a human form display,
> To those who dwell in realms of day.

Insofar as we see "a decay of beauty . . . in the past two centuries," it appears to have progressed under the auspices of a God of light and in neglect of the human form so beloved of Blake. At least that is the story I shall try to sketch now.

II

We begin with Wordsworth and the preface to *Lyrical Ballads,* which has dominated English-language aesthetic discourse since it appeared in 1800. This is a remarkable fact given the essay's notorious lack of intellectual rigor. Early traditionalists like Francis Jeffrey had an easy time ridiculing Wordsworth's theory and practice of "poetic diction," as it has come to be called. Coleridge, Shelley, and Byron — unhappily in the first instance, gleefully in the latter two — followed and elaborated Jeffrey's line of attack. Coleridge's is an especially interesting case. *Biographia Literaria* is — explicitly if also reluctantly — a long set of glosses on Wordsworth's brief polemic.

The *Biographia* is the first in a line of idealist responses to Wordsworth's novel explanation of poetry. René Wellek's contempt for the preface (in his *History of Modern Criticism*) is barely disguised. For him, pronouncements on aesthetic matters must at any rate *aspire* to a philosophical — if not a Kantian — coherence, the way *Biographia Literaria* aspires (a work Wellek can respect, despite its fractures and incompletions). The quest for a coherent *philosophy of* Beauty dogs the subject to this day, as James Kirwan's recent and very interesting book shows yet again. Wordsworth, however, like Byron on at least this point, is clearly indifferent to these kinds of systematic attitudes or aspirations. When he speaks of "the philosophic mind" he is thinking in aesthetic, not systematic, terms. The whole of the preface is framed as a contractual problem between poet and audience. It is an explanation of a new type of sympathetic cultural exchange. For all its personal rhetoric, *Biographia* is, by sharp contrast, a brief for ideas about the essential principles of poetry.

Let's examine Wordsworth's two key, and closely related, ideas — an idea about language and an idea about feeling. He proposes the language of "low and rustic life" as a measure for poetical discourse because he wants to make sincerity of feeling the central aesthetic issue. The focus of traditional rhetoric is on rules of decorum, not the language of the heart. This vantage gives it no ready means to study or anatomize its forms of expression. Consequently, these will be — as Gertrude Stein might say — always stanzas in performance, never stanzas in meditation. The show must go on.

Crucial to realize is the way Wordsworth's preface is installing a version of Schiller's myth of naive and sentimental poetry. Wordsworth proposes to make an aesthetic measure of "low and rustic" language as a means to rethink the grounds of art from an experiential rather than a synthetic or rational position. Whether such a language or such a culture actually *exists* is only heuristically important. Wordsworth means to imagine its existence — ultimately, to persuade us to willingly suspend our disbelief in its existence — in order to gain a fresh way of thinking about art, poetry, and culture. "The Idiot Boy" — which seems to me both the most ambitious as well as the greatest poem in the 1798 *Lyrical Ballads* — could not be more explicit in its demonstrative argument. In its world, things, animals, and people are all "bound each to each" in the natural piety of their immediate sympathetic relations, and their alliances comprise an exponent for Wordsworth's new poetical contract.

Sensations, feelings, emotions: these organize the world and the character of Wordsworth's poetry, which sets its face against the more customary signs of artistic action: wit, intelligence, beauty. The verse is replete with all three of those traditional signs of art, but they arise to our awareness — if they arise at all — only in forms of ruin, of which the idiot boy's ruined — that is to say, innocent — mind is the signifying monkey.

Lyrical Ballads and its preface thus originate a new rhetoric for poetry, one that is founded in — indeed, that culminates — the eighteenth-century traditions of sentiment and sensibility. So complete is Wordsworth's adherence to this recent moral and philosophical tradition that we will look in vain in the preface for any sign that beauty is a function of poetical or artistic practice. When Wordsworth speaks of poetry he gravitates to words like "sensation," "feeling," "pleasure," "emotion" and their cognates, *never* to any form of the word "beauty." The latter enters the preface only three times, in fact, and on each occasion it references a transcendental category of the natural world ("the beautiful forms of nature," for example, or "the beauty of the universe").

Those forms, however, have grown difficult of access. They are especially elusive to the eye of the picturesque tourist, who is Wordsworth's emblem of aesthetic decadence. One begins a passage to those "beautiful forms" — actually, to their precincts, not to the forms themselves — only through a felt confrontation with their desolated apparitions. Wordsworth himself says that the procedure is "indirect" (preface) — that is to say, it is symbolic. "The Ruined Cottage" and "Michael" were both written to make just that point. They are "the simple Wordsworth's" simplest statements of one of the momentous arguments of Romanticism: that when Beauty comes to us now, it comes disguised, veiled, or disfigured.

In Edmund Burke's more spectacular and political terms, the passage (back) to the Beautiful will have to be via its terrorized remains, the world of the Sublime. As James Chandler has shown, Wordsworth follows Burke's lead in a lower — a sublimated — register. Think of The Prelude, that great discourse on the subject of the recovery of Beauty. Wordworth's poem tells us how to regain his — our — Derwent origins, the world of primal Beauty, through a series of "self destroyings," "visionary dreariness," and a regular discipline of fear. We come into the world "trailing clouds of Glory" and pass from thence to darker circumstances. All this is the fallen world of Mountain Gloom and Mountain Glory, where we work out our salvation in fear and trembling. The world of Derwentwater, the world of Beauty, lies somewhere else — beyond, in some magical place where we are cradled in our nurse's or our mother's arms, as we are at the outset of The Prelude, or play children's games at the edge of the sea, as we do at the end of the "Intimations Ode."

This influential Romantic myth has many regenerated forms. All rest in the primary assumption — literally, the working assumption — that "Energy is the only life and is from the Body, and Reason is the bound or outward circumference of Energy." Human life begins not in a primal generative idea but in a primal sympathetic exchange — in a contract, as the preface assumes. This is why feeling and emotion ground every Romantic art: because the Romantic model for these processes of exchange is human and sentimental. They are incarnational and experiential processes, not inherited and transcendental.

Coleridge shared the general Wordsworthian view that poetry, properly executed, would lead one "to see into the life of things." "Imagination" was Coleridge's name for that revelatory function, and he declared that in point of imagination Wordsworth "stands nearest of all modern writers to Shakespeare and Milton" (*Biographia Literaria* chapter 22). He also agreed that "pleasure" was the immediate object of poetry and that the attainment of this object came through "a union of deep and subtle thought with sensibility; a sympathy with man as man."

But Coleridge also argued that Wordsworth's poetry had certain "characteristic defects" which reflected an ill-considered theoretical position. The sign of this deficiency was what Coleridge called Wordsworth's *"matter-of-factness."* The *Biographia* is a polemical effort to establish a correct view of poetry at a moment when its very (Wordsworthian) successes threatened to corrupt a clear understanding of its essential character. Wordsworth's idealization of the language of "low and rustic life" is, for Coleridge, what would later be called "the fallacy of imitative form." It leads Wordsworth into "a laborious minuteness and fidelity to the representation of objects" and "the insertion of accidental circumstances." The only justification for such irrelevant details, Coleridge thinks, is to provide factive grounds for Wordsworth's poetical representations (*Biographia Literaria* chapter 22). For in Coleridge's view, poetry is what Aristotle laid down: a discourse of imitative probabilities. Wordsworth's poems thus "contrav[ene] the essence of poetry," which "is essentially ideal [and which] avoids and excludes all accident" and circumstantiality.

Coleridge's attack on Wordsworth's facticities follows from his primary concern, which is to fence poetry from any theory or practice that would secularize its condition. Thus Wordworth's idea of a "primal sympathy" seems to Coleridge far too mortalized: Hartleian rather than Aristotelian; even, at times, pantheistic:

> And 'tis my faith that every flower
> Enjoys the air it breathes.

This way of thinking and writing tends to establish poetry on the secular ground of material embodiment. Wordsworthian sympathy emerges through what he famously called "a wise passiveness" before the "living forms" of other beings, both natural and human. But Coleridgean sympathy functions at a different — at what he regarded as a higher and more spiritual — level. It is the sympathy emblemized by the theoretical relation between the Primary and the Secondary Imagination, and thus between the eternal act of God's creation and its repetition in the finite mind. The Coleridgean imagination "struggles to idealize and to unify" its often "opposite and discordant" materials" (*Biographia Literaria* chapter 13) and create works that reflect the operation of its ideal origin, the way the natural world reflects the agency of its divine Creator. In Wordsworth, however, creation is an exchange function.

One final, crucial point must be observed. In praising the sympathetic structure of Wordworth's poetry, Coleridge says that this is "the sympathy . . . of a contemplator, rather than a fellow-sufferer or co-mate (*spectator, haud particeps*)." Because Wordsworth's pathos develops at a "meditative" remove from his subjects, the poetry exhibits "the gift of imagination in the highest and strictest sense of the word" — that is to say, of the imagination as Coleridge imagines it in the *Biographia*. Wordsworth stands to his poetry the way God stands to the world he is supposed to have created. Whether or not we agree with that deific view of Wordsworth's poetic practice, cultural history from Arnold and Bradley to Abrams, Bloom, and Hartman has followed that line.

III

However that may be, Romanticism also developed another major type of sympathetic structure. D. G. Rossetti gave it a name in 1848 (see also chapters 5, 6): he called it the "poetry of the inner standing-point." Its greatest exemplar was also its most famous, Lord Byron.

Byron's difference springs from the sympathy he kept with inherited forms — cultural as well as political — whose limitations and even decadences he was well aware of. In *Manfred* he calls this transcendental order "the dead but sceptred sovereigns who still rule / Our spirits from their urns." His transactions with that order, unlike Wordsworth's, took an agonistic form, as we see in the undertaking of *Childe Harold's Pilgrimage*. At the thematic level the poem reveals the ruination of the order of Beauty. The first two cantos come to argue that this ruin is a condition half perceived and half created. The poem's first installment tracks those ruins from England through the decadence of the

French Revolution on the Peninsula to Greece, the *fons et origo* of the Western myth of the "matchless" "Beauty" that Byron explicitly invokes at the beginning of the initial cantos ("To Ianthe"). Cantos 3 and 4 then resume the tale in a post-Napoleonic context in order to engage with various forms of sublimity, which for a Romantic is what remains when access to the order of Beauty has become troubled.

Byron's handling of the Spenserian stanza is perhaps the most striking index of how his verse cooperates in replacing the order of Beauty with an order of Sublimity. From Ariosto through Spenser and on to Thomson and Beattie, this stanza became a kind of emblem of a metrical form that could hold in balanced equipoise a great variety of poetical materials. Byron chooses the stanza and then forces it to perform unnatural imaginative acts. It is an astonishing virtuoso display. In Byron's hands the Spenserian stanza becomes not a thing of Beauty or a refuge of order but either a shirt of Nessus he must wear or a weapon he can wield. Indeed, neither this nor that, but both at once.

Wordsworth's project is slightly but significantly different. He writes his famous preface to install a new form of the Sublime — a psychomachia — in place of the model developed through the extravagant terrors and horrors of the Gothic. In the event Beauty fades from view, absented by the onset of "the picture of the mind" and its intense Glory. This is Wordsworth's way of turning the problem of Beauty — its disappearance and loss — into a *felix culpa*. In that redemptive transformation Beauty ceases to be a problem needing address. What occupies the poet is the need to investigate, map, and ultimately get possessed by the sensational dynamic he has discovered ("I recognize thy glory"). This is the fruit of the dialectic of pleasure, which may be intense and even alienating or, reciprocally, sympathetic and healing.

We do not, in Wordsworth's Romantic scheme, actually make contact with *to kalon*. Instead, we generate or contact a *feeling for* it. The feeling then stands as the emblem and sign of its alienated presence. For this Beauty, in such a romantic imagination, is always "moving about in worlds not realized." This Beauty is a transcendental category, something known only to the impeccable taste of God. Feeling, on the other hand, is quotidian, and Wordsworth will work to convince us that if we cultivate feeling and sympathy, rather than taste, we will position ourselves in as close a relation to the "beauteous forms of nature" as we might need or imagine in this world.

Now let's look again at Byron. Whereas Wordsworth does not struggle against the ideal of an alienated Beauty, Byron does.

> Of its own beauty is the mind diseased,
>   And fevers into false creation:— where,

> Where are the forms the sculptor's soul hath seized?
>   In him alone. Can Nature show so fair?
> Where are the charms and virtues which we dare
> Conceive in boyhood and pursue as men,
>   The unreached Paradise of our despair,
>   Which o'er-informs the pencil and the pen,
> And overpowers the page where it would bloom again?

> Who loves, raves — 'tis youth's frenzy — but the cure
>   Is bitterer still, as charm by charm unwinds
> Which robed our idols, and we see too sure
>   Nor Worth nor Beauty dwells from out the mind's
>   Ideal shape of such; yet still it binds
> The fatal spell, and still it draws us on,
>   Reaping the whirlwind from the oft-sown winds;
> The stubborn heart, its alchemy begun,
> Seems ever near the prize — wealthiest when most undone.
>   (*Childe Harold* 4 stanzas 122–23)

For Byron, the feeling for *to kalon* reaches perfection in a perfection of suffering and unpleasure. Like Laocoön toiling with his serpents, Byron wrestles and tears at the Spenserian form he has both inherited and chosen. As a result, Byron stages his use of the stanza as an emblem of what he elsewhere called, echoing Milton, the last infirmity of noble minds. *To kalon* is a "nympholepsy of some fond despair," "a faith whose martyrs are the broken heart." It defines this state of crucifixion because Beauty has emerged as a disease of human desire and imagination. But note that Beauty is not absconded, as it is in Wordsworth. On the contrary, Beauty in Byron is always being revealed, but revealed divested of its illusions.

Think of how differently Byron and Wordsworth conduct us on their touristic journeys. In "The Ruined Cottage" Wordsworth puts us in the hands of a guide who will instruct us in a forgotten piece of local history. "I see around me here / Things which you cannot see." In a first vision these things appear ruined, terrors and desperations to the feeling mind. But in a further view they emerge through those nightmares as signs of something else we can scarcely see or believe: natural harmony and "tranquil restoration."

That is one moral of the story. The other is that only a privileged Romantic eye has the visionary skill required to perceive this invisible salvation history. This eye has cultivated habits of sympathetic attention. Seeing through it we come to feel "the deep power of harmony" — Beauty's absent presence — in unimagined localities.

By sharp contrast, *Childe Harold's Pilgrimage* escorts us through a series of celebrated European places: nature reserves, on one hand, museums on the other. Nor is Byron a *spectator ab extra* tracking after or along "untrodden ways." So the poem assumes the fame of these famous places as emblems and touchstones of *to kalon*— that "ideal beauty" which possesses "all unquiet things" and moves them to "fever into false creation." Beauty is not an absent presence in Byron, it is fully apparent, known to all. As he moves through its famed localities, the forms of Beauty make an exhibition of their defeatures and illusions. This is the Byronic Sublime: the agony of Beauty in presence and in the present. The *agon* of Byron's Spenserian pilgrimage replicates that story from an inner standing-point.

IV

Byron's *Don Juan* style "turns what was once romantic" — the tormented narratives and pilgrimages — "to burlesque" — the comic manner initiated in the gossipy tale of *Beppo*. The change exposes certain undiscovered resources awaiting a Romanticism that works from an inner standing-point. In the comic procedures of the late poetry — their sources are, significantly, Sternean and Quixotic, not Spenserian and Miltonic — Byron becomes one of his own primary objects of amusement. "The moral of all human tales" is that every tale — *this* tale of *Don Juan* — is one of those tales, and they are all tales of defeat. They are also the teller's tale and, if the reader will agree not to stand aside, reading and paring his fingernails like a god or *spectator ab extra*, they are the audience's as well.

> I have spent my life, both interest and principal,
> And deem not, what I deemed, my soul invincible.
> (*Don Juan* 1 stanza 213)

That view of the matter will set the figure of Beauty on an important new footing. Byron's soul is vincible and, as a result, so will be the soul of his soul, his epipsyche, his art and its emblematic forms: those fragile creatures Julia, Haidée, Aurora Raby. These are the *figurae* of Beauty who preside over Byron's world, "the literary lower empire" which his poem exposes, satirizes, and participates in. The revelation of these splendid minor deities requires submission to the empire of the *Musa Pedestris*. Sublimity is abandoned in order to possess Truth and Beauty in a human register.

Here is one of Byron's restored incarnations of Beauty, a vision of spring in the winter of his Romanticism. He is setting the scene for the climactic feast on Lambro's island with a description of Haidée.

Of all the dresses I select Haidée's:
　　She wore two jelicks — one was of pale yellow;
Of azure, pink, and white was her chemise —
　　'Neath which her breast heaved like a little billow;
With buttons form'd of pearls as large as peas,
　　All gold and crimson shone her jelick's fellow,
And the striped white gauze baracan that bound her,
Like fleecy clouds about the moon, flow'd round her.

One large gold bracelet clasp'd each lovely arm,
　　Lockless — so pliable from the pure gold
That the hand stretch'd and shut it without harm,
　　The limb which it adorn'd its only mould;
So beautiful — its very shape would charm,
　　And clinging as if loth to lose its hold,
The purest ore inclosed the whitest skin
That e'er by precious metal was held in.

Around, as princess of her father's land,
　　A like gold bar above her instep rolled
Announced her rank; twelve rings were on her hand;
　　Her hair was starr'd with gems; her veil's fine fold
Below her breast was fasten'd with a band
　　Of lavish pearls, whose worth could scarce be told;
Her orange silk full Turkish trowsers furl'd
About the prettiest ankle in the world.

　　　　　　　(Don Juan 3 stanzas 70–72)

Such Beauty, neither an absent presence nor a disease of the mind, has cast out the spirits of symbolism. We are not asked to "see into the life of things," as if these exquisite surfaces were insufficient, nor are we led along by the fever of an "unquenched soul." But neither is the attitude anything like Wordsworth's famous "wise passiveness." The latter is a discipline of self-absorption, a method for regaining contact with blocked springs of feeling. Here, however, nothing seems blocked or concealed, the invitation is to discreet, meticulous attention. And so the actual action of the verse, fleet and delicate as Haidée, incarnates its ostensible, its ostensive, subject.

Of course in each case—Wordsworth's, Byron's—the style of address never ceases to be Romantic—that is to say, personal. *Don Juan*, like *Childe Harold*, fixes our attention on Byron and his acts of linguistic expression. But what we watch in *Don Juan* is Byron giving up his faith in unseen seraphs and pledging his allegiance to their mortal models. These are still what *Childe Harold* names "false creations," that is to say, beings fashioned from the mind's idealized and idealizing desires. The difference in *Don Juan* is that their irreality has become the measure of their Beauty rather than the sign of their absence or sublimity. The wonder of these wonderful stanzas rests in their exquisite simplicity and concern for small detail and pure appearance. "The mind's ideal shape[s]" emerge in the pace of the verse and its clear concern that every smallest feature of the language be rendered at something like full value. Every rhyme must be weighed out, every last lingual seen and sounded:

> With v*iands and* sherbets in ice —*and* wine

Syllables assume an absolute condition, even if it means that metrical rules might have to be bent or broken. The syllabic correctness of the line "The tables, most of ebony inlaid" prepares the lovely outbreak of the next line, where the three syllables of "I-vo-ry" insist upon full presence.

Or is it Byron who insists, as if answering the call for attention from these small worldly divinities? Reading the verse Romantically we should say it is indeed Byron who is charming us. But then we will also notice how the charm seems to slip into the language as such, as if Byron were wearing his words the way Haidée wears her clothing and jewelry.

This is verse with designs upon the reader and the reader's responses. The "feeling" in this poetry is no longer in the poem or the poet; it has been licensed to the reader. Is it Haidée's doing that she makes such a striking appearance? Well, presumably she *has* chosen her accoutrements. But that choice having been made — as we may willingly suspend our disbelief to believe — Haidée becomes an apparition, absolute, like an incarnate god. Which is why Byron, observing such a creature stepping—*mirabile dictu*— through his own text, remarks that "it would not be idolatry to kneel" before her.

Underlying this passage is the familiar dynamics of sensibility. But in this passage the dynamic has been arrested so that all its features may be examined. Byron's feelings do not measure this poetic action, as Wordsworth's feelings always do. That is why the poet speaks of "idolatry" in relation to Haidée. As a result, sympathetic exchange here turns to admiration and wonder, and the subjectivity of the Romantic ego is reciprocally objectified.

Haidée as mortal goddess thus comes to index the medium of which she has been made. The "conversational facility" of Byron's poem establishes and maintains its fundamentally Romantic style, which — like all Romantic styles — rides on what Wordsworth famously called "the feeling of my loss." In passages like this, however, we observe Byron using that style to (as it were) execute itself. When "feeling comes in aid of feeling" in Wordsworth, an exchange of human sympathy revivifies a faith in an absent god. *Don Juan's* verse, by contrast, has discovered an exchange of wonderment as the obverse of *Childe Harold's* exchanges of despair. A famous passage in *Beppo* describes Byron's discovery that "Truth and Beauty at their best" are actual human beings, what he calls "Love in Life!":

> Love in full life and length, not love ideal,
> > No, nor ideal beauty, that fine name,
> But something better still, so very real,
> > That the sweet Model must have been the same;
> A thing that you would purchase, beg, or steal,
> > Wer't not impossible, besides a shame:
> The face recalls some face, as 'twere with pain,
> You once have seen, but ne'er will see again;
>
> One of those forms which flit by us, when we
> > Are young, and fix our eyes on every face;
> And, oh! the Loveliness at times we see
> > In momentary gliding, the soft grace,
> The Youth, the Bloom, the Beauty which agree,
> > In many a nameless being we retrace,
> Whose course and home we knew not, nor shall know,
> Like the lost Pleiad seen no more below.
>
> > > (*Beppo* stanzas 13–14)

That this Beauty takes the form of a "Love in full life and length" is a tellingly mortalized view. Temporality rules, and it is transpsychic. The forms seizing Byron are not, as he thought in *Childe Harold*, "in him alone." They are "very real," and if he calls them "nameless being[s]" it is partly because he actually saw them in Florence — "leaning" from balconies, imaged in paintings by Giorgione — and partly to make the witty point that they are more substantial and wondrous than "ideal beauty, that" merely "fine name" for insubstantial things.

Byron's erotic reaction to these charming creatures becomes an emblem for his poetic method. Figured as a flirtation with the reader, this poetry develops a natural (nondivine) creation by sympathy of sexual liaison and attraction — a condition Byron repeatedly develops in the insistent and frank eroticism of his work. In the order of art this kind of creation is a reciprocating material semiosis where author and reader are engaged with each other at the inner standing-point of the poetry they have together undertaken.

While Romantic melancholy recurs through *Don Juan,* then, the poem celebrates creation's escape from its creator. The famous and much lamented nineteenth-century disappearance of god — the god of nature, the god of art — becomes here the locus of a neopagan order of Beauty, whose Real Presence leaves one at a loss very different from the loss felt in the absence of Beauty. The translation of Haidée into Beauty's figural form measures the textual effacement of the Romantic Lord Byron, who becomes, like Swinburne's Sappho, "now no more a singer but a song" ("Thalassius"). This effect — the translation of the Romantic ego into what Charles Bernstein wittily calls a "textual experience" — is the aesthetic gift of choosing to write at an inner standing-point.

The event, once again, contrasts sharply with equivalent Wordsworthian experiences, those spots of time that in a "flash [reveal] the invisible world." The very intensity of such moments effaces what the poet desires to perceive. Byron's Haidéean beauties linger awhile, if not for ever, as if meeting an obligation laid upon them by their remarkable mortality. For Beauty here insists that its particular material virtues be attentively marked. Responding to such Beauty, Byron's verse turns from pyrotechnics to precisions. The verse is more important than the versifier, the creature than the creator.

V

Blake warned his monotheist world against "choosing forms of worship from poetic tales." He was thinking about the way social institutions — thrones, principalities, powers, and dominions, as they are called in the New Testament — turn art into ideology. Byron's idolatry, however, is the reverse of that. In plain terms — and his poetry, like Thomas Paine's prose, cultivates plain speaking:

> I wish men to be free,
> As much from mobs as kings — from you as me.
> (*Don Juan* 9 stanza 25)

That view of freedom is "a vision not before communicated to man," as Shelley called another of Byron's great discourses on freedom, *Cain* (letter to

John Gisborne, January 26, 1822). The passage describing Haidée exhibits the
Beauty of that vision's Truth — as does her story, as do all the stories Byron
tells in *Don Juan*.

These remain to this day countercultural stories. "To what serves mortal
beauty," Hopkins famously asked, and his answer — that it serves to celebrate
the grandeur of God — sees poetry as a form of worship rather than a poetic
tale. Read that way, it is used — as Wordsworth is used, as Wordsworth *wanted*
to be used — to reify an idealist regimen and, more problematic still, an
abstract and moralizing approach to art and poetry.

Byron's answer to Hopkins's question would have been what Laura Riding's answer *was:* "Nothing" (*Anarchism Is Not Enough*). Mortal Beauty is not
in service. It is — for good and ill alike — absolutely free. It is an egg laid by a
free-ranging chicken.

This intellectual stance, like Byron's tomb, is located far from the center of
official culture. Indeed, its cultural displacement has been arranged through a
kind of preemptive strike against some of its key practitioners: Byron, Poe,
Swinburne, in the nineteenth century, for instance; Stein, Laura Riding, and
John Cowper Powys in the twentieth. The intellectual claims of Byron's work
are regularly discounted, even by his admirers. He is represented as a great
force of nature — Key West rather than the idea of Order thereat. So, "When
he thinks he is a child": this is what cultural mandarins like Goethe and
Arnold, impressive creatures in their own way of course, tell us about Byron.

They have worse things to say about Poe. Artists from Baudelaire to
Balthus and Borges understood the importance of Poe's art and ideas, just as
they recognized Poe's immediate Byronic source. Only when we take our
view from the anglophone academic center does that history fade out of the
light of common day. Its disappearance might be more lamented than the disappearance of god, so lamentable to the high priests of the imperium. The
fate of Beauty I've been tracing here — *its* crisis and apparent "decay" — is
precisely a *historical* phenomenon, and — more precisely still — the legacy of
a culture committed to choosing forms of worship over poetic tales. Worse
still, turning poetic tales into forms of worship.

"The death of a beautiful woman," Poe notoriously observed, is "the most
poetical subject in the world." This thought is strictly a poetic tale. A line of
feminist thinking, turned ideological and debased, has followed our early
modern moralists in reading that sentence through a set of realist conventions.
The move drags the sentence away from its wicked, brilliant, and (in several
senses) *original* context. There it forms a crucial moment in Poe's deliberately
anti-Wordsworthian manifesto "The Philosophy of Composition," where a
new type of "philosophic mind" is advanced for the artist. It is actually a mind

that reaches very far back. The mind once insisted on the beauty of the crucifixion of Jesus and of the suffering of St. Sebastian, and it demonstrated, despite all evidence, that nature is a Heraclitean fire and the comfort of the resurrection. Those remarkable poetic tales have remarkable nineteenth-century counterparts. Poe was right. The death of a beautiful woman *is* (*was*) the most poetical subject in that world. For better and for worse is this true.

How Poe's haunting mind fashioned such a poetic tale is a tale we shall have to tell. The tale haunts the margin that separates high culture from popular culture because that is where Beauty's tomb was built, at the public place celebrating her living defeat and death. The place is preoccupied with monuments — small ones like Rossetti's famous sonnet:

> A sonnet is a moment's monument,
> Memorial from the soul's eternity
> To one dead deathless hour. . . .
> (D. G. Rossetti, "The Sonnet")

— and great ones like Delacroix's amazing picture (of) *Freedom Expiring on the Ruins of Missolonghi*. Poe's mind proposed to raise up (and succeeded in raising up) a body of Beauty from the "wormy circumstance" — that comic and crepuscular phrase is Keats's — where Beauty found herself in the nineteenth century. Under the auspices of that mind, Beauty emerges like Venus from the brackish sea of nineteenth-century gift books and periodicals.

I close, then, by giving a few of the characteristic features of this beautiful mind — a "beautiful mind," let me add, about as far removed as one might imagine from a recent preposterous movie named with the same name.

The mind is fundamentally comic and self-aware. It works by a willing suspension of beliefs, not a willing suspension of disbeliefs. It is reverent of irreverence. It is responsible for the invention of the famous "religion of beauty" that flourished in the late nineteenth century. Also for the similar religion of beauty that flourishes today, the religion attended to in Johanna Drucker's superb recent study *Sweet Dreams*. When it thinks it *is* a child — but not in the sense that Goethe meant; rather, in Blake's sense. Like the god it displaces, this mind imagines itself master of a universe which, however, it knows to be fantastic. All its relationships are, as Wordsworth and Coleridge thought, basically sexual and, as Byron saw, as promiscuous as its lovers.

Finally, it cannot live without Beauty. It proves this by signing a contract to live, with others, in impossible worlds, the only truly possible ones, and to procreate there. As Keats knew — "a thing of beauty is a joy for ever" — its children cannot die.

CHAPTER 2

Romanticism, Post-Romanticism, and the Afterlife of Cultural Authority

Old man, 'tis not so difficult to die.

—Byron, *Manfred*

Here now in his triumph where all things falter,
Stretched out on the spoils that his own hand spread,
Like a god self-slain on his own strange altar,
Death lies dead.

—Swinburne, "A Forsaken Garden"

To address the question of cultural authority from the vantage of our early twenty-first century requires some basic historical recollections. We are dealing with a tale that began (more or less) in the 1790s — that is to say, at a moment when standards for cultural authority began to be articulated in the programs of Romanticism. These standards held sway until the beginning of the twentieth century, when the neoclassical turn that we call modernism consciously pivoted from the Romantic inheritance. By the last quarter of the twentieth-century another cultural shift became apparent in the emergence of what has been called postmodernism. This unhelpful term conceals, I think, what is most salient about the second half of the twentieth century: that it involves the first flowering of the Afterlife of Culture. The period has seemed to many more an emergency than an emergence because its ethos sidestepped a direct confrontation with the two previous cultural models, both of them salvation histories. Romanticism and modernism were aggressive movements, self-conceived as moral and cultural revolutions. But the spokespersons of our cultural afterlife inhabit what they take to be a heterodox space — in the innocent jargon of that moment, a heteroglossial field. That diversity made for a difficult passage through those strange days. As we know, postmodern culture is widely deplored for its relativist values, both social and personal.

Assessing the current state of cultural authority — this Afterlife of Culture — calls us to revisit and reinvestigate the commonplace narrative that I just briefly redacted. For the cultural history that unfolds between the end of the eighteenth century and the beginning of the twenty-first exhibits important and still largely neglected discontinuities. These discontinuities are the premonitory signs of the great cultural shift that began around 1930.

Let me try to retell the story. From a European vantage, at least until about the mid-twentieth century, Byron and Scott are the key, indeed the dominating, Romantic figures produced by England, whereas Wordsworth and Austen are barely visible. The English view of these four writers and their cultural authority is approximately the inverse of the European view. Or consider Poe and Whitman. The former is a touchstone and point of departure in a European view, whereas he has from the beginning run sharply against the North American grain. To this day he remains a contested figure in his own country. Although Whitman had his contemporary detractors and enthusiasts in America and abroad as well, he fairly quickly established himself as a great cultural authority in the United States, a position he held through the modernist reaction and into the present day.

These examples are important. They remind us that cultural authority resides in what Marshall Sahlins called "islands of history." Events concurrent in different islands may be, and usually are, perceived and understood very differently. Because History (with a capital *H*) is written by the apparent winners, as Walter Benjamin observed, these differences tend to get smoothed away or forgotten altogether. Who were the Savages (with a capital *S*) in the histories told about the European colonization of the New World or in the subsequent westward expansion of those colonists, then called Americans? What is the history of the Battle of the Little Big Horn? For that matter, of the Emancipation Proclamation? The Afterlife of Culture has helped us realize the important complexity of such questions. We begin to know what it means to see through a glass darkly — that it is not a damnation but an ancient and strenuous promise.

Let's revisit that promise by looking at a passage everywhere taken as exemplary of a Romantic idea of authority:

> What is poetry? is so nearly the same question with, what is a poem?
> that the answer to the one is involved in the solution of the other. For
> it is a distinction resulting from the poetic genius itself, which sustains

and modifies the images, thoughts, and emotions of the poet's own mind. A poet, described in *ideal* perfection, brings the whole soul of man into activity, with the subordination of its faculties to each other, according to their relative worth and dignity. He diffuses a tone, and spirit of unity, that blends, and (as it were) *fuses,* each into each, by that synthetic and magical power, to which we have exclusively appropriated the name of imagination. (*Biographia Literaria* chapter 14)

Coleridge himself glosses that magical Romantic word, Imagination, as "a repetition in the finite [mind] of the eternal act of creation of the infinite I AM" (*Biographia Literaria* chapter 13).

Note the progression of Coleridge's thinking. The definition of poetry hangs on the definition of a poem, and the latter is only to be determined by an explication of "the poetic genius." All too soon will the latter be equated specifically with what Coleridge here calls the "poet, described in ideal perfection."

The fame of this passage is so great that we want to be clear about what it is saying and doing. First of all, the phrase "the poetic genius" is not for Coleridge or his audience a synonym for a great or "ideal" poet. This is only a meaning that will emerge later, when Coleridge's polemics for the importance of poets and poetry get modified and culturally translated. Here "the poetic genius" is a term that means something like "muse" or what Plato signified in the term "daimon." "The poetic genius" is not the man or the woman writing poetry but the angel watching over the process.

Or rather, watching over the person undertaking the process. T. S. Eliot will attack the authority of Romanticism because the spokespeople for Romanticism located authority in a special individual person. While Eliot's idea of "tradition" traces its lineage to Coleridge's idea of "the clerisy," the difference between the Romantic and modernist ideas of authority gets sharply defined in this matter of the authority of the individual poet, that figure Eliot famously called "the individual talent."

I do not say the authority of the individual person but the authority of the individual poet. Romantic ideologues by no means celebrate the individual in anything like the way Whitman does. When touchstone Romantics like Wordsworth or Coleridge make arguments for authority, they call our attention specifically to the poet. If he is a man speaking to men, he is also something more exalted as well, as we saw in the passage from the *Biographia Literaria,* or as we see in this equally famous passage from Wordsworth:

What is a Poet? To whom does he address himself? And what language is to be expected from him? He is a man speaking to men: a man, it is

true, endued with more lively sensibility, more enthusiasm and ten-
derness, who has a greater knowledge of human nature, and a more
comprehensive soul. (preface to *Lyrical Ballads* [1802])

This stress on the cultural authority of the Poet (upper case) will persist well
into the twentieth century. Think again about Eliot's first full-strength attack
on Romanticism, "Tradition and the Individual Talent." Though a polemical
argument about a crisis in culture and cultural authority, the essay remains
Coleridgean in its commitment to poets and poetry as the source and end and
test of reliable authority. From Wordsworth through Arnold to Eliot the theme
is the same: if poetry is debased or ineffectual, if it loses its cultural authority,
the entire social body suffers. That is the situation meditated, threatened by
Tennyson in his exemplary "Lady of Shallot." Nor do any of these men use
the word "poet" in an extended sense, as to include for example writers of
fiction. From 1790 through 1930, if you want to examine problems of cultural
authority, you will — all but invariably — locate your discussion in the question of what Arnold called "The Use of Poetry." Not until 1884, when Henry
James published "The Art of Fiction," will what Coleridge and Arnold argue
for poetry be applied to fiction.

James's view — already well established in European culture — spread
quickly with the advent of modernism. But in framing his argument for
fiction's high cultural authority, James appropriated key features of Romantic
discourse. We see this clearly as James begins his final paragraph, the perora-
tion of his essay:

There is one point at which the moral sense and the artistic sense lie
very near together; that is, in the light of the very obvious truth that
the deepest quality of a work of art will always be the quality of the
mind of the producer. In proportion as that mind is rich and noble will
the novel, the picture, the statue, partake of the substance of beauty
and truth.

Fiction here gains membership with works of high seriousness. And while
James does not mention poetry in his catalog, he crowns the catalog with an
allusion to Keats's "Beauty and Truth," which by 1884 had become a sacred
cultural text. Finally, note that the determining criterion for judging fiction's
moral and aesthetic seriousness remains the Romantic subject. Entering this
discussion some thirty years after James and fifty years after Arnold, Eliot is
able to draw some new distinctions that neither Arnold nor James were yet
prepared to make. Eliot will eventually fold all "serious" works of art into a

single "history" and field of discourse, but in mapping that authoritative cultural space he still assigns to poetry a pride of place and privilege.

To appreciate the significance of Eliot's position we should look again at the grounds of his disagreement with the Romantic view of what poetry is, and hence of its cultural function. The difference appears when he investigates the Romantic ideology of affect: Wordsworth's "spontaneous overflow of powerful feeling," or even its lower-register form, "emotion recollected in tranquility." On the contrary, says Eliot, "Poetry is not a turning loose of emotion, but an escape from emotion; it is not the expression of personality, but an escape from personality" ("Tradition and the Individual Talent," *Selected Essays* 11). To approach poetry in this way is to exalt the individual rather than the work. And by the poet's work Eliot does not simply mean some particular poem or even some body of poetry. He means the social and moral effect that the poet's activities produce in the world. However he abhors their ideas, Eliot always writes respectfully of committed Marxists because he sees in them an honest and coherent moral purpose. By contrast, Romantic affect is for Eliot at best a distraction from high seriousness and at worst self-delusion. "What is Coleridge's Hamlet?" Eliot asks in "The Function of Criticism," and he answers with this severe and telling question: "Is it an honest inquiry as far as the data permit, or is it an attempt to present Coleridge in an attractive costume?" ("The Function of Criticism," *Selected Essays* 21–22).

Of course Coleridge might (and should) answer Eliot in this way: my *Hamlet* is attractive because I have ventured to demonstrate, as precisely and honestly as I can, why it causes such a depth of admiration in me. Coleridge's affective discussion is, so to say, the subjective correlative for the play's deep human truth. Coleridge's pleasure in *Hamlet* is then the affective correlative for the play's harmonizing greatness — its "balance and reconciliation of opposite and discordant qualities." And while Eliot also searches poetry for works that demonstrate the presence of this kind of aesthetic harmony, he dismisses Coleridge's judgments because they ground themselves in feeling. Eliot wants not subjective or affective correlatives, he wants — of course — objective correlatives. So when we ask the question "What is Eliot's *Hamlet*?" we are not surprised by the answer he himself gives in that superb and ornery investigation he published in 1920, "Hamlet and His Problems." Unlike Coleridge, Eliot is determined not to become a bardolator. "Our admiration of the poet," Coleridge argues, leads on "to our sympathy with the poetry." Just so, replies Eliot, which is why we want to approach poetry seriously rather than sympathetically. Poetry — Shakespeare's work itself — is too important to be approached under the guidance of feeling, least of all our own feelings. Judgment, the historical legacy of what he calls "tradition," must be the guide for our feelings, as Virgil was Dante's guide in his passage through Hell.

I think we are now positioned to ask the following question: What is so important about poetry that it should have dominated the discussion of cultural authority for so long? Eliot helps us to an answer.

> Tradition is a matter of much wider significance. It cannot be inherited, and if you want it you must obtain it by great labour. It involves, in the first place, the historical sense, which we may call nearly indispensable to anyone who would continue to be a poet beyond his twenty-fifth year; and the historical sense involves a perception, not only of the pastness of the past, but of its presence; the historical sense compels a man to write not merely with his own generation in his bones, but with a feeling that the whole of the literature of Europe from Homer and within it the whole of the literature of his own country has a simultaneous existence and composes a simultaneous order. [And] I mean this as a principle of aesthetic, not merely historical, criticism. ("Hamlet and His Problems," *Selected Essays* 4)

Like the long passage I quoted earlier from the *Biographia,* this one brings the whole soul of Eliot into activity and, more to the point, into an active promotion of ideas of order and coherence. Observe that the order is ultimately "aesthetic, not merely historical." Or as Coleridge might say, it is an order secured through "Imagination." In such a view, the only history that could count as serious or important would be poetical — "aesthetic" history, as Eliot says. Not history "in fact" but history in and as idea. For both Eliot and Coleridge, this idea of history is Christian.

I have spent a long time discussing these two great representatives of our recent poetic and cultural tradition, for two reasons. First, it's important to see that they stand to each other in a dialectical (as opposed to an evolutionary) relation. Each is committed to a defense of poetry as the engine that preserves the idea — and therefore "the reality" — of cultural order. On one hand this idea gets incarnated in individual subjectivity, on the other as an objective cultural inheritance that Arnold called "the best that has been known and thought in the world." Coleridge and Eliot thus define a cultural dynamic that Blake glimpsed early and defined with exquisite comic accuracy in *The Marriage of Heaven and Hell.* These opposite and discordant authorities, angel and demon, are balanced within a single self-regulating system. Blake could observe this system so acutely because he was, like Robert Burns, a kind of pre-Adamite sultan, gifted with the privilege of historical backwardness. The privilege licensed him to write the following observation, truly astonishing for its 1790 date: "These two classes of men are always upon earth and they should be enemies. Whoever seeks to reconcile them seeks to destroy existence."

As this balance was being negotiated during the nineteenth century, it would itself regularly get weighed up and be found wanting by the Cainite offspring of the marriage of heaven and hell. No one escaped this counterhistory, least of all the great exemplars — Tennyson and Browning for instance — of the more familiar history I've just recapitulated. But certain figures, dramatically recalcitrant, stand out. I want to examine a few of them now because their historical position is so significant. These figures step away or stand apart from modernity's productive war in heaven. They count, however, exactly because they were not easily accounted *for* by the historians who tried to map this cultural territory — Eliot preeminently, but Pound, Leavis, Richards, Blackmur, Brooks, Trilling, and so forth — their name is Legion — down to our last generation: Abrams, Bloom, Williams, Ellmann, Kermode, Eagleton. The Cainites are the auditors of the system in which they too participate. Their hallmark trait is honesty. If we mean to understand the cultural shift — the breakup of the marriage of heaven and hell — that emerged from its modernist demise, these are the key early witnesses.

The first and most obvious of these witnesses is Byron. Consider the following brief lyric:

> Sun of the sleepless! melancholy star!
> Whose tearful beam glows tremulously far,
> That show'st the darkness thou canst not dispel,
> How like art thou to joy remember'd well!
> So gleams the past, the light of other days,
> Which shines, but warms not with its powerless rays;
> A night-beam Sorrow watcheth to behold,
> Distinct, but distant — clear — but, oh how cold!
>
> ("Sun of the Sleepless")

Byron addresses the moon of Romantic Imagination in order to trouble and revise its recent cultural authority. This is not the familiar Romantic moon presiding over those magical landscapes conjured in, say, "The Idiot Boy" or "Frost at Midnight" or the majestic passage that opens the fourteenth book of *The Prelude*. This is not a moon created by a God but a moon made in the image and likeness of a man, by this very poet, as we quickly realize from the transferred epithet in line 2, so artful and self-conscious: "tearful beam." With

Romantic Imagination, one will, Wordsworth tells us, "see into the life of things." So it is here. But according to this poem, that life is human, self-knowing, finally equivocal. Imagination brings knowledge, as the ideology of Romanticism insists. But because the knowledge it gains is far from salvific, Romantic Imagination here flees from its grammar of assent and belief. Byron turns Imagination over for the pitiless study and inspection that it itself has licensed. As it happens, then, the greatest gift of this Imagination is not a Romantic "Joy" — that central term in high Romanticism — but an imperative to complete honesty and candor.

Affect is not dismissed from Byron's poem, however. On the contrary, the poem rides on a fully Romantic "feeling of my loss" which the moon / Imagination has exposed. The poem's Romantic melancholy then gets processed and transformed to a remarkable severity and resolve, so closely correlated with the economy of the verse movement. The message of the poem is thus more or less precisely the same as this passage from Byron's address to another iconograph of Romanticism, "Prometheus":

> Thou art a symbol and a sign
> To Mortals of their fate and force;
> Like thee, Man is in part divine,
> A troubled stream from a pure source;
> And Man in portions can foresee
> His own funereal destiny;
> His wretchedness, and his resistance,
> And his sad unallied existence:
> To which his Spirit may oppose
> Itself — and equal to all woes,
> And a firm will, and a deep sense,
> Which even in torture can descry
> Its own concenter'd recompense,
> Triumphant where it dares defy,
> And making Death a Victory.
>
> (45–59)

Verse of this kind and order proceeds directly from a Romantic ideology, from the authority of intense feeling that we've already talked about. It neither rests in nor abandons that ideology, however. It wrestles with it like Jacob in the wilderness or Byron's Laocoön. In that action it defines the authority of the Byronic countertradition that Swinburne would later identify as Byron's "sincerity and strength" (*Swinburne*).

Byron is especially important because so many who came after him were marked with his mark. His Everlasting Nay, a comical and exuberant cry, was heard but went largely unrecognized in Victorian England, whose exemplary poet — Tennyson — thought satire immoral. Not so in Europe, where Byron gets translated into various forms and languages, some satanic, some dandified, all one way or another — in Byron's terms — "mild apostates" or full-out renegades, "born for opposition." So far as English cultural history is concerned, however, Byron was fenced away and finally set aside until quite recently. Yet even in his exilic period he remained a poetic authority for many in the Anglo-American tradition: Thackeray and the Brontës; Clare and Beddoes; Clough and Swinburne and Wilde; Poe and Melville; closer to ourselves, Auden, Merrill, O'Hara, Veronica Forrest-Thomson, Charles Bernstein.

Other ways of troubling the authorities of the Great Tradition, Coleridgean or Eliotic, emerged throughout the nineteenth century. Nonsense verse (and prose), along with its fellow traveler, children's literature, is one of the most important. Carroll and Lear are key figures of the period, anticipating the full-blown turn to ludic forms that would occur in the twentieth century. The significance of these writers comes out precisely because they compose in minor keys. The poetic masterpieces in this line of work are, on one side, Christina Rossetti's "Goblin Market," and, on the other, one or another of Swinburne's works: the outrageously parodic "Dolores," perhaps, or his self-parody "Poeta Loquitur."

"Goblin Market" could be — has been — turned into a work of high seriousness, not least of all in our own day. But such a turn deadens the verve of this amazing poem. George Saintsbury acutely called it a "feast to the ears," but he was less acute to say that its "metre . . . may be best described as a dedoggerelised Skeltonic" (355, 353). That is a bad way of describing it, a way that flees from the poem's impish glories. Saintsbury had a superb prosodic ear and he was no prude. Nonetheless, he seems to have been slightly embarrassed that Rossetti's masterpiece should have been fashioned from nonsense traditions, children's verse, and sheer doggerel. It has its serious subjects to be sure: social, economic, religious, sexual. All get scored in the minor key lest they interfere with the serious work of the prosodic display, the poem's impersonal *tour de force*. And as a devout Christian Rossetti might have had good reason — good Christian reasons — to subordinate such worldly issues. A modest master, Rossetti did not want her poem read as an attempt to present itself in costumes attractive to strenuous moral Victorians. "Goblin Market" chooses "The Lowest Room" and triumphs in that characteristically Rossettian, that Christian, gesture. One thinks in our own day of Stevie Smith's superb verse or, for that matter, of Eliot's late little masterpiece, the *Old Possum's Book of Practical Cats*.

Or consider the comic line — parallel but different — pursued by Christina Rossetti's close friend and great admirer, the firebrand atheist Algernon Charles Swinburne. The preeminent Swinburne scholar Cecil Y. Lang regarded Swinburne as "the greatest parodist that English poetry has ever seen" (Lang 519). There is more to this judgment than one might realize since a great deal of Swinburne's work is clear parody. *Atalanta in Calydon,* for example, is a serious parody of Greek tragic drama, and most of the poems in the notorious *Poems and Ballads* are tours de force, and astonishing as such.

A poem like "Dolores," for example, strikes a balance at once delicate and forceful, moving as it does with outrageous ease between earnest and jest, as its own punning title declares. The poem's splendor falls from the ludic stance it assumes toward its Christian materials and their Sadean inversions. The implicit argument holds that the Christian and the Sadean economies are co-dependent functions of each other. "Dolores" is thus a triumph of the comic spirit over what Blake called "the wastes of moral law."

All this is plainly exposed in Swinburne's high-spirited letter to Charles Augustus Howell, written when he was composing new strophes for his snake of a poem. The letter is the best gloss "Dolores" has ever had: "I have added four more jets of boiling and poisonous infamy to the perennial and poisonous fountain of Dolores," Swinburne writes, sending along a sample of his infamies in a postscript to the letter:

> O garment not golden but gilded,
> O garden where all men may dwell,
> O tower not of ivory, but builded
> By hands that reach heaven from hell;
> O mystical rose of the mire,
> O house not of gold but of gain,
> O house of unquenchable fire,
> Our Lady of Pain!
>
> O lips full of lust and of laughter,
> Curled snakes that are fed from my breast,
> Bite hard, lest remembrance come after
> And press with new lips where you pressed.
> For my heart too springs up at the pressure,
> Mine eyelids too moisten and burn;
> Ah, feed me and fill me with pleasure,
> Ere pain come in turn.

A second postscript immediately follows: "Since writing the above I have added ten verses to D.— très infâmes et très bien tournés. 'Oh! Monsieur — peut-on prendre du plaisir à telles horreurs?' 'Tu le vois, Justine, je bande — oh! Putain, que tu vas souffrir'—" (Swinburne, *Letters* [May or June 1865]).

But the parodies Lang had mostly in mind were masterpieces like "Poeta Loquitur" and the *Heptalogia* exercises. All that is very high-order nonsense verse, which Swinburne also regularly practiced in private: in his unpublished flagellation farces, for instance, and in wicked and witty jeux d'esprit like his "Fragment of an address from S. Joseph to S. Mary":

> So this is your bloody religion —
> To father your kid on a pigeon?

The epigram is worthy of what Byron mock-seriously called "all those nauseous epigrams of Martial" (*Don Juan* 1 stanza 43). The couplet's domestic vulgate works the words "bloody," "kid," and "pigeon" into a critical travesty of the Christian economy and one of its central ideas: Jesus as sacrificial scapegoat.

Like "Dolores," "Poeta Loquitur" is parody raised to a higher power. Great parody, Lang observed, does not simply involve a critique of its source. It becomes in a sense one with that source, fused with it "like . . . anti-matter to matter." This type of fusion culminates in Swinburne's self-parodies "Nephilidia" and "Poeta Loquitur." Both propose to investigate the authoritative cultural idea that poetry should strive toward a perfect unity of sound and sense, of form and content. The verse executes that idea's comic realization. The consequence is an apparition of writing as pure performance, writing that seems — we remember Auden — to make nothing happen but itself. Playing that game with his language in "Poeta Loquitur," Swinburne achieves what few poets would dare to (or know how to) undertake: a critical satire of poetry itself constructed from an inner standing-point, that is, taking itself as exemplum.

> In a maze of monotonous murmur
>   Where reason roves ruined by rhyme,
> In a voice neither graver nor firmer
>   Than the bells on a fool's cap chime,
> A party pretentiously pensive,
>   With a Muse that deserves to be skinned,
> Makes language and metre offensive
>   With rhymes on the wind.

Mad mixtures of Frenchified offal
    With insults to Christendom's creed,
Blind blasphemy, schoolboylike scoff, all
    These blazon me blockhead indeed.
I conceive myself obviously some one
    Whose audience will never be thinned,
But the pupil must needs be a rum one
    Whose teacher is wind.

Hanging hard on the rent rags of others,
    Who before me did better, I try
To believe them my sisters and brothers,
    Though I know what a low lot am I.
The mere sight of a church sets me yelping
    Like a boy that at football is shinned!
But the cause must indeed be past helping
    Whose gospel is wind!

The theory of poetry at an inner standing-point — a theory Swinburne learned from his friend Dante Gabriel Rossetti — here discovers a kind of perfect form, one completely expressive and completely self-aware. Works like "Poeta Loquitur" at once demonstrate, argue, and perform autopoietic action. They make Nothing happen, they create ex nihilo "the nothing that is not there and the nothing that is." Swinburne thus achieves the comic overhaul and humanist recovery of the idea of the creative Imagination.

Comic writing is alone equal to that kind of task, whose ultimate purpose is to process transcendental categories and ideas — our idols of the cave — back into humane terms and human authority. With such translations comes the reminder that all gods reside in the human breast. Swinburne's poetic argument, simple enough, is yet utterly transformational when read in its historical context: Before Jehovah was, I am. That is not a Romantic idea in Swinburne, it is a neglected human proverb — vox populi, ancient wisdom.

Or consider the example of Dante Gabriel Rossetti, the man who imagined and organized the circle of the Pre-Raphaelites, which grounded the epoch of aesthetic innovation that climaxed in Pater, Wilde, Yeats, and Pound. An unusually self-aware figure, Rossetti conceived his life's work to be the renovation of English, and possibly even the whole of European, culture. As such, the project is founded on the recovery of Dante and the cultural Renaissance that poured out of late thirteenth- and early fourteenth-century Italy. Rossetti's first cultural move, therefore, is to transplant "Dante and his Circle" into nineteenth-century England via a massive act of poetical translation. At the center of this is his translation of Dante's *Vita Nuova*, "The New Life." The aesthetic of the inner standing-point drives the project. This aesthetic draws on several clear immediate sources, especially Keats and Browning: that is, the Keatsian poetics of "negative capability" and the derivate Browning made of it. Rossetti's work is a "Poetry of Experience" in extremis.

The most elaborate explication of the theory of the inner standing-point comes in Rossetti's commentary on his poem about prostitution, social as well as artistic: "Jenny." "The motive powers of art reverse the requirement of science, and demand first of all an *inner* standing-point. The heart of [the aesthetic work] must be plucked from the very world in which it beats or bleeds; and the beauty and pity, the self questionings and all questionings which it brings with it, can come with full force only from the mouth of one alive to its whole appeal" (Rossetti, *Collected Writings*), that is to say, from "one" plunged "alive" within the work's emerging aesthetic field. The clear antithesis to Wordsworth's "emotion recollected in tranquility," Rossetti's proposal is also nothing like "the spontaneous overflow of powerful feelings." Engulfment in Rossetti's work functions as a conscious and deliberated quest *for* an engulfment that one can also live to study: like the sailor in Poe's "Descent into the Maelstrom," like the "young and thoughtful man of the world" in "Jenny"; like the "Jenny"-poet Rossetti, who dares to ventriloquize the reflections of such a man. Negatively capable at an extreme Browning scrupulously avoided, Rossetti's poem invites us to read it as its own supreme example of the poem's central subject: prostitution and the fantasies that envelope it.

Through Rossetti come not only the dark equivalents of Swinburne's comic ecstasies. More important, perhaps, the work forecasts the ominous secret concealed in Eliot's work. For Rossetti's aesthetic program will get retranslated into even more desperate modernist terms. Like Tennyson's doomed Ulysses, the poet of the Last Days is called to become a part of all that he has met — with full conscious purpose and, in such an apocalyptic context, with full knowledge that the quest is Childe Roland's, literally hopeless, lost on all sides. The program is the aesthetics of historicism, as Eliot explicitly declared. But Eliot finesses the doom that awaits such a project, representing it instead as an ideal, if also a stern and demanding, task, "with a feeling that the whole of the literature of Europe from Homer and within it the whole of the literature of his own country has a simultaneous existence and composes a simultaneous order." Like Alfred Jarry later — like Dada, and the derivative Oulipians — Swinburne took this program ludically, which was the humane and sensible thing to do. Taken seriously, which was Rossetti's choice, it defines the Arnoldian condition of being caught between equally impossible worlds. It leads directly to what Keats called "a sort of purgatory blind":

> Or is it that Imagination brought
> Beyond its proper bound, yet still confin'd,
> Lost in a sort of Purgatory blind,
> Cannot refer to any standard law
> Of either earth or heaven?
>   ("Epistle to John Hamilton Reynolds")

Rossetti is a crucial authority, a cultural Jonah who escapes to tell us in appalling detail about the dangers lurking in the world of unbounded Imagination. Swinburne reports only on its glories, but Swinburne was blessed the way, for instance, that Michael Jordan or Shakespeare were blessed. Gifted arbitrarily as such persons are, from birth or from the gods, they set the measures of what can or might or should be done. For them there are no "proper bounds." But when Rossetti, that laboring, scrupulous student and technician, experiences at an inner standing-point, he gets compassed about with darkness and danger. Some of his greatest sonnets — "Life-in-Love," "Death-in-Love," "A Superscription" — are nothing but maps of the territory so seen. Or the remarkable sonnet "He and I."

> Whence came his feet into my field, and why?
>   How is it that he sees it all so drear?
>   How do I see his seeing, and how hear
> The name his bitter silence knows it by?
> This was the little fold of separate sky
>   Whose pasturing clouds in the soul's atmosphere
>   Drew living light from one continual year:
> How should he find it lifeless? He, or I?
> Lo! this new Self now wanders round my field,
>   With plaints for every flower, and for each tree
>   A moan, the sighing wind's auxiliary:
> And o'er sweet waters of my life, that yield
> Unto his lips no draught but tears unseal'd,
>   Even in my place he weeps. Even I, not he.

Extruded out of Romantic art and its conventions of sincerity, the sonnet uses aesthetic clarity, flaunted artifice, to transmute that inheritance. The change is signaled immediately in the first line's startling wordplay: "his feet." What feet, whose feet? Scarcely concealed by the sonnet is its parodic retelling of the scene in Genesis immediately after the fall, when the Lord God walks around paradise looking for Adam and Eve, who are hiding, ashamed of their sin. Those feet are clearly here.

But so are the feet of Eros, the god of Love, who often appears walking up and down the gardens and rooms — the stanzas — of "The House of Life," where this sonnet occupies a culminating position. The feet of Eros are also regularly metrical feet throughout Rossetti's sonnet sequence. The feet are as well the feet of Orpheus, another of Rossetti's familiar spirits. They are the feet of Dante too, as we know from the clear reference that the phrase "this new Self" makes to the Dantean New Life. And so forth. That characteristically aquarian pronoun "He" summons them all to this sonnet moaning round with the many voices of Eliot's intimidating aesthetic inheritance.

And what of that other aquarian pronoun, "I"? The poem sets it in a state of such pure Borgesian uncertainty that we wonder if this is not a drama of psychic dismemberment. Of course it is, but that is the least of the matter. For the pronominal ambiguities emblemize not secrets deeply concealed and buried but secrets flaunted, known, lived, exposed. Because there is no central Romantic self here, Romantic melancholy — Wordsworth's or Byron's — is both absent and beside the point. The tone is flat. Present instead are emblems of sorrow, a whole array of aesthetic objects that appear at once self-conscious and dreamlike.

Let us say what the sonnet appears to want us, reading it, to say: that a "new Self" *has* entered this highly cultivated field. Let us say that we recognize all of this new Self's accoutrements and proper names. What then? So eclectic is the aesthetic encyclopedia by the nineteenth century that even its dominant Christian myths begin to sink back into a more primitive, a more comprehensive, environment. Rossetti pursues this new Self by summoning Dante's late new Christian world. But even that Western world has its pagan sources, an unpayable debt and inexhaustible inheritance. Knowing this, Dante follows Virgil and finds a way to leave him behind. Rossetti then takes Dante for his guide only to discover — what else? — that a new Self emerges. Dante will not guide Rossetti into the new Afterlife he is glimpsing. Like the pagan gods, like the God of Genesis, like Orpheus: Dante and everything he represents is here becoming a part of all that the new Ulysses has met and will meet.

CHAPTER 3

The Life of the Dead: Laura Riding and the History of Twentieth-Century Writing

They became what they beheld.

—William Blake, "Jerusalem" plate 36

From Foolish Island Port Huntlady rose forbiddingly and temptingly above the fictitious emotions it inspired.

—Laura Riding, "Reality as Port Huntlady"

I

The vexed relation between academic and avant-garde writing defines the more or less extreme tension running through much of the past century's culture. In the face of such an antithesis, writing a history of the period's literature is difficult. The names Eliot and Stein divide a world between them, as the names Wordsworth and Byron did earlier, and the division is merely emblematic of so many others that persist to the present: Robert Frost v. H.D.; *Understanding Poetry* v. New Directions; Robert Lowell v. Jack Spicer; James Merrill v. Charles Bernstein.

The problem sketched here initially rose to my mind in 1961 when I read Alan Dugan's first and best book, entitled simply *Poems*. I had just come through college where I was taught that understanding poetry was a worthy and learnable skill. At the time my favorite poets were Lawrence Ferlinghetti and Allen Ginsberg. These were writers I had read on my own — they

weren't taught in (my) school. My favorite teacher at the time said their poems were ugly; this seemed true enough, though I liked them anyway.

Then I read Dugan and was shocked. Unlike my favorite poets, unlike the
modern writers I was taught to honor, Dugan's writing seemed repellent and
cruel beyond anything I had read before.

LOVE SONG: I AND THOU

Nothing is plumb, level or square:
     the studs are bowed, the joists
are shaky by nature, no piece fits
     any other piece without a gap
or pinch, and bent nails
     dance all over the surfacing
like maggots. By Christ
     I am no carpenter. I built
the roof for myself, the walls
     for myself, the floors
for myself, and got
     hung up in it myself. I
danced with a purple thumb
     at this house-warming, drunk
with my prime whiskey: rage.
     Oh I spat rage's nails
into the frame-up of my work:
     it held. It settled plumb,
level, solid, square and true
     for that great moment. Then
it screamed and went on through,
     skewing as wrong the other way.
God damned it. This is hell,
     but I planned it, I sawed it,
I nailed it, and I
     will live in it until it kills me.
I can nail my left palm
     to the left-hand cross-piece but
I can't do everything myself.
     I need a hand to nail the right,
a help, a love, a you, a wife.

PORTRAIT FROM THE INFANTRY

He smelled bad and was red-eyed with the miseries
of being scared while sleepless when he said
this: "I want a private woman, peace and quiet,
and some green stuff in my pocket. Fuck
the rest." Pity the underwear and socks,
long burnt, of an accomplished murderer,
oh God, of Germans and replacements, who
refused three stripes to keep his B.A.R.,
who fought, fought not to fight some days
like any good small businessman of war,
and dug more holes than an outside dog
to modify some Freudian's thesis: "No
man can stand three hundred days
of fear of mutilation and death." What he
theorized was a joke: "To keep a tight
ass-hole, dry socks, and a you-deep hole
with you at all times." Afterwards,
met in a sports shirt with a round wife, he was
the clean slave of a daughter, a power brake
and beer. To me, he seemed diminished
in his dream, or else enlarged, who knows?,
by its accomplishment: personal life
wrung from mass issues in a bloody time
and lived out hiddenly. Aside from sound
baseball talk, his only interesting remark
was, in pointing to his wife's belly, "If
he comes out left foot first" (the way
you Forward March!), "I am going to stuff
him back up." "Isn't he awful?" she said.

First of all, note the literal subject of the second poem. It seems remarkable that someone should have been writing about World War II and its veterans in this way in 1961. Perhaps Dugan's cynical view is partly displaced, for he is writing under the horizon of that first of our ugly imperial nonwars, the "Korean Conflict," and not World War II. In any case, until I read him I hadn't realized that either cruelty or ugliness could be deliberate features of poetry. Baudelaire, like Byron, wrote the romance of evil. Indeed, both just went to prove what I had been taught: that poetry, as another poet said, turns all things to loveliness. According to Matthew Arnold, that was one of its chief functions for the modern world. Dugan's poetry, however, didn't appear to work that way. Of course its technical skills were apparent, but the skillfulness only increased the shock of the verse.

What disorients one even now is the attitude of the writing. "Sweeney among the Nightingales" may be judged an *ugly* and even a mean-spirited poem — may be seen that way and still valued as poetry. Indeed, Dugan's work will help one toward such a view of Eliot in general. Unlike Eliot, however, Dugan's hostility isn't directed toward his human subjects. What Dugan attacks is the poetical contract itself, the marriage bond entered by poet and reader. The couple glimpsed in "Portrait from the Infantry" are not the object of the poem's wrath. Rather, they are left untouched by the poem, almost innocent, certainly unknown. As such they seem to judge both poet and reader, whose impulses to adopt some kind of moral posture toward the man and his wife are short-circuited by the text.

For its part, "Love Song: I and Thou" literalizes Dugan's view of the relation between the poet and his reader circa 1961. It summarizes his mordant interpretation of Literature (capital *L*) and Culture (capital *C*). The well-wrought urn, according to Dugan's poem, is at once marriage and crucifixion. That reading is not aimed at the poem's human subjects, however; its target is the instrument — poetry — that society in Dugan's time uses to see and "understand" those subjects.

Dugan is not attacking poetry "as such." Hindsight exposes the historical location of his view as the particular cultural form of modernism articulated through New Criticism's ideal of the well-made poem. A paradigm subject for New Critical readings — Dugan's poems are brief self-contained lyrics structured in irony — this antithetical writing functions as well as it does because it so perfectly parodies the object of its critique. Dugan's poetry is satire that has become what it beholds. Consequently, the very academicism of Dugan's poetry — so unlike the work of Ferlinghetti and Ginsberg — locates it as a type of postmodern "anti-aesthetic." Its countercultural reading of the documents of civilization is licensed by the intimacy of its relation to those documents. Like the antiquarian Benjamin, Dugan knows whereof he speaks. His *Poems* were first published as volume 57 in the Yale Series of Younger Poets.

Dugan interests me now because he throws the problems of the relations of modernism and its aftermath into sharp relief. Much contemporary writing sets "literature against itself," as Gerald Graff observed in 1979. In this sense Dugan is very much a postmodern writer. Yet in his writing procedures he seems worlds apart from recognized postmodern literary movements like Oulipo and Language Poetry.

I think we can illuminate these complications by reconsidering briefly the way modernism institutionalized itself in the late twenties and thirties. The central figure in this brief recapitulation of history is Laura Riding, who saw, more clearly than most at the time, that the culture of modernism was precipitating a set of crisis conditions for poets and their writing. Her decision to abandon poetry finished her critique of modernism — fundamentally a self-critique — which she had begun self-consciously in the mid-twenties. That critique and decision are important for understanding the subsequent history of poetry, especially in the United States.

II

In January 1927 Eliot reviewed four books for *The Nation & Athenaeum*, including Stein's *Composition as Explanation*, recently published (November 1926) by Hogarth Press. The subject of the books, and of the review, is "the future" of writing, of language, of art; in particular, the "postmodern" future that he sees lying beyond the cultural upheaval that had begun some twenty years earlier.

Eliot is not happy with the future he sees forecast in the books under review. One of them, John Rodker's *The Future of Futurism* (1926), imagines an epoch dominated by two kinds of writing: on one hand, "a pantheon of super-Mallarmés for a smaller and smaller public," and on the other "a completely Americanized" and "popular literature" (Eliot, "Charleston, Hey! Hey!" *Selected Essays 595*). Confronted with the example of Stein, however, Eliot sees no "warrant for believing [with Rodker] that our sensibility will become more 'complex' and 'refined'" when that new day comes. For Eliot, the future according to Stein is "precisely *ominous*" of "a future ... more simple and ... more crude than that of the present." Eliot ends his review in no uncertain terms:

> her work is not improving, it is not amusing, it is not interesting, it is not good for one's mind. But its rhythms have a peculiar hypnotic power not met with before. It has a kinship with the saxophone. If this is of the future, then the future is, as it very likely is, of the barbarians. But this is the future in which we ought not to be interested. (Eliot, "Charleston, Hey! Hey!" 595)

Eliot's review caught the attention of Laura Riding, who responded in the long essay "T. E. Hulme, the New Barbarism, and Gertrude Stein," the fourth part of which appeared in the June 1927 issue of *transition*, Eugene Jolas's new avant-garde journal. A brilliant appreciation of Stein's work, Riding's essay involves a critique of the contradictions of "high modernism." Her argument is simple: Hulme, Pound, Eliot, Joyce are all alike in holding to normative (classical) standards for art. That commitment, however, necessarily runs counter to "the devotion of the modern classicist to originality" — a devotion that Riding calls the "romantic weakness" of modernist aesthetics (Riding, *Contemporaries and Snobs* 185). A perpetual embarrassment, the contradiction produces the irony pervading modernist writing.

In Riding's essay, however, the irony is driven back on itself — doubled and double-crossed, as we see when Riding quotes Allen Tate's summary judgment on modernist practice. Here irony rides again, only this time — in Riding's repetition — its face is blank and pitiless as the sun: "the important contemporary poet [read: T. S. Eliot] has the rapidly diminishing privilege of reorganizing the subjects of the past" (Riding, *Contemporaries and Snobs* 182). By contrast, according to Riding, Stein "makes it new" by utterly depersonalizing her work, her writing being a plunge into the absolute of contemporary ordinariness.

> Everybody is unable to understand her and thinks that this is because she is too original or is trying too hard to be original. But she is only divinely inspired in ordinariness. . . . She makes [language] capable of direct communication not by caricaturing language in its present stage — attacking decadence with decadence — but by purging it of its discredited experiences. None of the words Miss Stein uses have ever had any experience. They are no older than her use of them. (Riding, *Contemporaries and Snobs* 188–89)

That is more than a superb "reading" of Stein, it is a judgment on recent cultural history. Residing, like New England's Emily Dickinson, at a cultural center, all men nonetheless said "What" to Stein — her brother, the reviewers, Pound, Eliot — and many still do. But as Riding's early essay shows, the perplexity or dismay over Stein's work reflects a critical inadequacy in her readers, not a failure of her work. This is why John Ashbery's 1957 review of *Stanzas in Meditation*, the poem finally published after twenty-five years, made a date with history.

A lot of remembering had to be done at that point. It would take another quarter-century for a momentum to be built for Stein's extraordinary achievements; nor was it Stein alone who had been lost to view, as the name "Laura Riding" itself declares. But now, after the work of Ashbery, William Gass, Lyn Hejinian, and a strong group of academic critics, we don't need lessons in reading Stein. What we require is a clearer grasp of her critical significance for modernism.

Riding's essay once again serves us well. More than a defense of Stein, it is a powerful early critique of Eliot and high modernism — all the more powerful for having come from such a central figure as Riding then was. Furthermore, the essay's own critical agenda stands apart from its dialectics of defense and attack. Consequently, as we read the essay now we discern the emergent outlines of four distinct postmodernisms.

The first is Stein herself. The second of these "first" postmodernisms is — modernism itself, or at least one version of it. The paradox of that statement is only apparent. By the late twenties the rich diversity of modernist writing had grown more volatile and entropic, as Eliot's review suggests. Artistic adventures began to be imagined as achievable programs, as if the practical work of imaginative writing were begging for greater ideological self-definition. The shift is very clear in Riding's essay, which frames its arguments in terms of distinct cultural constructs. Reading it now, we see with renewed clarity how much of the modernism that descends to us is a cultural reconstruction.

We "learned to be modern," as Gail McDonald has shown, in determinate ways. "High modernism" is one of our "first" postmodernisms: an academic line spun out of the Fugitives, mortalized in New Critical classrooms, and practically instituted in a network of writing programs. (Its great antinomy, as Riding saw, is that other "first" postmodernism called "Stein.") To many, of course, this massively influential academic line is modernism wearing its Easter clothes. Professional and fastidious, it would culminate and implode in our recently deceased Age of Theory, when the priesthood of culture, meditating its self-contradictions, has gone to war with itself and often, to its disgrace, with poetry and imagination as well. Eliot's 1927 review forecasts that war.

And then we have the world of the objectivists, a crucial "first postmodernism" in its own right. Rooted, like Stein, in early modernist writing, especially the work of Pound and Williams, the objectivists focus a long and complex tradition. So far as American writing is concerned, this is the postmodernism that — as Blake might have said — kept a divine vision through more than forty years of wandering in high academic deserts. From Zukofsky, Oppen, Reznikoff, and Rakosi to Black Mountain, the San Francisco Renaissance, the Beats, and the New York School: its defining moments are Zukofsky's An "Objectivists" Anthology (1932) and Donald Allen's The New American Poetry (1960).

This latter "first" postmodernism passes unobserved, perhaps necessarily, in Riding's essay, and I shall leave the subject to others. The importance of the objectivist project and aftermath, like the importance of Stein, is now in any case clearly realized. The same cannot be said of the fourth postmodernism sketched in Riding's essay — the postmodernism I name after Laura Riding.

In my view, this line embraces as well Nathaniel West, late Fitzgerald, writers of the 1930s like Kenneth Fearing, and Melvin Tolson's *Harlem Gallery*. It appears alternately played out and savage, pure or cynical, embrained and fantastic, and it even has a distinguishable academic presence: Lowell (particularly the early Lowell), Dugan, Berryman, Plath. Drawing attention to its disfigured features, the work constructs a special kind of writing against writing, an often morbid anti-aesthetic. Death is the mother of such beauties; but then Laura Riding was uncompromising in equating death with the truth of (modern) art.

This particular postmodernism interests me partly because it carries within itself important explanatory powers. Harry Mathews names Laura Riding as one of his angels of the presence, Charles Bernstein takes her as a point of departure. Those are eloquent historical facts, although some of Riding's oldest supporters regard them as monstrous facts. Whatever, they supply a missing piece in the complex puzzle of our fifth postmodernism — that is to say, the postmodernism of Ashbery, J. H. Prynne, Oulipo, and Language Writing, the postmodernism of Thomas Pynchon, William Vollmann, and Kathy Acker, of Crozier and Longville's English anthology *A Various Art* and Ron Silliman's American counterpart, *In the American Tree*. When we speak of postmodernism today this fifth column is what we probably have most in mind — at least if our dialect is writing rather than theory, and the art of writing rather than the writing of culture.

This fifth postmodernism is notably anti-aesthetic and often disfigured — a ludic world swinging between John Cage and Charles Bukowski, Hunter Thompson and Paul Auster. Kathy Acker's splendidly outrageous apothegm — "the demand for an adequate mode of expression is senseless" (Acker, *Empire of the Senseless* 113) — measures the distance this work puts between itself and our Kantian traditions of art and culture. Surrealism is an important precursor here, as we know from the work of Ashbery, Oulipo, and certain poets associated with Language Writing, like Michael Palmer. Equally important, however, is a stylistic feature that calls attention to itself: I mean the line's self-conscious acceptance of art's mortality and limits. The (dis)-figure of Parody presides — happily, for the most part — over this culminant postmodern scene.

Distinctive formations, these five postmodernisms are yet closely connected to each other, and the year 1930 marks an epoch. Current artistic disfigurings begin clearly to define themselves in the late twenties and early thirties. The key event is the Great Depression, which destroyed the international network of modernist culture, not least by scattering its people and closing its avant-garde instruments (most crucially, the culture of the small presses and little magazines that had fueled so much of the modernist movement).

Out of the real-time death of historical modernism began to emerge the lines of (postmodern) work I have sketched. All five maintain a close if antithetical relation with the complex modernities from which they were catastrophically disjoined.

These antithetical relations vary wildly, and the contradictions would only grow more severe as efforts were made to resolve them. *Understanding Poetry* constructed a magnificent Temple of Art out of the driving and wayward energies of modernist writing, a completed simulacrum of Pound's *Tempio Malatestiano*. In order to do this, a primer of modern heresies had to be written, and important figures like Stein excommunicated. Hence the emergence of my first two postmodernisms. *Understanding Poetry* and its associated texts — the books and academic journals that promoted the New Criticism — comprise the cultural equivalent of an ethnic cleansing — really, an ethnic self-cleansing.

That story is by now well known, and has been excellently exposed by a number of recent scholars, not least Marjorie Perloff, Cary Nelson, Peter Quartermain, and Allen Golding. A similar set of illuminating antitheses characterize the work of Laura Riding and the postmodernism she epitomizes. In this case we confront a congeries of writers — they are too various to be called a group — who lose or renounce their faith in the traditional missions of art. The attitude doesn't appear simply in renunciations that scatter themselves across the thirties scene. F. Scott Fitzgerald's late collection *The Crack-Up* (1945) is exemplary: "Now it's all as useless as repeating a dream," he writes (100), nor does he mean by this that some radical change has occurred in his work. Fitzgerald's crack-up is the fatal conclusion of a reckless and cynical career. This imagination of disaster will write and rewrite itself for decades to come in a stunning variety of dialects. The early Auden fashioned his own version of this dialect, and its summary statement, perhaps even its dead end, is probably John Hollander's superb self-devouring anti-aesthetic manifesto *Reflections on Espionage* (1976). So far as poetry is concerned, however, the line begins with Riding's amazing parable on the modernist scene, *The Life of the Dead* (1933), a work that in a happier world would be required reading in all courses on modernism.

III

To appreciate the radical and — if one's point of view is poetry as such — perhaps even the nihilist character of Riding's critical line, we have to recover the terms through which her work was defined. These are already apparent in her essay on Stein, where Riding sketches the problems that arise when "the meaning and the making of a poem become two separate elements" (*Contemporaries and Snobs* 143). "Criticism now actually precedes the demonic eloquence of

Nathaniel West or the political workmanship," Riding observes, and the consequence is a growing inclination among poets "to assume the position formerly belonging to philosophy." Poetry thus gradually converts itself "into a dogmatic science pledged to the refinement of . . . values" (*Contemporaries and Snobs* 143 – 44). The result of this philosophical turn, Riding shrewdly remarks, "has been to put an unnatural burden of faultlessness on the poem"(*Contemporaries and Snobs* 144).

This is a more polite version of what Kathy Acker will say about imaginative writing sixty years later: "The demand for an adequate mode of expression is senseless." In the latter, the word "adequate" is telling, for it implicitly defines the context to which both Riding and Acker are responding. "Adequate" reaches all the way back to 1857 when our modernist ways of thinking about literature and the world were initially formulated for us by Matthew Arnold. In his inaugural lecture in the Poetry Chair at Oxford, "On the Modern Element in Literature," forms of the word "adequate" run through the text, defining what is for Arnold the determinate characteristic of the "Modern Element in Literature": adequacy, and the "intellectual deliverance" it is supposed to bring.

But: what if this Arnoldian demand for an adequate mode of expression should be judged problematic ab initio — as it is so judged by Riding and Acker? Acker responds (negatively) to Arnold's demand — from outside and below normative cultural institutions. By contrast, Riding repudiates the Arnoldian demand for poetic adequacy in high cultural — that is to say, in Arnoldian — terms.

Like many others, Riding's is a story of a lapsed faith. At first she thought, following Arnold, that poetic form met the demand for an adequate mode of expression. Her thought is apparent in the series of books, poetical and critical, that she published between 1926 and 1930. Nonetheless, even in these writings she appears an equivocal advocate for poetry. By 1933, Riding's apostasy from poetry is a foregone conclusion, as one sees from those two remarkable works published that year: *The Life of the Dead,* a poetic tour de force, and *Poet: A Lying Word,* her last integral book of poems.

The crucial book in this history is, I think, the prose collection of 1928, *Anarchism Is Not Enough.* Like *Kora in Hell* and *Spring and All* earlier, Riding's book attacks the distinction between philosophy and poetry, thought and imagination. With *Anarchism Is Not Enough,* however, the attack comes by undermining the traditional distinction between fiction and nonfiction, stories and criticism. The book opens with a series of strange texts that read, for the most part, like literary criticism. These culminate in "Jocasta," a ninety-page critique of high modernism. The book then prints a series of story-like texts that seriously disorient the reading process, for they are woven into cryptic relations with what appear to be further critical essays. In the piece titled "An Anonymous Book," for example, the distinction between fiction and nonfiction turns into a game, and the work reads like nothing so much as a text by Borges or Calvino. The book concludes with a "Letter of Abdication," a literary (anti)manifesto whose genre status is completely equivocal:

> I have done all I could for you, but the only consequence is that you are the same as always. I had the alternative of ordering a general massacre, but I should then have had to go away anyhow. It is simpler to abdicate. It certainly makes no difference to the situation whether I leave you behind dead or alive. (Riding, *Anarchism* 209)

And so forth. Here and for the rest of this "Letter" the "I" and the "you" are open texts, unstable as to their identities. Remarkably, the prose could not be more sure of itself, more clear and directed, more self-identical.

> You do not know what you are. I will tell you, though it will not make the least difference to you, since you do not know what you are. You are a conceit. You are what you are not. You are a very fine point of discrimination. (Riding, *Anarchism* 209–10)

Texts like these cause one to reflect on the "essays" in the first part of the book. The major "critical" work of the collection, for example, is the piece titled "Jocasta," which at its most apparent level is a critique of certain representative high modernist cultural figures — primarily Spengler, Eliot, and Wyndham Lewis. The essay's title, however, disturbs its critical performance. If it observes the modernist scene as a play of "blindness" and "self-destruction" — and it does — this judgment comes to us under an ambiguous and self-critical sign. It is as if the "essay" (if it is an essay) were the self-conscious monologue of one of the principal characters anatomized in the essay. Not for nothing, we realize, does the book conclude with Riding's "Letter of Abdication." Her brilliant prose, like her equally brilliant verse, continually finds itself devouring itself. *Anarchism Is Not Enough* takes no prisoners.

In assuming the role of Jocasta — in writing criticism-as-story and story-as-criticism — Riding was inventing a distinctive postmodernism, a model for an anti-aesthetic. Riding's "essay" might be read as if it were not an essay at all, but a kind of "story" about the contemporary world. A woman poet-writer called Laura Riding names herself Jocasta, thereby turning her subjects —

that is to say, her readers as well as the nominal "subjects" of her critical essay (Spengler, Eliot, Lewis)—into Oedipal figures. These figures will subsequently be anatomized in the book's penultimate performance, the study of contemporary sex titled "The Damned Thing."

But this way of thinking and writing spells disaster for an Arnoldian view of poetry and culture. For poetry in particular, the skunk hour is at hand. Riding called it "the life of the dead."

> Poetry always faces, and generally meets with, failure. But even if it fails, it is at least at the heart of the difficulty. . . . (Riding, *Anarchism* 14)

> Poetry is defeat, it is the absolutism of dissatisfaction. . . . Poetry therefore seems idle, sterile, narrow, destroying. And it is This that recommends it. (Riding, *Anarchism* 36)

These kinds of dicta—they appear throughout *Anarchism Is Not Enough*—represent Riding's last Arnoldian ditch. They forecast her coming repudiation of poetry as an adequate mode of expression. But they also function as dark songs before the sunrise she always kept in view: a writing that would be equal to itself, no more and no less, a writing that would discover "perfection" by freeing itself from unnatural burdens of faultlessness.

> Only what is comic is perfect: it is outside of reality, which is a self-defeating, serious striving to be outside of reality, to be perfect. Reality cannot escape from reality because it is made of belief, and capable only of belief. Perfection is what is unbelievable, the joke. (Riding, *Anarchism* 15)

Like Dugan's infantryman, what Riding theorizes of poetry is the joke. This passage glosses the serious joke titled *Anarchism Is Not Enough,* all of whose texts are finally "unbelievable." Like Ashbery's "Impossible" Stein, like *Finnegans Wake* and the great thirties romances of John Cowper Powys, Riding's book is taking modernist irony to another level, one not easily defined but instantly recognized by anyone who has read Perec and Borges and Calvino, Harry Mathews and Charles Bernstein. Riding's work—like West's, like Fitzgerald's—announces the end of the (poetic, Arnoldian) world. It is a message others did not want to hear or believe. High modernists like Pound and Eliot were explicitly working to salvage the Arnoldian legacy—"these fragments I have shored against my ruins"—and if Pound ultimately arrived at a dark version of Riding's position (in the postmodern *Drafts and Fragments*), Eliot came to rest — so at least we are told by those who fashioned his postmodern monument — in the bosom of tradition.

To the degree that Riding's line gained currency within the Arnoldian academy, the priests of culture (and many of the poets as well) began to treat poetry as case history. This has been a typical way of making something out of Riding's idea that poetry is the "absolutism of dissatisfaction." It is a way, as we know, that Riding herself despised. Nonetheless, her work helped to license such a writing. The spectacular rise of psychoanalytic criticism in the thirties is another act of shoring up against the ruination that Riding's way of thinking seemed to entail. Kenneth Fearing's satire, self-inflicting as it is, forecasts those later poetic vocations that pledged their allegiance to Alfred Alvarez's savage god. If the manifest content of poetry seemed to grow increasingly nightmarish, its latent content might be critically reimagined to serve the needs of culture. The poet (as Jocasta, as Oedipus) might be healed and redeemed by the medicine man.

Riding herself did not of course follow either of the high modernist paths we call Eliot and Freud. Riding is important for us to remember just because she refused both civilization and its discontents. Her renunciation of poetry is not an act of pique or despair. Its nihilism is really just another Gay Science. Renouncing poetry was part of a highly self-conscious decision to address the problems of modernism in what she regarded as more fundamental terms.

IV

When Riding renounced poetry, she did not give up writing. She turned to her "stories," as she called them, to texts like those we saw in *Anarchism Is Not Enough*. In 1982 she collected a group of these splendid things in an augmented reissue of her 1935 collection, *Progress of Stories*. Her preface to this new edition, reflecting on what she originally had in mind, returns to her critique of modernism. The critique now takes the form of a distinction between the (modernist) view that poetry is an art, and preeminently an art of making — "make it new," "il miglior fabbro" — and her different idea that writing should be what she came to call "a telling." "The initiating impulses from which the stories issued were not impulses of *art*, not impulses to construct stories but to *tell* stories" (xxi–xxii).

"Make it new"; "tell it like it is." Riding's work hangs in the unbalanced history those two notorious phrases have come to define. This is why her ideas about poetry have begun to acquire such significance for us. Her view of writing-as-telling evolved critically from her initial view of writing-as-making. And this evolved distinction extrapolates her refusal of the modernist ideal of "faultlessness" ("adequacy" in the Arnoldian sense).

In its place Riding developed a fully articulated anti-aesthetic. The latter grows out of a foundational contradiction in her work: on one hand her insistence on the truth-function of writing; on the other her refusal of the ideal of poetic adequacy. In this situation the question arises: How can an inadequate art function as truth? For Riding, an answer to the question emerged when the truth of writing turned from something that might be *made* to something that might be *told*. If poetry is *made* into a corpus of (reified) ideas, its truth — including that very fact about itself — remains to be *told*, and may yet be told even by itself.

Riding undoes the conception of poetry as the dream of Adam. In her mind, one wakes from poetry — if one wakes — not to find the truth of its dream but the truth that it is traumatic illusion. In that discovery poetry begins to be read — begins to read itself — as a "telling" revelation of the inherited illusions of *poiesis:* the enacted truth of what she called the "Life of the Dead." To this truth and this life poetry in the twentieth-century would be supremely adequate. Writing (in her terms, "telling") became the horizon in which the ideals of adequacy and truth could function. In "writing" one could "tell" "the truth" about "poetry" as a twentieth-century event.

The figure of truth-as-telling recommends itself to Riding because it keeps the linguistic act in a conscious state of process, a permanent condition of impermanence. The writer as *homo faber,* a common twentieth-century figure, threatens to fetishize his own work. So poems may be turned into freestanding linguistic forms, as if living on their own. Moving against that modernist grain, Riding's thought anticipates Alan Davies's wonderful postmodern proverb: "Truth is lies that have hardened" (*Signage*). Writing that is a telling rather than a making keeps the work from being elevated in relation to the reader. Reciprocally, it prevents the reader from fetishizing the work.

One sees what Riding is about with special clarity in a work like *The Life of the Dead,* which is a reading of modernist writing as self-mystified and alienated from itself. The poem makes its argument wearing a grotesque and ludic mask, the outward and visible sign of an inward and spiritual (dis)grace. Nor can this act of writing be imagined — by author, by reader — as separate from its subject. The poem's modernist ironies, which elsewhere might have served to insulate the text from its own corrosive fires, are purposely driven to extreme forms. A Lord of Misrule, the poem thus delivers its Lukácsian judgments in a Benjaminian, perhaps a Kafkaesque, voice.

Such poetry is a historically located cultural form — a specifically postmodern form made possible, perhaps inevitable, with the collapse of the

Arnoldian aesthetic. The latter argued for the necessity of poetry in an age of science, as we know, and the argument depended on preserving poetry as a discourse set apart from the "multitudinousness" of immediate experience. Riding inherited that view and initially accepted it. As her career developed, however, she came to believe that poetry had become just another "wisdom profession" — along with religion, science, and philosophy. Assimilated to the purposes of official culture and the state, it could no longer seriously pretend to the critical function — "intellectual deliverance" — Arnold had set aside for it. Nevertheless, much modern poetry continued to entertain the Arnoldian pretension, and with the coming of New Criticism the pretension was taught as a dogma of the schools. In a perspective like Riding's, the contradiction within the cultural scene had thereby become absolute.

From these circumstances emerged that early postmodern antithetical form of reading "against the grain" epitomized in the Frankfurt School. According to that way of thinking, for example, the wasted land of *The Waste Land* is first of all the poem itself — which is exactly what William Carlos Williams thought; for the writing isn't to be taken as separate from its subject, it is to be understood as alienated from its subject. And one would want equally to show that the *Four Quartets* might just as well have been called *The Waste Land,* for in point of an alienated eloquence, the later poem is if anything even more extreme and self-mystified. Or call *The Waste Land* "Quintet for a Windy Night." Both are splendid works of poetry, but both are devastated, devastating; and never more so than when gazing, like the little girl in *Poltergeist,* into their hearts of light.

The faith — the bad faith — of Eliot's work can and should be traced through the culturally dominant writing practices of the next several decades. As more and more poets became institutionalized, the critical question for their work would become: if one writes out of the schools, what truths do you have to tell? One important answer turned out to be: "the life of the dead." Lowell's historical importance for twentieth-century poetry lies exactly in his understanding (a) that this was his great subject, and (b) that he took his subject from his high modernist forebears.

That, at any rate, was how Riding came to read the works of modernism. She is a humanist who would unburden writing from the illusions of art. For her, the truth of writing is measured in the opportunities offered by the language, rather than by an "art" that would come to the rescue of the language. As a story like "Reality as Port Huntlady" shows, creation is a game to be played, not a structure to be raised (unless we spell that word with a z). The story genre proved especially useful for Riding just because her cultural world continued to think about poetry in an analogy to a transcendental superstition (i.e., divine creation). Riding writes stories that are explicitly de-creative, stories that unravel the fictions of creativity and the superstition of the art of writing. Character, event, scene, topic, style: because in *Progress of Stories* all such textual features can't be separated from "the telling" that produces them, the true subject of her stories appears as the acts of writing itself.

And so we come back to Alan Dugan. "Love Song: I and Thou" is a poem "telling" truths about modernist art and poem-making that are not customarily told. An evident allegory, the text proposes a way of making poetry possible in a time and world wracked by self-deception. It is a critique of the well-made poem, and the poetics of the well-made poem, from the inner standing-point of the well-made poem. That it mounted this critique in the context of the forties and fifties, when New Criticism flooded the market of education, is crucial to remember.

For this writing has chosen to include itself in its critical assessment of culture. Dugan's infantryman — his "sound" baseball talk, his "awful" remark — are taken into the writing as a measure of truth-telling: so far as Dugan's poem is concerned, culture can gag on the escapist triviality of the baseball talk (which is yet one of this man's saving graces) and the savagery of an "awful" comment which in the poem turns as well to a mark of his fearful, complicit understanding. Here is a man of Dugan's world and time, "mon semblable, mon frère," and Dugan is not about to treat him the way Eliot dealt with Sweeney.

Nevertheless, Dugan is not celebrating his world, the way Williams celebrates Elsie, or Zukofsky his son. Altogether less romantic, Dugan "tells it like it is." That edged contemporary phrase seizes the day of Dugan's dark enlightenment. Not all postmodern writing is as pitiless as Dugan's or Plath's, of course. Even in a dark time there is a life of the living, but that was the subject of a different (post)modernism altogether: the (post)modernism, as Riding was one of the first to see, of Gertrude Stein, whose sweetness and light were to be inherited by writers like Lyn Hejinian and Alice Notely.

Riding's stories, especially her modern fairy tales, are part of this tradition, which is escapist in no pejorative sense. One wants to write above these texts the proverb out of Job: "And I only am escaped alone to tell thee" (1:15). The escape of such writing is a conscious fiction, and the sign of a spiritual emergency in the world beyond the writing. Stories like "Reality as Port Huntlady" supply an altogether different explanation for why "humankind cannot bear too much reality." To Eliot, we cannot because our natural condition is fallen. But Riding's view is that we cannot bear "reality" by definition, for Eliot's understanding and use of the word are inhuman. "Reality as Port Huntlady" is a telling of reality like it is: in this case, as a modern fairy tale for deconstructing realist illusions.

If, on the other hand, you choose to sojourn on the darkling plain or in the waste land — if and when that is the fiction of one's writing — then Dugan's work, like Larkin's in England, also tells it like it is. These are the tales from the dark side, tales not of fictive escapes fashioned in natural desires but tales of divine mercy and the cruel (or ludicrous) myth of historical redemption. "Love Song: I and Thou" fractures the fairy tale of the crucifixion.

That is Dugan's world, where modernist ideology — Dugan's inheritance — is weighed and found wanting. It is also the world raised up in much of the academic writing of the past sixty years, whether purposefully (as in Dugan's case) or not (I leave you to supply your own examples here). In this respect Dugan writes more like the Pound of *Drafts and Fragments* than the Pound of the *Pisan Cantos*. Both of these late, postmodern Poundian texts are indispensable resources, but whereas the work of 1947 is what Schiller would have called a "naive" poem, Pound's last text is clearly "sentimental": completely self-conscious about its modernist history and pretensions. *The Pisan Cantos* — the fiction of a recantation, a mythos of redemption — are important exactly for what they do not know about themselves: as if Pound could tell the postwar story of himself as the Suffering Servant and expect one to take that story seriously. These cantos got exactly what they deserved — the Bollingen Award, that Arnoldian imprimatur given to the best, the most shocking, American melodrama of 1947 (a play that includes the bestowal of the award as part of its text). *The Pisan Cantos* are great because of the monstrousness they have projected for us, for the cultured world they celebrate and epitomize. As poetry they are grotesque, a parody of their own miserable splendors. They are exactly what Riding had in mind when she wrote *The Life of the Dead*. For everyone working in the industries of culture — and that certainly includes ourselves — they issue a terrible warning.

Dugan's "Memories of Verdun" represents itself as another recollection of World War II, which it is. We might also read it as the postmodern commentary of a survivor of modernism. I'll spare you the details of such a reading, which you can work up on your own, if you like. I'd rather leave you with his poetry than with my prose anyway:

MEMORIES OF VERDUN

The men laughed and baaed like sheep
and marched across the flashing day
to the flashing valley. A shaved
pig in a uniform led the way.

I crawled down Old Confusion, hid,
and groaned for years about my crime:
was I the proper coward, they
heroically wrong? I lived out their time,

a hard labor, convict by look and word:
I was the fool and am penitent:
I was afraid of a nothing, a death;
they were afraid of less, its lieutenant.

PART TWO

Philological Investigations

CHAPTER 4

My Kinsman Walter Scott

In 1884 "The Art of Fiction" was not what it was in 1819, or what it would become in the late twentieth-century aftermath of James's celebrated modernist manifesto. For James the art of fiction is *unam, sanctam, catholicam,* as is clear in his dismissal of the distinction, authoritative since Scott, between novel and romance. "I can think of no obligation," James writes, "to which the romancer would not be held equally with the novelist." And why? Because the issue is a craft issue: "the standard of execution is equally high for each [and] it is of execution we are talking" (James, *Literary Criticism* 56). Fair enough, one thinks. But when we recall what James says about Trollope in the same essay, we realize there are many rooms in the house of fiction, not all of them to James's fastidious taste:

> Certain accomplished novelists have a habit of giving themselves away which must often bring tears to the eyes of people who take their fiction seriously. I was lately struck, in reading over many pages of Anthony Trollope, with his want of discretion in this particular. In a digression, a parenthesis or an aside, he concedes to the reader that he and his trusting friend are only "making believe." He admits that the events he narrates have not really happened, and that he can give his narrative any turn the reader may like best.
>
> Such a betrayal of a sacred office seems to me, I confess, a terrible crime [and] it shocks me every whit as much in Trollope as it would have shocked me in Gibbon or Macauley. It implies that the novelist is less occupied in looking for the truth . . . than the historian, and in doing

so it deprives him at a stroke of all his standing room. To represent and illustrate the past, the actions of men, is the task of either writer, and the only difference that I can see is, in proportion as he succeeds, to the honour of the novelist, consisting as it does in his having more difficulty in collecting his evidence. (James, *Literary Criticism* 46 – 47)

Although James calls Trollope to account, his real target is a far greater one, Walter Scott. Is it part of James's case for an art of discretion that he withholds the master's name at this crucial point? It's difficult not to think so. Scott's name seems written in invisible ink, that favored Jamesian medium, across this passage.

James's argument for a realist fiction, a Flaubertian argument, focuses on the artist's craft — on his ability to create verisimilar worlds that appear to stand on their own — looking, like Robert Browning's duchess, as if they were alive. So far as James is concerned, Scott's work must be at best charming, at worst crude, rarely rigorous. How could one possibly install an integral imaginative world with all those Jedidiah Cleishbothams and Peter Pattiesons, Drs. Rochecliffe and Dryasdust, who come to tell us in no uncertain terms that it is only making believe?

An equally authoritative proponent of the great realist tradition appeared a half-century after James to explain how Scott brought off this feat of art. Consciously anti-Jamesian and anti-Flaubertian, Georg Lukács argues that Scott's greatness is not the product of a "search for form" or some ingeniously contrived "skill" (Lukács 37). It derives from his insight into the precise and complex dynamisms of society and history. This repudiation of aestheticism comes with a critique of traditional, uncritical views of Scott. "What in Scott has been called very superficially 'authenticity of local colour' is in actual fact [the] artistic demonstration of historical reality. It is the portrayal of the broad living basis of historical events in their intricacy and complexity, in their manifold interaction with acting individuals" (Lukács 43).

In developing his case for Scott, Lukács makes two crucial moves. First, he insists that Scott has been mistakenly seen as a Romantic writer. On the contrary, Scott's work is "a renunciation of Romanticism, a conquest of Romanticism," and a repudiation of the "lyrical-subjectivist absolute" (Lukács 33 – 34) that defines the essence of a Romantic art. The latter is epitomized in the heroes of the Gothic and Byronic tradition, and Scott's heroes, Lukács correctly observes, do not get measured in such terms. The second move involves a kind of deliberate amnesia: Lukács says nothing about the elaborate comic apparatus that Scott created to support and transmit his novels to the public. This material seems to have struck Lukács as inconsequential to Scott's great project: the epic portrayal of human beings struggling within a "historical necessity . . . of the most severe, implacable kind" (Lukács 58).

And yet Lukács might have fitted his argument to the Shandean material scattered about the prefaces, postscripts, appendices, and notes of Scott's novels. Lukács, that is to say, might have pursued the implications of one of his most acute insights about Scott: that the books feed off a deliberate and "necessary anachronism." Unlike "post-1848" writers, Scott "*never modernizes* the psychology of his characters" (60), and Lukács shrewdly connects this commitment of the writing to Hegel's view that a true historical insight is only possible "if the past . . . is clearly recognized and experienced by contemporary writers as the *necessary pre-history* of the present" (Lukács 61). In this view of the matter one would have wanted Lukács to treat Jedidiah Cleishbotham, Peter Pattieson, et al. as fictional materials that define more precisely the historical divisions joining and separating the past from the present.

Why doesn't Lukács elaborate that argument? To answer the question I would return to James's critique of Trollope, and through Trollope to the whole line of fiction writers who "bare the device" of their artistic presence. In Scott, "the Author of Waverley" is a character of conscious make-believe; as such he is the determining focus of the fiction's recurrent patterns of comic spell-castings and spell-breakings. For his part Jedidiah Cleishbotham is a similarly fantastic creature, like his many framing and prefatory cronies. All are characters drawn from the contemporary historical setting that is as crucial to the historicality of these fictions as are the scenes and events called from the past. For James, of course, all are equally characters drawn from a primitive stage of the art of fiction.

For Lukács, however, these figures locate a serious problem. They implicitly undermine his key argument about the anti-Romanticism of Scott's work. Romanticism for Lukács is a phenomenon of localities and individuals, and its model is Byronism: on one hand the self-involved tumult of Giaours and Corsairs spinning to issueless exhaustion; on the other an airy or airless vortex, whether comical as in *Don Juan,* or brooding as in *Childe Harold,* Keats's *Hyperions,* Wordsworth's *Prelude.* Scott's work is perceived as different — a representation of processes of historical change whose accuracy stems from Scott's own conservative class and historical position. The "necessary anachronism" that Lukács sees there underpins a Hegelian/Marxist argument about history as a system of dynamic and progressive transformations. The historical dialectic traced out in the work casts what Shelley would call "the shadow of futurity" across a revolutionary history stretching from 1830 to 1930. That coming time is for Lukács both modeled and forecast in Scott's work. The novels comprise a Hegelian act of summation, a pivotal moment in the great historical shift from mercantile capitalism to international socialism.

And the novels might well have been precisely that—in a sense, they *are* precisely that—had Lukács's historiography proved true. In *truth,* however, his reconstruction of history must now seem to us in certain respects as quaint and idiosyncratic as Scott's history has often seemed to others. The quaintness is just inflected differently: in Scott it is antiquarian, in Lukács, theoretical.

Let me say here that these remarks make no pretense to a "higher criticism" of Scott, or for that matter of readers of Scott as eminent as James and Lukács. Scott's work is immense—like Shakespeare's, like James's own—and the history with which it is involved has not, of course, taken any final turn. Lukács's view may once again prove a great resource. But I find it helpful now to recover that early, originary view of Scott-as-Romantic, the view that Lukács was committed to oppose.

In a European perspective he and Byron were predominant cultural presences for almost two generations. They achieved this authority in large part because both constructed world-historical matrices for themselves and their work. They did this Romantically, however, that is to say, by keying their work to the idea of the individual—the cultural quanta named Byron and Scott. On one hand we have a romance focused in contradiction, on the other a romance focused in reconciliation.

If both James and Lukács were out of sympathy with those romances of Romanticism—each for good reasons—James seems to have had a clearer view of the functional presence of Scott's Romanticism in the art of fiction. Scott is not simply a kind of fantastical historian—the "Ariosto of the North," as Byron named him—he makes a parade of his imaginary moves. If, for James, this will never do, Scott nonetheless does it all the time, starting with the game he makes of his books' authorship. The famous act of self-concealment begun with *Waverley* leads directly to the games of the introductions, chapters preliminary, dedicatory epistles, and all their associated paratextual maneuvers. The introduction to the 1816 *Tales of My Landlord* is typical: elaborate, preposterous, and—so far as a Jamesian art of fiction would be concerned—wholly irrelevant to the two "tales" it prefaces. "TALES OF MY LANDLORD," it is headed, "*Collected and Reported by* / JEDIDIAH CLEISHBOTHAM / *Schoolmaster and Parish-Clerk of Gandercleugh.*"

> As I may, without vanity, presume that the name and official description prefixed to this Proem will secure it, from the sedate and reflecting part of mankind, to whom only I would be understood to address

myself, such attention as is due to the sedulous instructor of youth, and the careful performer of my Sabbath duties, I will forebear to hold up a candle to the daylight, or to point out to the judicious those recommendations of my labours which they must necessarily anticipate from the perusal of the title-page.

The comic absurdity of this should not obscure its fundamentally Romantic character. We are entering Never-Never Land in a self-conscious passage of style. More important, by choosing to begin this way Scott ensures that we shall only come to this place with full awareness that we are entering a house of fictions. This is romance at a second order, as it were: not the Romanticism of *The Prelude* or of Coleridge's conversation poems, but of *The Monk, Don Juan,* and "The Eve of St. Agnes." Readers join in this work through a conscious undertaking. That is the contract Scott insists upon.

Or consider the following passage. The voice this time is that of Peter Pattieson himself, rather than his editor and posthumous factotum. It is the opening passage of chapter 1 of *The Bride of Lammermoor.*

> Few have been in my secret while I was engaged in compiling these narratives, nor is it probable that they will ever become public during the life of their author. Even were that event to happen, I am not ambitious of the honoured distinction, *monstrari digito.* I confess, that, were it safe to cherish such dreams at all, I should more enjoy the thought of remaining behind the curtain unseen, like the ingenious manager of Punch and his wife Joan, and enjoying the astonishment and conjectures of my audience. Then might I, perchance, hear the productions of the obscure Peter Pattieson praised by the judicious, and admired by the feeling, engrossing the young, and attracting even the old; while the critic traced their style and sentiments up to some name of literary celebrity, and the question when, and by whom, these were written, filled up the pause of conversation in a hundred circles and coteries.

The wit of that kind of thing — Edward Bostetter called it "romantic ventriloquism" — seems to me beyond praise. The whole game of Scott's art is being put on display — indeed, is being drawn into the fictional space of the text. More wonderfully still, readers everywhere, readers of every kind, are already here as well, imagined into this fiction before they ever knew they were, and awaiting their inevitable encounter with themselves when they undertake this passage. Not every reader of the book in 1819 would have seen and heard Walter Scott within these words of Peter Pattieson — the fiction of Scott's anonymity was still officially intact. But every 1819 reader *was* already involved with "the question when, and by whom the *Waverley* novels were written." Besides, after five years of intense curiosity the truth was spreading that Scott was the "Author of *Waverley*." He wrote this passage explicitly to play with, and on, the rumors, and thus to engage different readers at different levels of awareness. In 1819 Byron was one reader who read that ventriloquized passage knowing its author was Scott — a knowledge he did not have in 1816. Whatever the reader's case in 1819, it would not be long before all would have complete access to the pleasure of such texts.

This kind of writing — so replete in Scott — installs neither a truth of fact nor a truth of fiction but the truth of the game of art. It is more than make-believe, it is conscious make-believe. Scott wants to draw his audience into his fictional world by assuming and playing on his reader's distance and disbelief. His Romantic reconciliations therefore begin in an imaginative deployment of a nonfictional idea of truth and reality. There can be no Romantic escape to imaginary worlds unless there is first of all a real world, or rather the idea of a real world, from which to escape. Scott's game of authorship forms a crucial part of his elaborate method for imagining the audience's idea of the real world and integrating it into his fiction. More than that, the game largely organizes his general method for directly involving his audience in a social, a cooperative venture of fictional making. Ultimately this encompasses more than the epical creation of past history, it necessitates the invention of the present as well. Scott doesn't create that history by himself, however. His fictions become the means by which individuals, isolated readers, are led to become willing participants in this large cultural enterprise.

A full apparatus of complex narrative-framing did not appear until 1816 when the "Author of *Waverley*," with three novels out, initiated the "Tales of My Landlord" series. Nevertheless, the rhetoric of this Author's fiction is operating from the start. *Waverley* begins with an "introductory" chapter in which the (unnamed) Author discusses his fictional procedures with the reader. It is important to the book that this chapter is not separated from the main body of the tale as prefatory or paratextual matter. So here we discover as a first order of fictional business that the book's title, subtitle, and narrative genre are part of the fiction called *Waverley; or 'Tis Sixty Years Since*. We also discover that the Author and his reader have been incorporated into the fiction as assumed presences, quasi characters. The complete continuity of these materials is clear from the first sentence of the embedded tale that the Author has set out to tell — the first sentence, that is to say, of chapter 2. Having informed us about his book, what it is and how it got made, he ends

"Chapter I. Introductory" and begins "Chapter II. Waverley-Honour. A Retrospect" thus: "It is *then* [my emphasis] sixty years since Edward Waverley, the hero of the following pages, took leave of his family to join the regiment of dragoons in which he had lately obtained a commission." "Then" signals the time of the Author's book whose clock was set going in the previous chapter. But this Author is no mere rhetorical device, he is — according to his own text — a historical personage. We see this from another shrewd deployment of the word "then." It comes earlier, in chapter 1: "By fixing then the date of my story Sixty Years before this present 1st November 1805, I would have my readers understand . . ."

1st November 1805! But, gentle reader, here and now it is 1814, 'tis nine years since what you are reading was written.

The telling of this tale and its reading, the writing of it, the publishing of it, the printing of it (think of its famous and crucial title page): all have been incorporated into the work, which emerges as a complex textual condition. Sixty or so years later James will deplore a fictional imagination that could so bare its own artifice as to produce such regular, casual demystifications as the Author's reference to "the hero of the following pages."

Some of the most distinguished Scott scholars have urged readers to forgo these paratexts and begin further along, where the text picks up the actions of the core characters — for instance, with *Old Mortality,* in chapter 2, "The Wappenshaw." Disagreeing with scholars like Angus Calder, Jane Stevenson, and Peter Davidson isn't easy to do, but on this matter I must disagree. To enter this great book at chapter 2 means you will not read Jedidiah Cleishbotham's "dedicatory epistle" to the first of the *Tales of My Landlord* series or Peter Pattieson's introduction to *Old Mortality* and the oral narratives and anecdotes comprising the archive of his materials.

Why are these matters and materials important? Simply, they establish the basic narrative terms of Scott's fiction. These are Rabelaisian, not Jamesian, terms. They are terms that have far more in common with works like *A Glastonbury Romance, At Swim-Two-Birds, If on a Winter's Night a Traveller, Gravity's Rainbow,* and *Lanark* — that is to say, they make the subject of tale-telling an explicit and governing preoccupation of the fiction. The first series of *Tales of My Landlord* comes in four volumes headed with Jedidiah Cleishbotham's "introduction" where we are introduced to Scott's complex scene of tale-telling. The key figures here — others will be invented later — are Cleishbotham and his "young friend" Pattieson, the "now deceased" recensor of the tales. Then come the first two stories, *The Black Dwarf,* in the first volume, and *Old Mortality,* which makes up the next three volumes. Each of the stories has a chapter "preliminary" where Pattieson gives "a short introduction," as Cleishbotham explains, "mentioning the persons by whom, and the circumstances under which, the materials thereof were collected."

All this is simply — simply?— to put the reader in the most self-conscious relation to the whole fictional enterprise that the books are unfolding. *The Black Dwarf*'s preliminary chapter literally italicizes its purpose here with a series of passages that are set off from the main body of roman print. The first of these comes at the point where the subject of the Black Dwarf gets raised in an adventitious way, as a mere rhetorical flourish in the speech of a character whose name we never learn and who figures not at all in the tale his casual remark will provoke. Cleishbotham's interest is piqued, and Pattieson's narrative records the moment: "'The Black Dwarf!' said *my learned friend and patron,** Mr Jedidiah Cleishbotham, 'and what sort of personage may he be?'" The phrase in italics, *my learned friend and patron,* is asterisked to the following "note by the publisher":

> We have in this, and other instances, printed in italics some few words which the worthy editor, Mr Jedidiah Cleishbotham, seems to have interpolated upon the text of his deceased friend, Mr. Pattieson. We must observe, once for all, that such liberties appear only to have been taken by the learned gentleman when his own character and conduct are concerned; and surely he must be the best judge of the style in which his own character and conduct should be treated.

So we are dealing with a text, with a tale, where the boundaries between fiction and fact have been made as porous as possible. Characters in the tale revise the text and its publisher turns out to be himself a minor character of its fiction.

Scott's framing personages pass from our ken throughout the core narrative treating the Black Dwarf, but they return in a new and even more remarkable way when the tale of *Old Mortality* begins in volume 2. Here the preliminary chapter comes with another witty typographical signal. Printed entirely in inverted commas, the chapter explicitly mediates Pattieson's narrative through the editorial devices of Cleishbotham, Pattieson's "worthy and learned friend and patron." This is how the chapter begins:

> "Most readers," says the Manuscript of Mr Pattieson, "must have witnessed with delight the joyous burst which attends the dismissing of a village-school on a fine summer evening. The bouyant spirit of childhood, repressed with so much difficulty during the tedious hours of discipline, may then be seen to explode, as it were, in shout, and

song, and frolic, as the little urchins join in groups on their play-ground, and arrange their matches of sport for the evening. But there is one individual who partakes of the relief afforded by the moment of dismission, whose feelings are not so obvious to the eye of the specta-tor, or so apt to receive his sympathy. I mean the teacher himself, who, stunned with the hum, and suffocated with the closeness of his school-room, has spent the whole day (himself against a host) in controlling petulance, exciting indifference to action, striving to enlighten stupid-ity, and labouring to soften obstinacy."

The narrative now comes with a series of footnotes authorized by the pub-lisher and signed by Cleishbotham, who annotates a text he seems to have scripted from Pattieson's original manuscript. But if the inverted commas tell us this text is a verbatim report of Pattieson's original, they also, by that very move, raise a question about their textual status. Why put all this material in quotation marks at all, why not simply give Pattieson's "preliminary" exposi-tion as it was given to us in The Black Dwarf? That text's series of minor scrip-tural interpolations "may [here] be seen to explode, as it were, like restive schoolchildren, into a condition of indeterminate freedom." Just how faithful is Cleishbotham's recension to Pattieson's original? Scott works to provoke that question here for the same reason that he plays on the public mystery of his authorship at the beginning of The Bride of Lammermoor. He is urging his readers to attend to the artifice of the work before them.

From such attention comes awareness of the reflexive character of this chapter's own small narrative. Quasi-allegorical in form, it draws an explicit set of parallels between Old Mortality, on one hand, and Peter Pattieson on the other. Both cultivate a knowledge of the past and work to preserve it from effacement. The education of society being the purpose of what they do, the running references to schoolmasters and schoolchildren are much to the point. Both are, moreover, irregular kinds of instructors, operating with their tales outside the schoolroom. If all of these relations are easy enough to regis-ter, they prepare us to see others of equal, perhaps even greater, note. Putting the entirety of the chapter in quotation marks underscores the further paral-lel, never far from our attention in any case, between the recensor Pattieson and his literary agent Cleishbotham. And that equation entirely "explodes" the Chinese box structure of the narrative as a whole. The legendary figure of Old Mortality dissolves and mutates into the invisible Author of Old Mortality, "renewing . . . the half-defaced inscriptions of the past" with his fragile fictions.

Framed as they are in this way, Scott's narratives regularly, if also randomly, break out of their narrative enclosures into the freedom of self-conscious romance. Often the moments are brief — for instance, in chapter 23 of *Quentin Durward*. Having been fitted out in disguises by the Syndic Pavillon and his family, Quentin and Lady Isabelle set off from Liège. Two brief paragraphs intervene at that point before the narrative returns us to the central characters.

> The instant her guests had departed, Mother Mabel took the opportunity to read a long practical lecture to Trudchen [her daughter] upon the folly of reading romances, whereby the flaunting ladies of the Court were grown so bold and venturous, that, instead of applying to learn some honest housewifery, they must ride, forsooth, a damsel-eranting through the country, with no better attendant than an idle squire, debauched page, or rake-helly archer from foreign parts, to the great danger of their health, the impoverishing of their substance, and the irreparable prejudice of their reputation.
>
> All this Gertrude heard in silence, and without reply; but, considering her character, it might be doubted whether she derived from it the practical inference which it was her mother's purpose to enforce.

The passage inevitably turns our attention to Scott's own novel, whose core situation Mother Mabel has simply summarized. The text all but demands that readers be prepared to formulate the response that Gertrude did not give. What *is* the point of romance fiction, of reading *this very book*? For Scott that is precisely a historical question and problem. There are fifteenth-century answers to the question and there are nineteenth-century answers, as this very text reminds us. And in our time as well we have to address and respond to that question all over again.

Scott's books are all conscious efforts to reflect on this question, if not to answer it directly and definitively. The problem is vigorously brought forward in *Kenilworth*. Lounging in her barge on the Thames, Elizabeth starts a conversation among her courtiers about the relative merits of bear-baiting and play-going as civil entertainments. When Shakespeare's plays come to focus the issue, the scene immediately turns reflexive. To an 1821 reader the debate initially seems comical, a moment for the reader to stand back from the tensions of the romance narrative and observe for a brief space from a cool and amused distance. But the Author of *Waverley* is at his ventriloquist games once again, most plainly, I suppose, when he uses Elizabeth as his mouthpiece in the following text:

> And touching this Shakespeare, we think there is that in his plays that is worth twenty Bear-gardens; and that this new undertaking of his

Chronicles, as he calls them, may entertain, with honest mirth, mingled with useful instruction, not only our subjects, but even the generation which may succeed to us. (2.5; chapter 17)

The text says "this Shakespeare" but it (also) means the "Author of *Waverley*."

But the scene involves far more than a diverting moment of reflexive comic relief. When the queen asks for some serious judgments on the question, Sussex begins by debunking the "nonsensical bombast and irreality of the theatre," arguing that blood-sports are more effective means for training a vigorous citizenry. Leicester responds "in behalf of the players" by arguing that the "rants" and "jests" of the theater are useful means of social control. The plays

keep the minds of the commons from busying themselves with state affairs, and listening to traitorous speeches, idle rumours, and disloyal insinuations. When men are agape to see how Marlow, Shakespeare, and others, work out their fanciful plots . . . , the mind of the spectators is withdrawn from the conduct of their rulers.

Cutting as it does into the fanciful plots of Scott's own fictions — of *this* fiction even now being transacted by the reader — Leicester's argument seems highly equivocal, and not least because Leicester is himself at this point deeply involved with a fanciful and labyrinthine plot of his own. So when the queen quickly responds, "We would not have the minds of our subjects withdrawn from consideration of our own conduct," the remark applies as much to the immediate technical management of Scott's fiction as it does to his work's social and educational aims.

The stakes are raised further when the Dean of St. Asaph's weighs in against the theaters in a puritan diatribe that carries, for later readers, the substance of historical prophecy — that is to say, the coming closing of the theaters. Shakespeare and his fellows promote lewdness, profanity, social discontent — "blaspheming heaven . . . slandering . . . earthly rulers [and] set[ting] at defiance the laws both of God and man." The queen answers by drawing a distinction between moral and immoral artists, and she closes her response with the passage, quoted earlier, about how artists like Shakespeare bring "useful instruction [to] the generation which may succeed to us." In this highly reflexive moment, that remark comments as much on the work of Scott and Byron as on Elizabethan theater. Unlike Byron, Scott is not like those artists denounced by the Dean of St. Asaph's, he is the contemporary avatar of Shakespeare. This passage is the fictional equivalent of Scott's view of Byron's ideas about "religion and politics." Nor is it the first time he would use his fiction to mount a critique of his famous contemporary and close acquaintance. The judgment on King Richard that comprises the final paragraph of *Ivanhoe* involves a concealed reference to Byron. When Scott ends by (mis)quoting Johnson's "Vanity of Human Wishes,"

> He left the name at which the world grew pale,
> To point a moral, or adorn a TALE.

one can scarcely *not* recall Byron, as "rash and romantic"—these are Scott's words—as the crusading king the words describe. For it was Byron who reclaimed those lines for his age when he reworked them at the end of *The Corsair:*

> He left a Corsair's name to other times,
> Linked with one virtue, and a thousand crimes.

It is important to remember that these reflexive interludes in Scott's work are rarely disengaged from the central plot action. This scene, for example, takes place when Leicester's duplicity toward the queen has thrown him into a dangerous position. Caught in his own web of deceit and the complicating intrigues of the court, he almost decides not to join the river party. "Go, say I am taken suddenly ill," he tells Varney, "for, by heaven, my brain can sustain this no longer." But politics forces him on, and throughout the scene we are kept as much aware of the extreme tension and anxiety in his mind as of the external events transpiring before us. As is almost always the case, Scott explicitly gives us the formula governing the fictional events: "Leicester . . . endeavoured to divert his thoughts from all internal reflection, by fixing them on what was passing around . . . abstract[ing] his thoughts and feelings by a strong effort from every thing but the necessity of maintaining himself in the favor of his patroness." This formula explains why "what was passing around"—the eventualities of the action—here serves primarily to index Leicester's mental state and "internal reflection." And by giving the formula so explicitly Scott ensures that his readers will not lose themselves in the psychology of the characters and forget what is passing around—forget, in other words, that we are transacting the passages of this text. Leicester's behavior is a textual signal indexing Walter Scott in 1821—as involved in the current issues raised by his tale-telling as his characters are in the events of the plot.

This reflexive inertia persists in his work to the very end—I mean, to late works like *Count Robert of Paris,* a preposterous undertaking that yet involves a remarkable feat of style. The book opens with a series of reflections on the decadent world of the Byzantine Empire, which will be the scene of the action, and in particular on the euphuistic style practiced at the court. In attempting to re-create that world for his tale, Scott moves to become what he beholds, as it were. And so we get the remarkable chapter 4 where Scott lays out a pastiche of the decadent and all but unreadable prose of the Byzantine historian Anna Comnena.

The event is comic both at the textual and at the narrative level. It is also boldly reflexive given the way Scott has put the issue of Byzantine style at the foreground of his tale. For Scott's own style has over the years grown increasingly elaborate and formulaic. To pastiche Comnena's prose at this point is to fashion a critical measure of his own.

That second-order awareness is written large in the reception history, though perhaps not exactly as Scott himself would have liked. For readers have closed the book on Scott's book as a stylistic disaster. That judgment, plainly correct, also seems to me not correct enough. *Count Robert of Paris* isn't a good book, a "neglected work." It *is* all but unreadable. But the book, and in particular its opening chapters, involves an important and characteristic feat of style: the pastiche of Comnena's notoriously decadent prose. The move turns reflexively on Scott's own tale, suggesting that we might register certain equations between Comnena and Scott.

Of course many great writers — Wordsworth, for instance — have no ability or even interest in that kind of self-conscious art. It is as essential to Scott as it is to Byron, however, which is why the last book I want to talk about, *Ivanhoe,* is such a key work. In the perspective I am taking here, it is clearly Scott's masterpiece.

Consider again, briefly, the Johnson quotation that ends the book. The witty contemporary reference to Byron is grounded on another, more immediate turn of wit. For the name of King Richard isn't simply, in the context of *Ivanhoe,* a proverbial figure. He points a moral in *this* work and he is *this* tale's adornment. It is as if the ultimate point of Richard's spectacular career would only be reached when he was turned into a character in Scott's novel.

That way of conceiving his book, as if it were the measure of history's meanings and events (and not vice versa), is written into every line of Scott's text. And Scott is explicit about this matter, though his forthrightness comes in his usual comic ways. Laurence Templeton in his dedicatory epistle tells Dr. Dryasdust that he makes no pretense to "historical accuracy in his details," whether large or small, for his interest in the past is driven by his concern for the present and the future. Part of his present concerns, of course, involves a desire to make contact with Great Britain's historical inheritance. But for Scott this always means renegotiating our relations with the past. Simply, Scott's histories — the eventualities of the past as well as the textualities of the present — are all living inventions.

So one of *Ivanhoe*'s chief concerns is that we never lose sight of its inventiveness. To measure its success in this regard, think of the main line of attack the book drew out. None of Scott's fictions treat their historical details so cavalierly or break so far from the conventions of novelistic realism. The following sequence of passages typify Scott's manner of proceeding:

> Our history must needs retrograde for the space of a few pages, to inform the reader of certain passages material to his understanding the rest of this important narrative. (chapter 28)

> Our scene now returns to the exterior of the castle, or preceptory, of Templestowe, about the hour when the bloody die was to be cast for the life or death of Rebecca. (chapter 43)

> A flight of steps . . . leads up to a low portal in the south side of the tower, by which the adventurous antiquary may still, or at least could a few years since, gain access to a small stair within the thickness of the main wall. . . . (chapter 42)

This is the sort of thing that provoked James's dismay. To read texts of this kind, he says in his condescending 1864 review of Scott's work, we have to become like children at sunset listening to bedtime fairy tales (James, *Literary Criticism* 1199–1204).

And perhaps we do, though not in the sense that James intended. For what *Ivanhoe* requires is a reader with the understanding and conscious intelligence that Scott calls for in these very passages. The passage from chapter 28 continues, for instance, like this: "[The reader's] own intelligence may indeed have easily anticipated that, when Ivanhoe sunk down, and seemed abandoned by all the world," and so on. Or when, in chapter 40, Scott tells us that it "becomes necessary to resume the train of [the Black Knight's] adventures," he addresses us directly: "You are then to imagine this Knight, such as we have already described him . . . , mounted on his mighty black charger. . . ."

Such a reader is summoned, as usual in Scott's works, at the outset of the book, in Laurence Templeton's fictitious dedicatory epistle. One of the most artful of Scott's imaginary introductions, it comes to present the case for *Ivanhoe* as a work different from the "idle novels and romances of the day." Templeton's fussy prose wanders in and around that issue until he finally admits that he has only written a "romance," or fictitious narrative and that its admittedly "slight" character "might not suit the severer genius of our friend Mr. Oldbuck." So instead of contradicting the charge of idleness, Templeton craves the reader's, and Dryasdust's, indulgence:

> If, therefore, my dear friend, you have generosity enough to pardon the presumptuous attempt, to frame for myself a minstrel coronet, partly out of the pearls of pure antiquity, and partly from Bristol stones and paste with which I have endeavoured to imitate them, I am convinced your opinion of the difficulty of the task will reconcile you to the imperfect manner of its execution.

Representing himself as a pasteboard minstrel, Templeton develops a dialectical figure composed of a modest and unassuming author on one hand, and a perspicacious yet indulgent reader on the other. But that rhetorical figure, like the character Templeton, flaunts its own pasteboard condition, as we see in the very next passage where Templeton closes his introduction with a discussion of his tale's principal archival source, the "Wardour MS." At this point the structure of Scott's textual masquerade comes into full view, for Sir Arthur Wardour, the owner of the precious MS, is none other than a character we have already met, not in ordinary factive history, but three years earlier, in 1816, in the fictitious realms of *The Antiquary*.

All this is amusing and artful enough, but when we enter the history proper called *Ivanhoe*, we find Scott driving us to negotiate the text as a consciously imaginary realm. The texts already cited underscore this urgency of the tale, but its self-conscious fictionality is coded far more deeply and thoroughly. Several times in the book, for example, all at strategic and widely separated points, the Author of *Ivanhoe* recalls us to his archival sources. The first comes to authenticate the decorative details of the tournament at Ashby, in chapter 7. A second, halfway through the book, supports the representation of De Bracy's barbarous treatment of Rowena. In this case the Wardour MS is a second-order authority attesting the truth of another text, the legitimate *Saxon Chronicle*. What is especially interesting here is the way Scott's text calls attention to the imaginary status of its own principal source text:

> Such and so licentious were the times . . . recorded by Eadmer; and we need add nothing to vindicate the probability of the scenes which we have detailed, and are about to detail, upon the more apocryphal authority of the Wardour MS. (chapter 23)

In Scott's fictional world, vindicating probabilities is not the function of spurious texts like the Wardour MS. It is rather an authenticating sign — a true index — of Scott's powers of historical invention. So it is that details "given at length" in the Wardour MS become the authority for winding up various narrative threads in the last chapter of the book.

As the romantic history of Ivanhoe, Rowena, Rebecca, and Bois-Guilbert develops, the book puts more and more of its fictionality on display. The narrator's outspoken interventions, noted earlier, are relatively muted in the first half of the book, but with that famous "blast of a horn" before the gates of Torquilstone at the end of chapter 21, Scott explodes his fictional spaces and makes the making of the book one of his least disguised central subjects. From the horn blast to Ulrica's ominous chant of death at the end of chapter 31, the entirety of the book's central action moves through a series of reflexive turns that emphasize the constructed character of the narrative. The horn blast and its narrative consequences signal how involved Scott means to be in the fortunes of his tale and how attentive to that involvement his readers are expected to be. Scott, it seems, takes his fictional art every bit as seriously as James. Only the touch is lighter, perhaps less pretentious.

Consider just a few of his most wonderful acts of creation. His two chief comic characters, Gurth and Wamba, compose and deliver a formal "letter of defiance" to Front-de-Boeuf and his allies that tranforms a central chivalric ceremony to low comedy (chapter 25). The Magician of the North then manages a parodic resurrection from the dead (in three days no less!); and at the climax of the action, when Ivanhoe rides against Bois-Guilbert to decide Rebecca's fate, Scott brings off his most brazen conjuring trick. The Templar unhorses the wounded hero with his "well-aimed lance," an "issue of the combat all had foreseen" since it's clear Ivanhoe has no possible chance of defeating Bois-Guilbert. But though the Templar's shield is barely grazed by Ivanhoe's lance, Bois-Guilbert nonetheless "reeled in his saddle . . . and fell in the lists," dead. "'This is indeed the judgment of God,' said the Grand Master, looking upwards, '*Fiat voluntas tua!*'" Scott's will indeed be done. This belated trial by combat doubles and completes the work begun in the lists of Ashby — that "passage of arms" whose meaning is here fulfilled to the law of the letter: "In the beginning was the deed."

Which is to say — after Goethe, after Scott, after Derrida — "the pen is mightier than the sword." In the death of Bois-Guilbert — at once a Regency and a Romantic event — we see precisely how it is that a god takes a hand in every stroke.

Like *Don Juan*, so admired by Scott, the world of *Ivanhoe* aspires to Brechtian transparency. Behind both lie other favorite texts: *Tristram Shandy,* of course, but *Don Quixote* and the Rabelaisian corpus even more. All are the works of gods whom we may learn to look upon and live. But generous and good-natured as they are, these greatly illusionistic works suffer few illusions. The two chief parts of *Ivanhoe*, we want to recall, each end in scenes that cast premonitory shadows across the triumphs they bring. The climax of the victory at Torquilstone comes as Ulrica's song of death, whose dark formula hurls this prophecy at the histories of the aspirants of power: "All must perish." And the marriage of Ivanhoe and Rowena, the book's finale celebration, is turned into a literal anticlimax when Scott decides to end his tale with Rebecca's visit to the newly married Rowena. The scene reminds us that while Rowena and Ivanhoe inherit their world, it is Rebecca who represents whatever moral authority that world might hope, however vainly, to possess. This is why, when Rebecca refuses Rowena's well-meaning but absurd invitation to become a citizen of that world, we realize how nicely Scott measures out his sympathic judgments. Rebecca turns away from Rowena, "leaving [her] surprised as if a vision had passed before her." History, Scott is telling us, will pursue that vision for ever — as it will for ever move in fear and trembling of the vision of Ulrica, Rebecca's darker double.

Scott's book also tells us where those two visionary forms, dream and nightmare, may be most helpfully engaged: in the imaginary fields of books like *Ivanhoe*. Pagan and Jew will not truly find a place in English culture until James Joyce and John Cowper Powys have imagined ones for them. The expectation of such a future defines the Romanticism of Scott's work. Cutting across such a Romanticism, however, is what I might label (lamely enough) Scott's "postmodernity": the ironic awareness with which he constructs and pursues his Romantic quest, the awareness that forbids him from turning his poetic tale into a form of worship. Is that complex vision the reason that Victor Hugo, speaking for many, declared *Ivanhoe* "the true epic work of our age?" I'm not sure. But I do know that when Lukács, quoting Hugo (Lukács 77), defined the epic character of Scott's work, he saw it in a very different way. And I suspect, as we all work to recover and re-understand this remarkable writer, that we might begin all over again further back, with Hugo and the other pre-Jamesian intelligences whose readings we might now once again find useful.

CHAPTER 5

Tennyson and the Artists of the Beautiful

> Tennyson . . . the saddest of all English poets, among the greats in Limbo, the most instinctive rebel against the society in which he was the most perfect conformist.
>
> —T. S. Eliot, *In Memoriam*

I

Tennyson is a Victorian sentimental poet. For readers who remain in the or-bit of our great Victorian antithesis, modernism, that fact about his work be-comes a problem. Perhaps even more problematic, Tennyson is a poet who embraced the official culture that made him its laureate. I'm not talking about poems to be (we may think) safely slighted or ignored: the Wellington "Ode" or "The Charge of the Light Brigade," say. The problem infects the core triad of Tennyson's masterpieces — *The Princess, Maud, In Memoriam*. All three are historically inflected in the sharpest way, and the last — which will be my chief concern — carries as well the marks of Tennyson's deep personal in-vestment in what the poems say and do. Those personal and historical inflec-tions, however, created the problems in the first place.

About twenty years ago an interesting strategy for reading Tennyson's his-torical works began to appear. Picking up on Christopher Ricks and especially Eliot, these procedures try in various ways to reconcile structural themat-ics — like those of the New Criticism and its many formal inheritors — with new historicist procedures (broadly conceived). Herbert Tucker's useful 1993

Critical Essays on Alfred Lord Tennyson rightly sets Isobel Armstrong's 1980 essay on *In Memoriam* as a key point of departure. For Armstrong, Tennyson's monumental elegy is powerful and engrossing not because it is, as many besides the laureate himself complained, too pat and "hopeful," but because of its poignant and unresolved contradictions. Armstrong sets out to explain what Eliot left in description: Tennyson's "blackest melancholia," his poetry of "doubt" and "despair" (290, 294). "There is a fundamental anxiety in *In Memoriam*" that Armstrong traces to Tennyson's fear for "the dissolution of language altogether" (137). "The poem recognizes its need for simple longings and consolation while continually investigating and complicating these desires" (151). Following that line, Herbert F. Tucker gave it normative expression in his splendid book *Tennyson and the Doom of Romanticism.*

This "anxiety" is not just a narrowly aesthetic or linguistic problem. Armstrong and Tucker were succeeded by critics like Eve Sedgwick and, most recently, David Riede in an explication of the broadly based social and political issues that are a function of Tennyson's anxiety. We now see pretty clearly, as Riede succinctly remarks, that "Tennyson's 'Poetry of Sensation' is not an emanation of his autonomous essential genius, but a social construct very much dependent on England's contemporary 'imperial' mission" (675). But seeing that, what do we make of Tennyson's distinguishing poetical feature, his famous melancholy? Tucker reads this as primarily a reaction against "the Romantic imperial self" rather than as a function of an anxiety about "political and cultural empire" (28). But as Riede, quoting Alan Sinfield, points out, Victorian imperialism feeds on Romantic aesthetic ideology: in Sinfield's words, "The poetic spirit [as Romantically inflected] is the advance guard of capitalism and imperialism, and cannot escape this involvement" (53).

I think we can help to clarify the issues here by asking: how could Tennyson have escaped this involvement? By *not* being an inheritor of Romanticism? Who of his period refused that legacy? Of the poets, perhaps Praed, but none of the major ones; and among the novelists, perhaps Trollope. But then who would say that either Praed or Trollope escaped the same involvement by setting Romanticism aside? We might rather say that both had no wish to escape the ideologies of their place and time.

But Tennyson did have that rebellious desire, as all his readers know. Armstrong's reading gained its persuasiveness exactly because she grasped Eliot's point about Tennyson being at once the "instinctive . . . rebel" and "perfect . . . conformist" of his age. In this contradiction, Eliot went on to say, Tennyson "express[ed] the mood of his generation" (291) as no one else did. When Armstrong demonstrates that Tennyson's alienation can be traced to an anxiety and despair about language itself, she is glossing why Eliot was right to use the superlative, "blackest," when speaking of Tennyson's melancholia.

Maud is a poem driven by Tennyson's instinctive rebelliousness, *The Princess* is one driven by his "perfect conformity." That is to say, they each organize themselves around those two contradictory and even dialectical forms of disequilibrium. Eliot found the former flawed but powerful, the latter "beautiful but dull" (289), and he decided that *In Memoriam*, like Mama Bear's porridge, was just right. But despite what emerged through his own masterpiece *The Waste Land*, Eliot's Romantic attachment to neoclassical ideas left him out of sympathy with work organized around states of radical disequilibrium, as both *Maud* and *The Princess* are. We do not forget Eliot's greatest and most distinctive piece of critical malfeasance and error, "Hamlet and His Problems." *Maud* has *Hamlet's* problems.

The problems of *The Princess* are different. Eliot's lack of sympathy in this case arises because the work centers in the contradictions of what Eliot liked to call "serenity." The word "serenity" is a psycho-ideological counter for Eliot signifying an idea of perfection. Had he a better appreciation for the traditions of sentimental literature and philosophy, or even a more sympathetic attachment to the quotidian world, he might have thought differently about a poem haunted and even terrorized by its own serenities. But then, as we know, Eliot never understood what a writer like Gertrude Stein was doing.

I pause to reflect on these literary-critical issues for the cautionary tale they involve. Eliot's essay on Tennyson is perhaps the single finest essay ever written about the poet. The supreme conformist rebel of his own age, Eliot was perfectly placed to write about a poet like Tennyson. Equally facilitating was Eliot's programmatic neoclassicism, which gave him access to Tennyson's technical virtuosity. Seeing these things we also see that his essay is as much or more an essay about himself and his own work as it is about Tennyson. But that is something Eliot does not see — or if he does, he works to suppress it beneath his characteristically Olympian mode of address. And so one begins to realize that in this essay about a great poet of doubt and uncertainty, Eliot affects to speak as if he were free of Tennyson's unfortunate religious quandaries. He affects to *know* Tennyson; more than that, he affects to know how to know. That is Eliot's most important message. In delivering it about Tennyson, however, Eliot's essay exposes its own buried life to a critical analysis.

Critical blindness, we have been taught, is a function of critical insight. And Paul de Man always said that his program of deconstruction was directed against the critics and the philosophers, not the poets and the artists. What we were not taught by deconstruction was the generic difference between ideas as they are expressed in expository prose and ideas as they are expressed in forms of imagination and mimesis. The ideal of the one is an adequate generalization, the ideal of the other is *le mot juste*. To write expository prose about poetic forms is thus fraught with peril and illusion; which is why such prose should never be read without wary attention. Eliot's prose report on Tennyson is thus important for its distinctive understandings and misunderstandings. And so is Alan Sinfield's, who writes about Tennyson's failed escape from Romantic illusions as if Sinfield himself knew how to make an escape, or how Tennyson might have. Indeed, so committed is Sinfield to a program of critical enlightenment that his prose affects to have escaped the ideological complicity he finds in Tennyson's verse. But of course no one ever escapes. There is only the effort and expectation and desire for that escape whose margin fades for ever and for ever as we move.

II

I borrow those words from two famous melancholy poets, the first in certain ways Tennyson's precursor. But Tennyson's melancholy is more acute than Wordsworth's or — Tennyson's other immediate precursor — than Byron's precisely because he does not write under the sign of a real, personal guilt, as both Byron and Wordsworth did. Both can and do point themselves toward personal losses and failures for which they know themselves to be responsible. Wordsworth hides his guilt, Byron wears it as a badge of honor and a disguise. Whatever, the torment and the triumph of their Romanticisms emerge from a self-knowledge they both possess and repossess in every poem they write. Those poems are what Byron calls mirrors of the heart. To write them is to observe oneself disposing elaborate acts of disguise, secrecy, and displacement.

Fortunately and unfortunately, Tennyson did not have any *felix culpa* to focus his attention. Nor does his despair commence with the death of Hallam, as we know. Not that Hallam's death could explain this gigantic melancholy — this "cherished madness of the heart." Like Eliot's Hamlet, Tennyson's melancholy seems "in *excess* of the facts as they appear" (125). It is an abyss, an empty place, a void. And so readers speak of a Virgilian "lacrymae rerum" and metaphysical Angst as if Tennyson had tapped into "some divine despair," whatever that might be. Like the despair of Keats's "grey-haired Saturn" perhaps? But of course *that* despair is not divine, it is very very human. And so is Tennyson's.

But it isn't personal in the usual sense of that term. When by an evil fate Hallam's death enters Tennyson's prevenient and indurated melancholy — the mythical black blood of the Tennysons — the event supplies a poetic fiction of personal loss in which Tennyson can willingly suspend his disbelief. Tennyson seizes the chance and begins a seventeen-year investigation of his sorrow. Whatever we make of that amazing and tenacious pursuit, we want to keep clearly in mind two crucial matters: first, at the end of the poem the melancholia remains as bleak as ever — indeed, seems even more bleak given the marriage Tennyson uses to set a finale to his poem; and second, while Tennyson makes an overpowering representation of his sense of loss, he remains to all appearances as guiltless as ever. He will reproach himself in his poem for cultivating his sorrow but we know, as he knows, that he has no poetical recourse but to be perfectly assiduous of his grief. Indeed, guilt for Tennyson would enter this situation, this poem, if he relinquished his grief and turned to make his way down the ringing grooves of change. His greatness and importance as a poet hang on that everlasting nay.

What is involved here is best explained through Baudelaire and his theory of "le poésie lyrique anonyme." Baudelaire associates this poetic ideal specifically with Byron and Tennyson — a connection that at first seems startling until we realize what Baudelaire has in mind by an anonymous lyric. Although Cleanth Brooks probably borrowed his notion of the "poem nearly anonymous" from Baudelaire, the thinking of the two men runs along very different lines. Brooks's thought means to evacuate all biographical and historical particulars from the poetic space. Baudelaire, on the contrary, is describing a certain kind of lyrical theatricality. "Lord Byron cuts a figure but he is not figurative," Keats famously remarked, thus calling attention to Byron's deployment of cultivated and dandiacal posing as a stylistic device. What Keats deplored, however, Baudelaire counted a supreme poetic virtue as well as a notable innovation. Baudelaire is clearly reading Tennyson as a consciously masking poet.

How apt that reading is comes clear when we compare Tennyson's use of dramatic monologue with Browning's. With some few notable exceptions — for example, "How It Strikes a Contemporary" — Browning does not put on masks when he writes in dramatic monologue. Or, rather, he does not make his masking procedures a forward and conscious feature of the poetical surface. To find Browning in his dramatic monologues you have to subject them to a severe — virtually a deconstructive — anatomy. Why Browning should cultivate such invisibility is an extremely interesting question that I hope scholars will discuss some time. For now I set it aside to attend on Tennyson, who clearly behaves very differently in his poems.

In England the person who has the most interesting things to say on this subject of lyrical anonymity is D. G. Rossetti. His comments emerge in 1871 when he is defending his dramatic monologue "Jenny" from Robert Buchanan's critical abuse. The poem, Rossetti says, is written from "an *inner* standing-point," which he calls one of "the motive powers of art." Rossetti had introduced the theory of the "*inner* standing-point" more than twenty years earlier, in an unpublished note to his pastiche poem "Ave." In 1847–48 the theory of the inner standing-point relates directly to Rossetti's interest in early Italian art and poetry.

Like those other two urban artists Poe and Baudelaire, Rossetti at the time was much involved with projects that cultivated escaping the contemporary world. "Ave" and the associated "Songs of the Art Catholic" were magical texts written to open a passage whereby Rossetti could plunge into a lost land of his heart's desire. To manage this feat he elaborates various kinds of "*inner* standing-point" procedures. He composes pastiche works like "Ave" and "Mary's Girlhood," quasi-pastiche works like "The Blessed Damozel," conjuring prose tales like "Hand and Soul" and "St. Agnes of Intercession," and the ventriloquizing translations from Dante and other early Italian poets. In each case the crucial move does not abstract Rossetti away from his texts — which is Browning's object and great achievement — it involves Rossetti in his own poem's dramatic action. "Ave" is a special kind of dramatic monologue where an "*inner* standing-point" is constructed and then occupied simultaneously by the writing/composing Victorian poet Rossetti and his imaginary Catholic antitype from the fourteenth century.

When a poetics of the inner standing-point is undertaken in a poem of contemporary life such as "Jenny," the results are very different from those gained when Rossetti wrote "Ave." The world of "Jenny" is no lost spiritual dreamland, it is an all-too-present nightmare. Readers to this day argue about whether the "young and thoughtful man of the world" is offered for our judgment or our sympathy, and about Rossetti's relation to his imaginative figure. Their ambivalences, which reflect Rossetti's own description, are well summed up in John Ruskin's comments on the poem.

> The character of the speaker himself is too doubtful. He seems, even to me, anomalous. He reasons and feels entirely like a wise and just man — yet is occasionally drunk and brutal: no affection for the girl shows itself — his throwing the money into her hair is disorderly — he is altogether a disorderly person. The right feeling is unnatural to him, and does not therefore truly touch us. I don't mean that an entirely right-minded person never keeps a mistress: but, if he does, he either loves her — or, not loving her, would blame himself, and be horror-struck for himself no less than for her, in such a moralizing fit. (*Ruskin Rossetti Pre-Raphaelitism* 234)

Though Ruskin meant this for a negative comment on the poem, it merely restates in judgmental terms Rossetti's own comments on his "young and thoughtful man of the world." Ruskin is uncomfortable with a poem that presents its volatile materials in these equivocal terms.

The subsequent reception history of the poem, with its wildly varying interpretations of "Jenny," replicates the poem's textual condition at its originary historical moment. Judged "from without" rather than engaged from within, the poem appears an unhappy artistic performance, replete with what Ruskin calls "doubtful" events, feelings, ideas. Ruskin's brief commentary locates a few from the indefinite number of others that might as well have been chosen. The "young and thoughtful man of the world" objectifies this pervasive structure of doubtfulness within the "framework" of the poem. But the poem itself *incarnates* that structure in the sense that it troubles every effort to judge or understand either the poem or its subject "from without." Biographically inflected readings of the poem — they are common — underscore this situation. The more explicit of these readings range between praise for Rossetti's enlightened or brave undertaking in the poem to sharp criticism of his sexist and pornographic illusions.

Rossetti's theory of the inner standing-point involves a major rewriting of the sympathetic contract poetry makes with both its subjects and its readers. Romantic sympathy in its most authoritative cultural form displays — as Keats famously put the matter — "the holiness of the heart's affections." In this view, because the poet is imagined to have clearest access to that holy place, the poetic act becomes a moral and spiritual standard. Arnold would authorize this set of attitudes when he argued that poetry would replace religion for persons living in the modern world. His sonnet "Shakespeare" represents this set of ideas about the transcendental status of poetry:

> Other abide our question. Thou art free.
> We ask and ask, thou smilest and art still,
> Outtopping knowledge.

That is the romance — really, the Romanticism — of an art conceived as some still point of a turning world. Rossetti's aesthetic move called such a view into radical question. Or perhaps one should say, Rossetti exposed the bad faith on which it had come to rest, for the authority of Arnold's sonnet is pure illusion, as Arnold himself showed in other of his poems, especially a devastating work like "The Buried Life." In Rossetti's wonderful story "Hand and Soul" the exposure comes when Chiaro dell Erma, Rossetti's surrogate, poses this question for himself and his art: "May one be a devil without knowing it?" If the heart and its affections are that problematic, the ground of sympathy will only be gained through what Tennyson called, in one of his most darkly witty moments, "honest doubt."

> There lives more faith in honest doubt,
> Believe me, than in half the creeds.
>   (*In Memoriam* 96.11–12)

The lines arrest our reading exactly as we get arrested when we read this in Wordsworth:

> Enough of science and of art;
> Close up these barren leaves;
> ("The Tables Turned," 29–30)

Is Wordsworth's poem a set of barren leaves? Or how do we fashion a grammar of assent out of Tennyson's flaunted and paradoxical assertion?

In such moments the lyrical voice turns rhetorical. We are thrust out of the Romantic artifice of absorption, as Charles Bernstein calls it, and begin to see the poet in quasi-Brechtian terms. This effect is a function of what Baudelaire means by lyrical anonymity and what Rossetti means by adopting an inner standing-point. It can take either of two reciprocal forms. In a lyrical space that is inflected subjectively — "The Tables Turned," *In Memoriam, Childe Harold* — the effect shifts the poem from the figurative to the figural and the voice of the poet begins to be heard — rather than overheard — in the land. In a dramatic monologue like "Locksley Hall" or "Maud," *The Lament of Tasso* or "Jenny," the fiction of a speaker who is not the poet dissolves into a theatrical palimpsest and the image of the poet in propria persona begins to appear. In each case we are made to witness the distantiation of a poetic illusion — on one hand, of the spontaneous Romantic voice, on the other of a poetical text uninflected by the poet's subjectivity.

III

Let me now return to the problem of Tennyson's melancholia. It seems to me that Baudelaire and Rossetti provide us with helpful instructions for reading the laureate's work. "May one be a devil without knowing it?" Rossetti asks this late Romantic question in his story "Hand and Soul" through his alter ego, the painter Chiaro dell Erma. When he does, the question gets addressed to the possible moral culpability of the artist. In foundational Romanticism the demons are well-fed Porlockian wits who propagate "the world's slow stain." The point is to retreat from the too-much-with-us world. You see into the life of things "when the light of sense goes out" in the blinding flash of unconscious revelation.

Baudelaire's (and Rossetti's) late Romantic variation on this Romantic faith is not the first to expose the ambivalent character of the heart's affections — Blake, Byron, and Coleridge had already done that in graphic ways. But it also demonstrates that this ambivalence must not be read as a purely personal moral affair. The fiction of the purely personal is what Baudelaire reveals as the shared hypocrisy of the Romantic poet and his audience. That fiction — already unstable among the first Romantics — cradles Tennyson into his poetry, as we see most clearly, I suppose, when the self of "The Palace of Art" quotes its soul's confession of solipsism and guilt. The evil consequence is the felt loss of a great cultural heritage, which will open for reappropriation, we are told, only "when I have purged my guilt." We are not told how that happy event will come about. What the poem offers is the candid display of "a poem . . . divided against itself" (119), as Tucker remarks. This division pervades its basic structure, its first-person monologue of a self and soul. That formal procedure creates a strange hybrid grammar, an impersonal (not at all a plural) first person.

The typical Romantic procedure is very different. When the first Romantics study their guilt and error, they speak in propria persona: "wearied out with contraries," *Wordsworth* "yielded up moral questions in despair" (*The Prelude* 1.304–5); fencing his "errors with defensive paradox," *Byron* himself is "the careful pilot of my proper woe" ("Epistle to Augusta" 22–24). So far as Tennyson is concerned, the guilt in "The Palace of Art" is not specifically his own or indeed any one's. It is rather a kind of inheritance, and we might think of it as original sin were it not clearly far less metaphysical than that ancient idea. The guilt in the poem develops and spreads through specific institutions ("palaces," for instance) and cultural works ("art").

The undefended paradox of this poem and others like it — "The Lady of Shalott," for example — is that solipsism is measured not as a personal but a social function. The speaker of "The Palace of Art" has no identity; like Mariana in her moated grange, he suffers in a condition of extreme alienation. Tennyson's famous turn from a poetry of Romantic solipsism to a deliberate engagement with social questions and problems is very much a continuation of the Romantic pursuit and exploration of the self, Blake's lost little boys and girls. In Tennyson this lost self typically has no name and so it assumes masks, fictional names, and surrogate identities. The dramatic monologue is the defining poetic genre of the period because it is self-alienation's adequate late Romantic form.

Byron's poetry of masks and masquerade begins to expose the social character of self-alienation. In elementary terms, he becomes famous, a mere "name," as he often laments. But the lament is what Baudelaire will define as a conscious hypocrisy, for Byron — as he himself knows and says — has been "cunning in his own overthrow." Byron's poetry thus forms an ironical conspiracy of alienation with his audience. To make a drama of this conspiracy is to develop a type of the anonymous lyric.

In Baudelaire's view, Tennyson's poetry begins at that point and develops another type of lyrical anonymity. To adopt an inner standing-point in the personal style of high Romanticism threatens to obscure the precise character of that standing-point. It deflects attention away from what Fredric Jameson famously called the political unconscious and the degree to which any individual is possessed by it. Tennyson's melancholia is the affective condition of the impersonal first person, who is what Mikhail Bakhtin calls "the hero" of Tennyson's writing.

That alienated character appears regularly in third-person narratives from Byron, Pushkin, and Lermontov down to our own day. Tennyson's originality was to have invented ways to give lyrical expression to an experience of identity-loss and psychic fragmentation and to define it in clear sociopolitical terms. *Maud* is of course the paradigm case of that experience, but we often forget that the paradigm *state* of the experience comes in the poem's conclusion, when the hero plunges from his torments into his final "moral abdication" (429), as Tucker calls it. That conclusion takes the measure of *Maud*'s companion poem of brightness visible, *The Princess*, whose central theme Tucker has also well described as "instinct in the toils of culture" (357). Here is "The Palace of Art" in a clear Victorian reincarnation, and Tennyson returns to it in mid-career for the same reason he went there in the first place: precisely because its impersonal first-person guilt has *not* been purged. To observe that "a finicky narrative apparatus . . . diffuses authorial responsibility for the plot" (Tucker 351) is to locate the work's brilliant lyrical anonymity. Tennyson's style represents the ideological condition of the individual in a well-meaning privileged society — Vivian-place, one of Felicia Hemans's stately homes of England. The condition is rebellious conformity, a paralytic state whose realization always issues in Tennyson's hallmark melancholy tone.

Tucker rightly observes of *The Princess* that in the end it leaves its "affairs pretty much where they stood" (351) at the outset. Pursuing its famous "strange diagonal," it stands from first to last in its "betwixt" condition, unable to please anyone, a fence-straddling poem of the first order ("Conclusion" 25–28). To say this simply redescribes the poem as it describes itself. Tucker speaks in passing of the poem's "bad faith," but we should not take that phrase as a negative aesthetic judgment. For who can better represent the disfunctions of a social order than the artist who knows them from the inside, proving them on his pulses by giving his heart to them? Even Louis Althusser mistakenly imagined that "art is not among the ideologies," a view initially sanctioned by Marx himself when he represented the art practice of the ancient world as prehistorical. On the contrary, art is, after religion, the supreme form of ideology and always has been. It not only holds a mirror up to the world, it raises that mirror from its worldly vantage. As Maurice Merleau-Ponty acutely observed, "After all, the world is around me, not in front of me" ("Eye and Mind" 138). Art therefore approaches "hypo-criticality" when it realizes its hypocritical and compromised position.

IV

Tennyson's greatest work in this remarkable poetic mode is *In Memoriam*. Its immediate and enduring success testifies to how completely the poem realizes what the acculturation of the individual entails. That "the poem . . . trades in clichés" (Tucker, *Tennyson* 378) once seemed the very emblem of its irrelevance for a culture committed to Making It New. But the poem grips all of its essential particularities through these clichés. Some are Romantic or Victorian commonplaces, some Christian pieties, some the diction of a poesy rubbed smooth by long and ancient usage, or by more current imaginative fashions. Byron, Shelley, Keats, Wordsworth: each moans round in a poem moaning with many other voices, all deliberately called upon and meant to be heard, as the opening lines of section 1 let us know:

> I held it truth, with him who sings
>> To one clear harp in divers tones,
>> That men may rise on stepping-stones
> Of their dead selves to higher things.

Tennyson will question and complicate his initial Goethean "truth"; for *In Memoriam*, it turns out, is less interested in securing that initial "truth" than in studying the divers ways it has been or might be written or thought about. The words "harp" and "stepping-stones" are *so* telling: the one a poetical archaism, the other a core proverbial term. That kind of diction litters the poem because Tennyson's lyric voice is seeking to merge with the voice of a mighty nation at the lyric or personal level. Or rather, he is seeking to represent how the individual person gets interpellated by that national identity.

The interpellation is managed through a shared ideological discourse — in this case, through a poem that addresses its reader in terms that are the sentimental analogue of Baudelaire's ironies. Were *In Memoriam* to have an epigraph it would be something like: "O sensible lecteur, mon semblable, mon frère." Tennyson will repeatedly break out of his overheard reverie poems to address this reader directly, as in section 124 when he tells us how he was sustained in his moments of religious doubt. "If" he saw himself being called to a faithless despair,

> A warmth within the breast would melt
>   The freezing reason's colder part,
>   And like a man in wrath the heart
> Stood up and answered "I have felt."

This is the Tennysonian version of Wordsworth's legacy whereby feeling comes in aid of feeling. In Tennyson, however, Wordsworth's tables are aggressively turned from musing to rhetoric. Horses of wrath here demonstrate the holiness of the heart's affections.

Section 85 is especially interesting in this regard, for the passage cunningly manipulates imaginative dialogue, first-person direct address, and third-person exposition. Tennyson is addressing someone directly in this section — a reader who is both a particular person, perhaps Edward Lushington, as well as any reader, including ourselves. This reader's self-conscious attention is arrested in the first quatrain when Tennyson quotes his own poem — the famous lines from section 27: "'Tis better to have loved and lost / Than never to have loved at all." The section proceeds to lay out the elegy's rationale, an explanation of the mechanics of the "sad mechanic exercise":

> Whatever way my days decline,
>   I felt and feel, tho' left alone
>   His being working in mine own,
> The footsteps of his life in mine; . . .
>
> And so my passion hath not swerved
>   To works of weakness, but I find
>   An image comforting the mind,
> And in my grief a strength reserved.
>
> Likewise the imaginative woe,
>   That loved to handle spiritual strife

Diffused the shock thro' all my life,
But in the present broke the blow.

My pulses therefore beat again
   For other friends that once I met
   Nor can it suit me to forget
The mighty hopes that make us men.

I woo your love. . . .

(41–44, 49–61)

Characteristically, Tennyson expresses this argument in terms that invite multiple applications. For instance, lines 53–56 might be describing either a psychic or a social poetic therapy — an apt ambiguity since the poem is written both for Tennyson personally and for the social body at large. He woos multiple persons — most immediately, the dead Hallam and the poet's living audience — in order to establish the broad bond of sympathy that is the object of the whole exercise. The love bond, forged through seventeen years of elegizing verse, has been instantiated in *In Memoriam* itself, where a general diffusion of Tennyson's shocked feelings prevents what would, he says, otherwise occur: a complete breakdown "in the present."

But this diffused pain has another peculiar characteristic: it defines an elegy that does not bring emotional solace. Tennyson's affect after the final wedding is as low as it ever was in the earlier time-marking Christmases and anniversaries. The happiness he says he sees all around him defines the dark difference he makes. So in the end he leaves the reveling company to pursue his primal sad isolation. As with *The Princess* (and, for that matter, *Maud*), *In Memoriam* leaves matters — that's to say, its emotional matters — pretty much the same at the end: in a diffused state of shock.

That is the condition of indurated sorrow, or what Freud famously called "melancholia." It is a sorrow in excess of the facts as they appear — a kind of *surplus* sorrow cherished precisely for its excess and the privilege that excess defines. Tennyson represents this privilege in aristocratic figures and clichés ("I was *born* to other things," 120.12), as if an order of beings existed beyond class and economic differences, beyond the long- and short-term temporalities of biology and history. The poem calls its readers to that order, and the order is established when the call is answered. Tennyson's *In Memoriam*, the poem as written, is a reader's model — a user's guide — for how one might answer the call.

The poem's fundamental paradox is that this superior order should be signed with melancholia. That paradox reflects the social contradiction on which it rests. For no such order exists except in the imagination that calls it from a desperate dissatisfaction with the state of the social order as it actually stands. But one cannot utter Baudelaire's cry "anywhere out of the world" or speak Tennyson's desire for a far-off divine event except from the negative world elsewhere, this world — ultimately, this poem. *In Memoriam* reflects that negative world in displaced terms, as if it were a world defined by the absence of Arthur Henry Hallam. But Hallam is only a sign, fashioned in Tennyson's poem, of a grief that dare not speak its name. And indeed Hallam himself is not named in the poem: his identity is purely fantasmal, or as we poetic interpreters like to say, "symbolic." Hallam is a symbol that stands for the order of the symbolic itself, that's to say of a world "felt" as devoid of human sympathy and social connection. Why does Tennyson leave the wedding feast of his sister and friend, why is he everywhere so blindly at strife with apparent blessedness? Because the tents of prosperity are not what they appear. They are illusions, simply symbols.

In Memoriam proposes to make physical contact with symbolic realities on their own terms, not as they are judged "illusions" by presumptively enlightened minds — in Tennyson's terms, by "freezing reason's colder part" (124. 14) — but as actual, *felt* mystifications and fetish objects. Section 95 climaxes this proposal, but it happens throughout the poem. The event's lowest common denominator is the poem's pattern of clichés, which realize the life of the dead at the poem's elemental linguistic level. The poem's melancholy is thus the residue of the poet's decision to execute its ideological task.

This is properly registered as a kind of *heroic* agreement in the fullest equivocal sense of that term, for two reasons. First, Tennyson represents as catastrophic a loss that is no more than an ordinary misfortune — common in an individual's life, scarcely remarked in society at large. The discourse of sensibility implicitly looks to bring a more sympathetic notice to these quotidian things — sorrowful events like that meditated in Hemans's "The Image in Lava," or pleasurable such as Barbauld describes in "Washing-Day." The style of address in these kinds of poem is typically modest and unassuming, in contrast to the large claims *In Memoriam* clearly makes for itself. Second, although *Childe Harold* and *The Prelude* changed all that, explicitly identifying the personal with the political in the most grandiose ways, both of those works transform suffering into triumphs of Romantic assertion. In *In Memoriam,* however, Wordsworth's benevolence and Byron's defiance have become Tennyson's melancholy. In this sense *In Memoriam* is far more honest and disillusioned than either of those romantic masterpieces. Tennyson has not only become what he beheld, he has done this deliberately — enlightened eyes wide shut, disillusioned heart laid bare.

An enlightened consciousness is by definition and aspiration a mastering consciousness. It cannot know the illusions it proposes to identify or attack, it can only think to see them. It assumes it is critically removed from those illusions. That remove, sometimes called "objectivity," is enlightenment's badge of honor, the sign of its innocence (both moral and intellectual), the source of its confidence and self-satisfaction.

Tennyson's poetry, and especially *In Memoriam,* is different. In enlightenment terms, it is an art of complicity that makes what J. G. Ballard would call an atrocity exhibition of itself. Its illusions and complicities are atrocious, but then there is its art, which is to suffer consciously through its own atrocities. For Tennyson, the worst of these is not the propagation of the faith of suffering; it is the *poetical* propagation of that faith, the betrayal of the Keatsian illusion that "a thing of beauty is a joy for ever." Or rather, it is the exposure of that illusion, according to Blake's severe proposal: "That he who will not defend Truth, may be compelled to / Defend a Lie, that he may be snared & caught & taken" (*Milton* plate 8:47–48). *In Memoriam* is a melancholy poem.

V

If a poetic tone can be legion, melancholy is. It dominates what we call in America "workshop poetry." It is the characteristic tone of a writing troubled by its own complicity in a culture of conformed rebellion. In the United States, the paradigm moment of such writing came in the so-called confessional work of the fifties and sixties: the work of Alan Dugan, John Berryman, Anne Sexton, Sylvia Plath. While avant-garde poets often disdain this kind of verse, each case has to be judged on its own merits, as Tennyson spectacularly shows. Verse that aspires to critical awareness — Pound's, say, or Riding's, Reznikoff's, or Oppen's — runs great, even terrible, risks. The event will decide if the risks were worth taking. What is certain is that only bad-faith complicity gives access to certain kinds of reality and modes of experience.

What difference does it make that Berryman and Plath, for instance, wooed and won a savage god? Each to himself or herself must be the oracle for such a question. But if poetic candor is something that matters, then John Hollander's *Reflections on Espionage* (1976) has outsoared, it seems to me, the shadows of their night battles. It is, like *In Memoriam,* a poem about poetry and society, each at once the other's mirror, at once and alike brilliant and appalling. Charles Bernstein and Susan Howe, stronger poets than Hollander in my view, could never have written such a poem. Their cultural complicity is too imperfect and uncertain. In *Reflections* Hollander puts his technical skills on display in order to locate himself as a secure (if modest and perhaps secondary) servitor in America's late-twentieth-century palace of art. Where Tennyson turns his complicity into a drama of melancholy, Hollander makes his a one-man game of wit. Hollander wraps poetry's secret ideological services to the state in metaphors of code, as if the metaphors were "just poetry" and not, as George Lakoff would say, metaphors we live by, as if the making of such metaphors in this very poem were not self-reflexive. But this splendid code-maker traps his own poem in its terrible self-destructive logic by following the logic of his professional virtuosity, by adhering strictly to the code.

Academic poetry like Hollander's is often ignored outside the academy, or disdained, within and without, by those who register its institutional complacencies. But as Blake acutely saw and bravely showed, the authority of the artist is not dependent on some moral function or expectation. The moral guidance we look for changes with time and circumstance, shifts with the sands of history. Nothing shows this fact so well as the reception history of Byron — that supremely moral poet, which is to say that supremely ideological poet. His words about another laureate are much to the point here: "All are not moralists, like Southey, when / He prated to the world of 'Pantisocrasy'" (*Don Juan* 3, stanza 93). There are many mansions in that house of ideology, the palace of art. Poetry's great public service comes exactly because the poet is, as Plato thought, an unreliable citizen. Poets will betray the palace secrets that they know because their whole vocation is endless imitation. Some of the worst traitors — some of the greatest poets — are the most patriotic. Like Tennyson.

CHAPTER 6

Beauty, a (Nineteenth-Century) User's Manual

I

For printed and scripted work, language and meaning unfold through the reader's transaction with visible phenomena. In recent years, this view has energized a resurgent body of bibliographical scholarship grown increasingly aware of its foundational position in any interpretive act. As a result, scholars now take for granted that the meaning of cultural objects like poems and stories is a function of their material characteristics. Or, as Marshall McLuhan famously said a half-century ago, "the medium is the message."

Despite these understandings, however, few scholars of textual objects regularly engage the question of meaning at the most primitive textual levels — that is, in the foul rag and bone shops where type meets ink and kisses paper and where paper gets gathered and bound for glory.

The difficulty is not theoretical; it is practical in a very specific sense. Even where a work clearly, and as we might say "deliberately," aims to integrate message and medium, the ideative contribution of the most elementary textual materials usually slips past notice or gets short shrift. The case of Stéphane Mallarmé's *Un coup des dès* is exemplary: for while the poem has drawn to itself a large body of interpretation, the explications almost always seek to resolve themselves at levels of meaning above the level of the types and the *mise en page*. Those interpretations implicitly declare that the signifiers are vehicular forms — not incarnations of meaning but hired bearers. On the other hand, the case of William Morris shows how the full significance of visible language gets lost at the other end of the interpretive schedule. Commentators on

Morris so foreground the artisanal scene of his writing that they turn it into a spectacle of Work and Beauty, as if a record of vital statistics obviated any need for those nuanced critical reflections so characteristic of Mallarméan studies.

We need to *execute* in regular ways our theoretical views about the material and performative character of textual works of imagination. Theory will not take us very far, as the history of scholarship for the past fifty and more years has proved. Roland Barthes's work set forth all the required theoretical lines, and others since have refined and reiterated them. Despite these things, and despite much lip service to materialist and phenomenological ideas, interpretive method today remains largely committed, at the practical level, to referential and vehicular, rather than to incarnational and performative, models of meaning.

Real change will come about when we develop a set of regular interpretive procedures that command attention to the textual action that takes place at the signifying system's most primitive levels. We have come pretty far, especially in the past twenty years, in developing explication procedures for a work's production and reception histories. Even the best of these, however, tend to organize their data at so-called higher order frames of reference. While such moves are necessary, even crucial, they compromise their own critical strength when they fail to pursue a fully articulated interpretational representation at the craft level of the signifying process.

No one now knows how to do this, and if history is any guide, as it usually is, we will only learn through the continuous efforts of many persons over some period of time.

Here I propose to take a small step in a direction we might go by looking at a particular book — Herbert Horne's *Diversi Colores*. The book seems to me especially useful, in the interpretational context just set forth, because (a) its principal subject is bookmaking's relation to poetry, and (b) it makes itself the focus — the performative and material focus — of that larger subject. Unlike *Un coup des dès* or *The Earthly Paradise*, Horne's book tries to regulate its orders of meaning, including its cultural and ideological orders, in bibliographical aesthetics.

Before we look more closely at what Horne did with *Diversi Colores*, let me recall briefly the book's context. First of all, Horne was not primarily a poet, and *Diversi Colores* is the only book of verse he ever published. He wrote more poetry than appears in this book, but his interests were primarily in book design, in typography, and later in architecture and art history. He designed three different typefaces and he wrote an important work on bookbinding. In the late 1880s and 1890s — the immediate context of *Diversi Colores* — Horne's interests were focused on the aesthetics of the book and he established himself as a major figure in the British "renaissance of printing" movement. He was — in all but name until 1893 — the editor of that key arts and crafts periodical, *The Century Guild Hobby Horse,* and he seems to have been indispensable in organizing the meetings of the Rhymers Club. He himself, it appears, never read any of his own poetry at those famous gatherings, though he was a regular participant.

When we locate *Diversi Colores* in that general context we can see very clearly the difference Horne's book makes with other books of aesthetic and decadent poetry. His corpus is not a sequence of volumes of his own verse, as it is with "Michael Field," Michael Davidson, Arthur Dowson, John Gray, or Lionel Johnson. Horne's corpus is a designer's corpus — a series of books, mostly books of verse, one of which prints his own verse. *Diversi Colores* is the second in a series which climaxes in 1895 in the splendid book of Lionel Johnson's *Poems,* published by Elkin Mathews.

When poets write poems, part of the writing is a quest to explore and develop their own resources. The same is true of artists, and in this case we trace a clear line of advance in Horne's powers as a book designer. Simply in point of book design, Horne's work in 1895 is more certain and accomplished than it was in 1891 when he put his own book of poetry together. Because the texts in *Diversi Colores* are Horne's own, however, that book provided him with a unique opportunity. Somewhat like Blake one hundred years before, even more like D. G. Rossetti a few decades earlier, Horne took comprehensive control of his book's principal expressive features. In doing this he fashioned an aesthetic manifesto for an art of the "total book" quite as interesting in its way as that pivotal manifesto of the immediately preceding period, Rossetti's "Hand and Soul." But whereas Rossetti constructed a contemporary historicist argument via his fictional tale, Horne's book proceeds as a demonstration of method. It lays down his aesthetic precepts by setting an example of how to carry them out. Consequently, in *Diversi Colores* graphic design is not a bearer of other meanings, it is meaning's informing principle: to borrow a figure from the Christian lexicon so central to *Diversi Colores,* the book's "outward and visible signs" incarnate its "inward and spiritual condition." That idea pervades the book in recurrent forms of what Horne calls in one of the book's poems "the secular image."

The argument begins on the title page, which is printed entirely from a woodcut (see fig. 1). The presence of woodcut textual forms is a notably self-conscious initial move — partly a historicist allusion to pre-fifteenth-century printing, partly a reminder that books and texts can be printed in diverse ways. This title page is also a virtual emblem for aestheticism as the Religion

Figure 1. Herbert Horne, *Diversi Colores* (1891), title page.

of Beauty, although the emblem is by no means transparent. In that respect it signals a procedure of obliquity that runs through the book as a whole.

Several things on the page are especially significant. The central flower ornament, a woodspurge, deliberately recollects Rossetti's poem "The Woodspurge," where the poet makes his remarkable argument for emptying natural forms of their religious symbolism in order to restore their primary value as secular images. Furthermore, heading an 1891 letterpress book with a woodcut makes a clear aesthetic gesture, a move underscored by the reference to Chiswick Press. William Morris had issued his first call to an arts and crafts revival in the 1850s by having his own work printed at Chiswick, which represented an antithesis to the age's commercially driven butcher printing.

These are not transparent signs, though they are perhaps more recondite now than they were in 1891. Most striking of all, however, are the least transparent features of this page: its title and author line. These primary informational elements are, in one case, secretly coded, and in the other, invisible. They are, in short, conventional signifiers that call attention to themselves by *not* functioning in their customary informational way.

I will shortly comment in greater detail on the specific historical character of the book's aestheticism. But first let us consider the way meaning is withheld or obscured on the title page. The page arranges an ensemble of reading difficulties that command a heightened level of attention to the material signifiers. It thus sends forward, into the body of the book, a signal to the same effect. Unlike Horne's title page, however, where the privacy of the book is emphasized, the typographical main text lays down an inherently more public and accessible set of signifiers: not just the letterpress characters but, in the case of a book of poems, a set of well-established presentational conventions. The ideal of a noise-free channel of message delivery controls most printed texts, which have usually toggled off their reveal-codes option. Such books do not want to draw attention to their typographical and bibliographical codes lest the vehicular division of signifier/signified collapse into what has been called a "symbol standing for itself." Such books solicit readers who expect a transparency of the signifier.

Horne's book also solicits these kinds of readers, but not in order to satisfy their customary expectations. *Diversi Colores* is organized to short-circuit a vehicular transaction (and theory) of its texts in order to make an argument — it is also a demonstration — of a very different approach to textuality.

What is most notable about Horne's book is the simplicity of means he chooses to make his argument. The famous displays of complex textuality that lay in the future of *Diversi Colores* — for instance, *Un coup de dès, Caligrammes, La Prose du transsibérien,* or Pound's *Cantos* (especially the first two installments) — are far too spectacular for Horne. Equally removed are those elaborate private adventures in textuality that preceded Horne's work: Blake's illuminated books, which Horne knew and admired, the Brontës' fantastic worlds of Gondal and Angria, the "sumptuary" textualities spun from Emily Dickinson's scripts. Had he possessed Alfred Jarry's ebullience he might have sought a more startling or crazed typographical surface. But Horne's imagination, though acute, ran to spareness and reserve, not to styles of excess, as the book's small and modest format makes very clear (the book is 16 cm tall). In that miniaturized textual world he is able to foreground

the material signifier — or rather, the integrated system of material significa-
tions — by playing relatively simple variations with roman and italic type
across a book space (as opposed to a page space) carefully organized in three
distinct parts. Aside from the title page, he deploys only one other type of
textual manipulation: a special *mise en page* procedure in the first section of
the book.

Let's look more closely at how Horne's book design works. Although no
table of contents signals individual poems and no sections of the book are separately marked, *Diversi Colores* falls into three distinct parts. Leaving the divisions unmarked puts a special demand on the reader's attention. If these unmarked parts are not observed, one will entirely miss a key expressive feature
of the book. The first section, running from pages 7–16, holds four pastiche
works; the second, pages 17–40, shifts to a series of poems that exploit a first-
person style. Note that both of these sections end on a verso and face the recto
of the section to follow. The third section, pages 41–47, unfolds an integral
sequence of six numbered poems presenting themselves as a kind of homage
to Robert Herrick.

To appreciate the importance of the sectioning, consider the poem that
opens the second part. I offer it here as it appears on the recto side of its bibliographical "opening" (see fig. 2). Forget about the poem on the left for the
moment and read only what New Critical exegetes used to call "the poem itself." This is the poem whose meaning emerges from the book space of a
single page. Despite the lucid syntax and the clear arrangement of images, this
text by itself is surely quite enigmatic. The problems begin with the title:
"Vigilantibus" must mean either "By the Watchers" or "To the Watchers" —
whoever they are. The difficulty ripples through the second-person pronoun
as well as the poem's implied first person. Who are they, what do they have
to do with each other? Similar elementary questions proliferate: is the imperative of the last two quatrains addressed to the "you" named in line 7? How
do we read the references to the sleep of the body and the sleep of the soul
and the temporal relations between them?

"The poem itself" does not resolve such problems. The difficulty here calls
attention to a more general issue of textual interpretation that needs some
comment at this point, though it bears only indirectly on the immediate issue.
That is to say, the very concept of a "poem itself," or indeed of any kind of self-
identity in any textual unit, distorts our apprehension of the signifying mechanism of poetical textualities. Like all critical deformations, of which "the
poem itself" is this century's most famous and successful, the New Critical
method can serve useful critical purposes so long as, applying it, we bear in
mind that the method *is* a simplifying distortion. Forgetting that, we will only

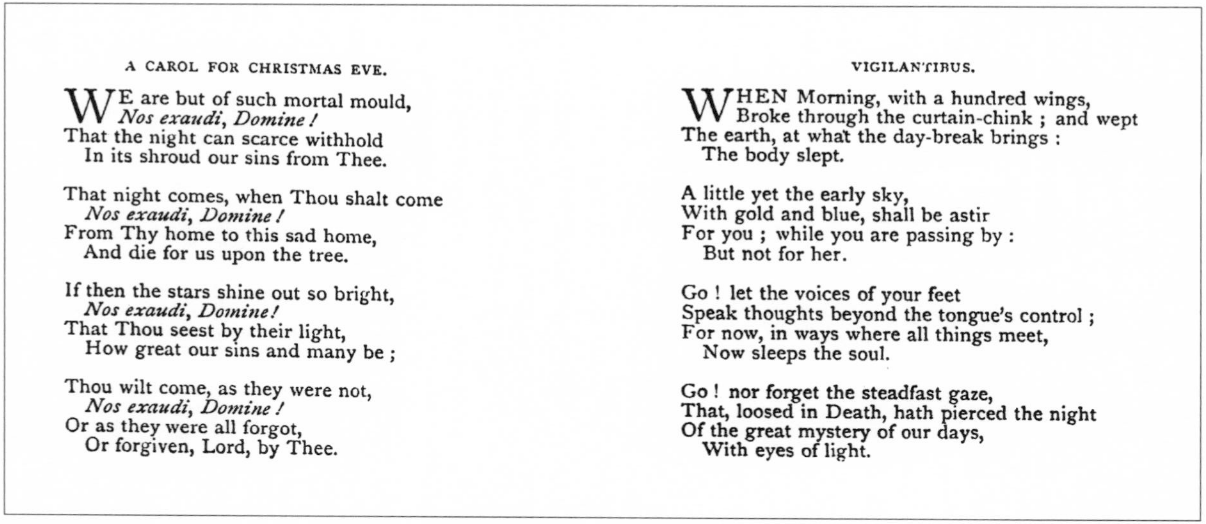

A CAROL FOR CHRISTMAS EVE.

WE are but of such mortal mould,
  Nos exaudi, Domine!
That the night can scarce withhold
  In its shroud our sins from Thee.

That night comes, when Thou shalt come
  Nos exaudi, Domine!
From Thy home to this sad home,
  And die for us upon the tree.

If then the stars shine out so bright,
  Nos exaudi, Domine!
That Thou seest by their light,
  How great our sins and many be;

Thou wilt come, as they were not,
  Nos exaudi, Domine!
Or as they were all forgot,
  Or forgiven, Lord, by Thee.

VIGILANTIBUS.

WHEN Morning, with a hundred wings,
  Broke through the curtain-chink ; and wept
The earth, at what the day-break brings :
  The body slept.

A little yet the early sky,
  With gold and blue, shall be astir
For you ; while you are passing by :
  But not for her.

Go ! let the voices of your feet
  Speak thoughts beyond the tongue's control ;
For now, in ways where all things meet,
  Now sleeps the soul.

Go ! nor forget the steadfast gaze,
  That, loosed in Death, hath pierced the night
Of the great mystery of our days,
  With eyes of light.

Figure 2. Herbert Horne, *Diversi Colores* (1891), pages 16–17.

flay the poem alive, stripping it to some thematized death, or what Blake might have called "A Poetic Abstract."

Setting that matter aside for the moment, however, let's look again at the text — this time by restoring it to its position in the book. For we want to keep in mind that bibliographical position is a key element in any book's three-dimensional coding system. The poem is the first poem of the second section and lies on the recto side of an opening. The verso opposite carries another poem whose four quatrain text makes a visible rhyme with the four quatrains of "Vigilantibus." The opening thus draws a connection between two parts of Horne's book that are, in other crucial respects as we shall see, utterly different. The opening, in short, makes visible a *hinge* moment in the book, turning us from one part to the next and signaling the turn not through some conventional section marker (say a half-title) but by a far simpler, far more discreet gesture. The discretion of the move issues a metadeclaration about the cognitive importance of bibliographical position and the special functional opportunities licensed at a page opening for any bibliographical field.

The connection between the first two sections of the book is reinforced in the way Horne deals with the physical presentation of the poem's title. Printed in roman small caps, it rhymes with the other titles in the book. But the book also locates the title in relation to italic types, for a presentational rule holds that whereas all of the central poetic texts will be roman, all paratexts (like marginalia), most of which are Latin texts, will be italic. That differential in the typefaces exposes the wit secreted in the title "Vigilantibus." The word names those vigilant readers who can trace through the discourse of typographical signs to locate the reference of the title. The word "Vigilantibus" references the *"Voces vigilantium"* of part 1 of the book, those characters marginally printed — which here means "named" — in the second poem of *Diversi Colores.*

That reference takes us to the center of the book's opening section, where *Diversi Colores's* second most important nonsemantic semiosis is deployed. The four works printed on pages 7–16 all emerge from their textual condition as what we now call shaped poems. Each of the texts, but especially the first two, are presented as if they were found texts of the late sixteenth or early seventeenth centuries here presented in a late nineteenth-century orthography. But whereas Horne appears to have modernized the spelling of the texts, he also appears to have preserved an antique rather than a modernized typographical design. The entire scene is a pastiche exercise that recalls nothing so much as certain of Rossetti's works (like "Ave"). Rossetti never carried his imitative forms so far as Horne does here, however — that is to say, he never attempted to install pastiche at such an aggressively nonsemantic level.

Horne's shaped poems are nothing like Apollinaire's or e. e. cummings'. But we will be much mistaken if we register these texts as merely ornamental or antiquarian. At an initial encounter they call attention to themselves precisely because their code of signals is far in excess of the apparent (the transparent) religious meanings borne along with the poems. No pastiche is needed to deliver the Christian message of these texts. What then is the function of such textual redundancy? That is the question haunting these four strange poems — the first and the last Christmas songs, the second and third dramatic scenes from the legend of the Resurrection of Jesus.

As with "Vigilantibus," deciphering these poems hangs on our ability to draw bibliographical connections between them and other parts and elements of Horne's book. For *Diversi Colores* is finally not a book containing a set of poems containing their subsets of semantic messages. On the contrary, it is a carefully organized arrangement of differential signifiers of various kinds, some of which we have yet to examine. Horne presses our attention on his book's nonsemantic features to break the spell of the sign's transparency. The arrangement is a demonstration of the communicative power of the material signifier *as such,* and the demonstration requires the reader's active participation. Estranged from the easy semantic transfers of a customary textual economy, the reader is asked to reengage with the text as a whole by a fresh passage through its most primitive elements. The book then marshals that process of reexamination toward a general demonstrative argument about the dynamic structure of textual formations.

II

I am now going to shift this commentary into a different mode because an explication of nonsemantic signifiers presents peculiar but very interesting interpretive problems. Let me explain.

Like the alphabet, graphical and bibliographical codes work by patterns of difference, and the emergence of meaningful formations waits on the appearance of some governing form or dynamical rule. The marks and forms do not "mean" anything by themselves. Furthermore, deciphering these textual elements and their molecular (so to say) arrangements requires a reader, and the reader — whose name is Legion — has to decipher by further encoding. We recognize this as a process of textual supplementations, and traditional interpreters have worked out procedures for unfolding them. Because the procedures typically focus on the semantic text, however, the reader engages the text — recodes it — at an equivalent systematic level. We can't easily do the same with nonsemantic elements.

DIVERSI COLORES.

꒡ꔷ   ꒡ꔷ   ꒡ꔷ

A MORNING SONG FOR
CHRISTMAS DAY:
FOR MUSIC.

1. AKE! what unusual light
   doth greet
   The early dusk of this our
   street?

2. It is the Lord! it is the Christ!
   That hath the will of God sufficed;
   That, ere the day is born anew,
   Himself is born a child for you.

Chor. The harp, the viol, and the lute,
   To strike a praise unto our God!
   Bring here the reeds! Bring here the flute!
   Wake summer from the winter's sod!
   Oh, what a feast of feasts is given
   To his poor servants, by the King of Heaven!

3. Where is the Lord?
2.   Here is the Lord,
   At thine own door.   'Tis he, the Word;
   He, at whose face, the eternal speed
   Of orb on orb was changed to song.
   Shall he the sound of viols heed,
   Whose ears have heard so high a throng?
   Shall he regard the citherns strung,
   To whom the morning stars have sung?

Chor. Then wake, my heart, and sweep the strings,
   The seven in the Lyre of Life!
   Instead of lutes, the spirit sings;

7

Figure 3. Herbert Horne, *Diversi Colores* (1891), title page 7.

At a certain point in any exegesis of nonsemantic forms, therefore, the reader has to situate them in a general reading program that is coded as an explanation rather than as a demonstration or an execution. This explanatory move must not be taken to imply, however, that the nonsemantic forms are the vehicles for semantic meanings. On the contrary, the semantical recoding that we call interpretation is itself the servomechanism for advancing the reader's engagement with the totality of the text. In the present case, it will help to clarify the presence of a network of graphical elements and their relations.

Look at the first text page of Horne's book (see fig. 3).

How do we know that we are not to read this as a doctrinal work centered in Christian liturgy? More than that, what makes us realize that the page signals the reader to make secular translations of certain key phrases like "the Word" and "changed to song"? That's to say, to read both phrases much more literally, as referencing not "Christ" and "the music of the spheres" but this text, the "MORNING SONG" named in the title line?

We know this because the book lays down a diverse pattern of textual phenomena, ranged across its whole length, that (a) trouble or resist the offered transparent meanings, and (b) passively invite such aesthetic transformations as alternative readings. The case here is at bottom no different from the case of "Vigilantibus," or indeed of the recondite title page. Essential to Horne's performative argument is that he not *declare* these procedures for the reader but that he leave their execution to us. Essential to my exegetical argument, on the other hand, is to supply at a certain point a general framework for licensing reading procedures that, if applied anywhere in the book, will find their truth-conditions satisfied by a specific interpretive move.

Let me begin to sketch that framework by looking at another resistant text — the title of Horne's book. It hides its reference to a relatively obscure verse in the Vulgate Bible, 1 Chronicles 29:2. Here is the King James text — though as we shall see, Horne's Latin title is far from a mere stylistic affectation.

> Now I have prepared with all my might for the house of my God the gold for things to be made of gold, and the silver for things of silver, and the brass for things of brass, the iron for things of iron, and wood for things of wood; onyx stones, and stones to be set, glistering stones, and of divers colours, and all manner of precious stones, and marble stones in abundance.

The passage makes the book's initial coded announcement of Horne's aestheticist ideas and intentions. Horne's editor's introduction to the Janu-

ary 1889 *Century Guild Hobby Horse* is our common reference point for his beliefs — they can scarcely be called anything less — about visible language and
ornamental integrity in writing and bookmaking. These convictions are of
course famously executed in the design features of that quintessential aesthetic periodical of the period. The title of *Diversi Colores,* however, indicates
the precise devotional character of Horne's position.

I say "precise" and "devotional" because Horne's devotions are, like Rossetti's before him, *precisely* secular. Orthodox commentators, religious or not,
too often mistake, or condescend to, the fin de siécle's "religion of beauty."
Certainly many at the time embraced this central period idea in loose, un-
clear, or even slovenly ways. Horne was not that kind of person, and one of
the most important critical features of *Diversi Colores* is the exactitude with
which it illustrates this key aestheticist conception.

As the root meaning of the word indicates, religion binds one to a set of
practices. These practices will or should mark all aspects of the devotee's life,
and when the person is involved in devotional exercises as such, precision
is the watchword for behavior. Equally important, a religious practice is directed away from the self. It is a practice aimed toward the praise and glorifi-
cation of the object of devotion. In this case, Horne devotes himself to glori-
fying Beauty by making a beautiful thing.

The book's recurrent Latin texts all either quote from the Vulgate or imitate medieval textual usages. This kind of thing is common in decadent and
aesthetic poetry, as we know, but rarely is its programmatic function so
clearly exposed. The layout of the poems gives them to us in an ornamental
display, as their titles emphasize: "A Morning Song for Christmas Day: For
Music"; "Hic Incipit Resurrectio Domini Nostri Jesu Christi, Qui Nos
Dilexit"; "Ego Sum Primus et Novissimus, et Ecce Sum Vivens in Saecula
Saeculorum, et Habeo Claves Mortis, et Inferni"; and "A Carol for Christmas
Eve." No style of personal inflection — Horne in propria persona — appears
in these poems. They are dominated by various impersonal or named voices
who get identified and framed through obsolete bibliographical codes. The
first poem has four numbered voices and a chorus; the second has various
characters named "Vigilantes," "Maria Magdalene, Joanna, Maria Jacobi et
ceterae mulieres," a prima, secunda, and tertia "Vox," and an "Angelus." The
third poem is spoken by the resurrected Jesus, the fourth is an impersonal
carol. The opening four poems thus emphasize their material textuality and
subordinate their original Christian semantic meanings to an aesthetic display. As typology yields to typography and the *mise en page,* we find ourselves
caught up and even secretly addressed by these dead signs, as if they and we
too were coming back to a strange new life: "Wake! What unusual light doth

greet / The early dusk of this our street." Like Thoreau in *Walden,* although here the style is severely impersonal, Horne's book is moving to wake its neighbors up. Page design works to evacuate the texts of their residual Christian significance and release them to secular construal:

> If ye would be the heirs . . .
> Follow ye me . . .
> All I have overcome,
> For I have risen
> Out of the jaws of Sin,
> Out of the toils of Sloth,
> Out of the death of Lust,
> Out of the grave of Self:
> Therefore now I am made
> Even the Son of God;
> He that is risen;
> He that was dead, and is alive again.
> ("Ego Sum Primus et Novissimus . . ." 51, 53, 56 – 65)

This is nothing less than the modernist dictum "Make It New" cast in an aesthetic inflection, as the Latin title of the poem suggests. As a dramatic monologue this poem follows the impersonal rhetoric of the two preceding poems, which have no first person at all. They speak themselves dramatically, through characters (in both senses, we now realize) and the signs of voiced sounds. But since the texts flaunt themselves as pastiche documents, all of these characters collapse into figures of pure textuality, as if the poems were what a later poem in the book describes as "absolute" ("Upon Returning a Silk Handkerchief"). So the passage above translates into an allegorical revelation of a newborn poetry. The poem appears to be speaking itself.

Not without reason, therefore, are Dante Alighieri and Dante Gabriel Rossetti two of the book's key poetic/artistic presences. A heroic model in the pages of *The Century Guild Hobby Horse,* Rossetti is twice explicitly invoked — on the title page, as we've seen, and in "Lines Written in the Glen at Penkill." Both Dante and Rossetti are called to attention in "Upon Returning a Silk Handkerchief," which invokes Beatrice via a deliberate pastiche of the translational style Rossetti made famous in *The Early Italian Poets* (1861). Rossetti used that volume to translate Dante's performative argument about a renascence of poetry. That is also to say, Rossetti translated Dante's *Vita Nuova* into an argument for a new nineteenth-century life for poetry. Like *The Century Guild Hobby Horse, Diversi Colores* is a conscious move to extend that argument.

This new poetry means to break free of Sin, Sloth, Lust, and Self, and the rest of Horne's book will try to show how that escape comes about. Christian sinfulness, especially lust, is abandoned in the pursuit of an erotic ideal that consciously recalls Rossetti's famous declaration: "Thy soul I know not from thy body, nor / Thee from myself, neither our love from God." Sloth yields to the book's display of elaborate care in its making, and the ideal of an impersonal address and procedure unfolds as this very text and all its companions.

If we return to "Vigilantibus" now, we shall be able to read it in the context that Horne's book has created for itself. The title reaches back to the second poem, "Hic Incipit Resurrectio Domini Nostri . . . ," which opens with a speech by a group of "Vigilantes." After thanking God for the daybreak, they worry that the promise of glory will, as another poet famously lamented, "fade into the light of common day." "Vigilantibus" makes an explicit reprise on that earlier passage in *Diversi Colores* and in so doing explicates its own strange title. That's not to say it settles the question of whether the case of the word "Vigilantibus" is dative or ablative, only that both cases function equally well. If the poem is "to" the watchers, then it promises to answer their earlier apprehensions. If it is "by" the watchers, it illustrates that they have overcome those apprehensions.

Who *are* these watchers? The secular allegory established in the four opening pastiche poems settles that question nicely. They are those who watch for the coming of the new day or who, as in the passage from 1 Chronicles, prepare the house of the coming Lord. They are, in short, artists like Horne and readers like those he solicits. The poems of these vigilant persons are themselves "Vigilantes," as we see in lines like the following, which are addressed to the poem itself, quite in a Dantean *stil novisti* manner: "Go! Let the voices of your feet / Speak thoughts beyond the tongue's control." That kind of wordplay, recurrent in the book, reminds us of the impersonality of Horne's poetry. "The voices of your feet" are textual voices being addressed by other textual voices.

III

The fifth poem in *Diversi Colores,* "Vigilantibus" turns the reader over to the book's second section of erotic and secular pieces cast in a first-person address. Some of these are quasi-pastiche poems, like the brilliant *stil novisti* exercise "Upon Returning a Silk Handkerchief," others adopt a more traditional first-person address. All are focused on the central issue of *poiesis,* as we see in the recurrent invocation of earlier poets. Catullus, Dante, Blake, Shelley, Keats, Swinburne, and especially Rossetti are all called into presence. They comprise a group of secular saints, on one hand revered for their devotion to their craft, and, on the other, for their awareness that a worthy craftsmanship must be measured by an ideal of self-extinction.

The dramatic and presentational poetic method established in the first section of *Diversi Colores* passes its influence over to section 2. Here a romantic first-person style comes in twenty-three poems that appear less as spontaneous overflows or tranquil recollections than staged examples of those modes of poetic address. As in Pound's *Hugh Selwyn Mauberly* or Stevens's "Thirteen Ways of Looking at a Blackbird," each poem takes up the same theme from a slightly different perspective. The poems consider the problematic relation, in a purely secular world, of artistic work that aspires to a devotional impersonality.

We see this most clearly, perhaps, in the second section's sonnet "To an Unknown Lady," one of the most arresting pieces in the book. The sonnet is Italian in form and done after the manner of Rossetti. It represents the thoughts of a first-person speaker — let us say Horne — studying a drawing by Raphael. Horne uses his poem to address the "unknown lady" in the picture. He surmises that her visage was transformed to this "secular image" when Raphael saw the actual woman "face to face" one day "within this very place / This Umbrian valley" now visible to Horne, centuries later and in another country, in Raphael's picture. The locution that climaxes the octave, "face to face," is biblical and suggests a divine or transcendent encounter.

As the sonnet turns to its octave Horne imagines that the lady has forgotten this meeting — perhaps because she is dead, perhaps because she incarnates a being who was rapt away in her own immediate act or ecstasy of living. Horne's Raphael, however, has not forgotten, which is to say that his picture "holds the calm features" of the lady in a daily and ceaseless flowering. Horne reserves for the sonnet's final tercet a startling turn of wit: the revelation that if this (imagined) ordinary woman from Umbria were to look at the portrait Raphael drew, she would behold, not herself, but "the face of Mary, mother of thy [i.e., her] God."

Two things about this poem are particularly important. First, we want to notice the act of imaginative wit that joins this poem to the order of the book conceived as a whole. The connection is made through the secret and devoted artifice of "the secular image" — that is to say, through a linguistic equivalence registered at the level of the signifier. When the pastiche Jesus of "Ego Sum Primus et Novissimus . . . " declares that "I live for evermore," he is translating part of his own poem's title: "Et Ecce Sum Vivens in Saecula Saeculorum." Horne's book reconnects that biblical locution for eternal life, *in saecula saeculorum,* to its root mortal meaning, "secular."

Second, we want to see that the sonnet's first person is turned by "his" own poetic action from a living being into an aesthetic character. The "poet" here addresses a frankly imaginary creature and makes no effort to develop a reflective psychomachia. Those alternatives define the limits of an expressivist and Romantic style: spontaneity of expression, on one hand, sincerity of thought on the other. In refusing either alternative the poem realizes an impersonal zenith of subjective expression. Like Swinburne's Sappho in "Anactoria," the first person here has become "now no more a singer but a song."

The first-person voices in the book's second section thus appear not to see or know themselves as voices. They come before us in diverse emotional states, all of them either troubled or — as in "To an Unknown Lady" — unaware of their aesthetic location. The function of the second part of the book is to stage the Romantic program as an aesthetic drama, thereby subsuming it to secular translation and transcendence.

The book's final section completes the process by a marvelous pastiche of Herrick's Cavalier style, as we see so clearly on the section's opening page (see fig. 4).

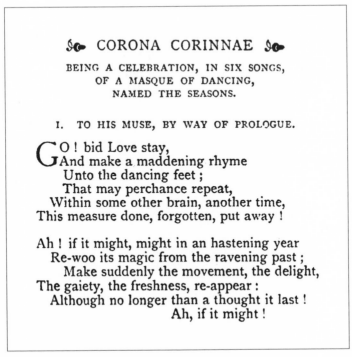

Figure 4. Herbert Horne, *Diversi Colores* (1891), title page 41.

As in section 1 of the book, layout here defines the way this corona of poems will be seen and read. We think of shaped poems in relation to concrete poetry, to various works by cummings and Apollinaire, or to famous texts like Herbert's "Easter Wings." But this page is clearly another example of Horne's shaped verse, with page layout raising up the ghost of Herrick's Cavalier poetical world. The effect is to translate the text and all its elements into an abstract and aesthetic condition. The "maddening rhyme," "the dancing feet," "this measure done": here these figures become Horne's "absolute images," symbols that stand for themselves and the dance of their purely literal action.

That literality seems to free the poem from the "hastening year" and the "ravening past," which are the enemies this work is proposing to escape. Pastiche cancels the fleeing present and the flown past by collapsing them together. That this action comes simply as an immediate bibliographical apparition only enforces the sense of an escaped temporality. In the spatial form of this page, the antique title ("TO HIS MUSE, BY WAY OF PROLOGUE") transforms the first poem into a kind of found object. As in any number of Renaissance poems that follow similar formulae, the poem itself appears to issue the imperative of its first stanza and the subjunctive of stanza 2. In such a case the referent of "HIS" doubles itself to signal both Herrick and this speaking poem, who work under a single inspirational form ("HIS MUSE").

Horne's *mise en page* thus supplies the "magic" needed to realize this text's "thought" as a demonstrative and immediate action. The effect makes one think forward to Stevens. If Beauty is fitful and momentary in the mind, "in the flesh it is immortal." Horne's bibliographical codes make his poems' words flesh in a sense very like the one Stevens was pursuing. Alike in the flesh, they differ in the spirit. Horne's neoclassical stance leaves him no room for Stevens's wonderful textual comedies. Nonetheless, both were well practiced in the religion of beauty and its "secular images."

CHAPTER 7

Mr. James and His Discovery

In an epoch like our own, where the limits of knowledge are mapped onto models of language, the special character of historical criticism (as opposed to literary hermeneutics) may be clarified by asking the following question: must we regard the channels of communication as part of the message of the texts we study? Or are the channels to be treated as purely vehicular forms whose ideal condition is to be transparent to the texts they deliver? How important, for the reader of a novel or any other text, are the work's various materials, means, and modes of production? Does a work's bibliographical existence, for example, seriously impinge on its symbolic form and meaning?

Such questions return upon us with special force when we examine the strange case of Henry James and the textual problems of *The Ambassadors*. Those problems locate more than a textual crux in James's novel, more (even) than a set of very difficult questions for editorial method and theory. The issues put into question the very grounds of critical reflection as such. They suggest as well the possibility that we might be called now to recover certain pre-Enlightenment and even pre-Socratic views about the work of *poiesis*.

I. The Facts in the Case of Mr. James

We locate these issues in terms of an astonishing textual mistake. Here is the story, or at least my version of the story.

In 1950 Robert E. Young published a famous essay in American Literature, "An Error in *The Ambassadors*." The essay argued that chapters 28 and 29 as printed in the first American edition (Harper's, 1903) and its "definitive" successor, the 1909 New York Edition of James's complete works, were printed in the wrong order — specifically, in reversed order. Young argued his case on the grounds of the novel's internal chronology. His point was that when one read these chapters one found that the events they narrated seemed to involve impossible narrative sequences: for instance, the narrative seemed to refer to events before they ever happened. Young said the reversed chapters had been preserved and reprinted in every subsequent edition of the novel.

Young made his discovery when he was an undergraduate student of Yvor Winters at Stanford. This is an important fact to know because Winters had become a prominent critic of James's so-called late style, of which *The Ambassadors* was taken to be a good example. According to Winters, James's prose had become increasingly byzantine as his career developed, and the New York Edition was for him little more than an ornate basilica enshrining that debased style James had come to serve. Following Winters's general view in this respect, Young concluded — after giving a schedule of the chronological contradictions he found in the two chapters — that the reversal occurred because James's style had grown so complex the author himself could not follow its paths.

Young had to seize some such general argument because he knew that James had corrected the New York Edition of his works with extreme care. That fact, however, was all the more useful for Young's purposes. The real "error" concealed in the title of his essay — the "error" that most interested Young (and Winters) — was less the reversed chapters as such than the style of writing that seemed to produce such a textual mistake.

The publication of Young's essay came as the proverbial bombshell, and it drew a number of immediate responses. The most important of these were the two written by Leon Edel, who in 1950 was the most influential James critic in the world, and the acknowledged authority on James's texts. Edel's responses were to prove decisive for installing the textual mistake that Young's work had — there is no better word — created.

Edel made no effort to question or refute the factual "error" that Young described. Edel accepted Young's basic position: that people — himself included — had been reading the novel for nearly half a century without realizing chapters 28 and 29 were in reverse order. Edel let this go, I think, because he (correctly) saw that the real thrust of Young's essay was to ridicule James's late style. So Edel assumed as his task the defense of James as a writer. In doing this, he marshaled his historical and bibliographical knowledge — materials that Young had virtually no awareness of or perhaps competence with — in order to argue that the "error" was not James's fault.

Edel made sure that the scholarly world understood how ignorant Young was. He noted (rather imperiously) a significant factual mistake that Young had made in saying all the editions printed the reversed chapters. The first English edition (Methuen, 1903), which preceded the Harper's edition by a few weeks, actually had the chapters in the order that Young said they ought to follow. From Edel's vantage, then, Young was wrong on an important matter. In place of Young's unbroken tradition of mistaken texts, Edel produced two distinct printed texts at the initial moment of production. Furthermore — and this became Edel's position — what seemed to have gone wrong in the Harper's edition (and its crucial descendant, the New York Edition) had not gone wrong in the Methuen edition. The latter was in fact the very first book printing of the novel, and the first text in which the two chapters appeared together. As it happened, all subsequent texts followed Harper's, so that only one textual line reproduced itself. The Methuen text stood at the beginning, but it stood alone.

Edel thus positioned himself to argue that James got the order "right" in the first edition. His task then became to show how James could have overlooked the "error" in the Harper's edition and, most troubling of all, in the New York Edition.

I shall not rehearse the details of Edel's arguments. Suffice it to say that Edel's general view was (a) the complications of proofing and printing the first two book editions created great confusion for James and his two publishers (Methuen in England, Harper's in the United States); and (b) the printers and publishers were the chief culprits in allowing the confusion to obscure the textual problems. What was "correct" in the first book printing thus got fouled in the second, both in 1903.

This position left Edel with the problem of the New York Edition. The problem was twofold: why did James choose the (presumably imperfect) Harper's edition as his copytext for the New York Edition? And why, having made that choice, did he miss the "error" when he was correcting the text — especially since James had (once and even initially) gotten the sequence right, in the Methuen edition? In truth, Edel does not have any good explanations for these anomalies. Although he concedes that James worked scrupulously on his revisions for the New York Edition, he argues that at this (late) point in the project James was paying little attention to the kind of details that would expose the presence of reversed chapters. In short, Edel says James simply missed what he ought to have seen.

Edel's responses to Young had a double effect. On one hand they supplied a weighty scholar's confirmation of Young's critical and reader's view of the "mistaken" text. On the other, they smartly challenged Young's more general point about James's bad late style. According to Edel, it was not the master who was at fault, it was the house servants. They put the dishes in the wrong cabinets, after the master had first shown them where they ought to have been put.

As it turned out, Edel's account of the early textual history was itself not accurate. He argued that printing complications created problems for the Harper's edition, which had the chapters in the (now presumed to be) wrong order. But although there were indeed printing problems, they plagued not the Harper's edition but the Methuen edition. This fact was brought out only much later by Brian Birch, who in 1965 finally did what ought to have been done at the beginning of the controversy: he collated all the relevant documents. This operation revealed the actual truth of the printing history: that the Methuen edition was forced to print from various imperfect materials and had to work under difficult transatlantic transfers. The Harper's edition was produced without any of the problems faced by the English publisher.

Edel mistook the initial textual situation, I think, because its true history is counterintuitive. Methuen was the first book printing, after all, and James was living in England when the novel was going through press. One would naturally expect that if problems arose in transmitting copy, they would appear on the American side, not the English. But although the Methuen text was published first, the Harper's edition is more authoritative from a textual point of view. This happened because Harper's printed the novel first — not as a book, but in serialized form in the *North American Review* (January–December 1903). Harper's thus received its copy directly from James, whereas Methuen got its copy at second hand. (The problem of the "reversed" chapters does not arise for the serial text because that text does not print chapter 29.)

If one takes Birch's important article as a point of departure, one realizes that neither the 1903 Harper's edition nor the 1909 New York Edition are anything but what they should be, from a textual point of view. Furthermore, one also sees that the Methuen edition — which prints the chapters in Young's so-called correct order — is a highly problematic text: badly supervised, and printed from uncertain copy in crucial places.

As it turns out, an unpublished letter (which Edel knew and read) from James to Mrs. Humphry Ward (December 16, 1903) shows that James was aware that the Methuen text had what he called "a fearful . . . fault . . . which . . . no one has noticed & which nothing will induce me now ever to reveal not at least till some one does spot it." Edel not only missed the importance of this letter, he didn't print it in any of his editions of James's letters.

The letter is crucial for two reasons. First, it shows that James was aware of a serious textual problem in the Methuen edition. Second, it partly explains why the problem of the novel's text remained unrevealed for so long, and why it continued to be obscured even after Young's essay lifted the subject into public view. James never had to reveal the textual problem in the Methuen text because, when he came to edit the New York Edition, he simply ignored the Methuen text and worked from Harper's edition. And after Young's essay, James's letter to Mrs. Ward was not closely attended to. Only a small excerpt from it was published (by Edel) and that excerpt was misinterpreted (also by Edel).

The truth is, then, that a mistake had indeed occurred in the early printing of *The Ambassadors*, and that it involved (among other things) a reversal of chapters 28 and 29. Robert Young did not discover this mistake, however, and neither did Leon Edel. Henry James did, in 1903. Young read the correctly printed (Harper's) text and — because he had trouble making sense of its narrative — he decided the chapters were reversed. Edel came along and confirmed Young's hypothesis that Harper's printed the two chapters in the wrong order. But the order of the chapters was not wrong in Harper's edition, at least from James's point of view. It was wrong in the Methuen edition.

The final irony in all this, however, is what Young's and Edel's mistake now exposes for criticism generally. A return to Young's reading of *The Ambassadors* shows how he came to his conclusions about reversed chapters in the Harper's edition. Simply, he misread a demonstrative pronoun in the first paragraph of chapter 29 — misread the word "that" as referring to one evening in the plot when it ought to have been read — if one wants to preserve the novel's plot continuity — as referring to another evening. Chapters 28 and 29 deal with events over a two-day period. Young took the phrase "that evening" in the first paragraph of chapter 29 to be referring to the evening of the second day. But the plot continuity of the Harper's and New York editions requires that the phrase refer to the evening of the first day.

If we do not take the phrase to be referring to the evening of the first day, a whole structure of narrative incongruities will rise up before the reader of the novel. Young's 1950 essay raised up that structure. But if we don't read it as Young did, then the narrative offers no problems and we then understand how readers for forty-one years must have been reading the novel without encountering narrative anomalies.

Or do we?

The problem here is the speed with which Young's view established itself as "the truth" about the text. Would Young's (and Edel's) position have gained such authority so quickly if readers had been clear about how to read James's demonstrative pronoun at the beginning of chapter 29? It seems unlikely. That Young's new and startling idea gained currency without protest or challenge suggests that readers of the novel could hardly have been paying much attention to the pronoun at all. Young gave a precise meaning to that pronoun and in doing so exposed a deep problem in the text. What he did not see was that his precise meaning was only one reading option.

We are not dealing here simply with an ambiguous pronoun. The word "that" is in fact open to two different readings in the context of James's novel, and the ambiguity may be mapped onto the divergent textual and reading histories I have been summarizing. What is shocking in all this is not the ambiguity, however, or the fact that readers of the novel were variously inattentive to the text. What is shocking is the coherence of randomness in the novel, which the ambiguous pronoun, seen now from our vantage, reveals. Read the word *that* one way and the Methuen text seems to have chapters 28 and 29 in the "correct" order; read it another way and Methuen suddenly has the "wrong" order, but Harper's and the New York Edition have the "correct" order.

The novel, that is to say, has two perfectly good structural sequences embedded in its language. Each can be materially invoked by simply changing the order of two chapters. It is as if the novel had hidden within it structural protocols that could be set in operation arbitrarily in this case, by releasing the logical options of a pronoun whose ambiguities were no part of James's program for his novel. It is as if the language of the book had its own authorities, as if its highly deliberated and particular form concealed stochastic energies. The text suddenly (if I may randomly appropriate an inapposite text from Matthew Arnold)— the text suddenly "seems / To lie before us like a land of dreams." It suddenly seems a text that, while it can't mean or be made to mean everything at any time, might mean or be made to mean anything at every point in time. It becomes a kind of quantum text.

Let me return to James's letter where he reveals his awareness of the problems of his text. I shall quote exactly what he says:

> The book is, intrinsically, I daresay, the best I have written in spite of a fearful though much patched over fault or weakness in it (which, however, I seem to see no one has noticed & which nothing will induce me now ever to reveal not at least till some one does spot it.)

Earlier I discussed the problem of the ambiguity hidden in the fateful pronoun "that." The question now arises, is James here — in this letter — talking about a problem of reversed chapters or about a problem of a pronoun? It makes a great difference. If the letter is referring to his awareness of an error in the Methuen chapter sequence, then James must be reading the pronoun for the meaning that Young did not see. But suppose the "fearful though much patched over fault or weakness" indicates James's awareness of the pronominal ambiguity as such. In that case his letter indicates an awareness that the two chapters might be put in either order, that one could choose between them. As it happens, when James wrote this letter both of the early editions were in print and a copy of the Harper's edition could have reached him in England. Mrs. Ward certainly read the Methuen edition, but James may at this point have seen both texts and may have discovered the discrepancy between them.

We can't know precisely what he found so "fearful" about his work's "fault or weakness." We certainly don't know what he meant by "much patched over" — given what we have of the surviving documentary evidence. Perhaps he was referring here to the whole of chapter 29, which he (perhaps) added to the *North American Review* version of the novel (perhaps) to clarify the events as they were unfolding at that crucial point in the plot. Or perhaps he was referring to the first paragraph of chapter 29, which (perhaps) James wrote to "patch over" the chronological difficulty created by the addition of his new chapter. We don't know.

And what of the "fault or weakness"? It might be that James saw a "wrong chapter sequence" in the Methuen text, it might be that he saw the fateful pronominal ambiguity, it might be that he even saw how that ambiguity permitted two distinct chapter orders. Or should we imagine that James glimpsed the most disturbing consequence of the bibliographical situation: that at this textual moment James's linear narrative revealed a hidden quantum structure? We may read, that is to say, as if both linear sequences are to be apprehended simultaneously — because both sequences are present simultaneously, are objectively present.

II. Two Roads, Both Taken

To read in that way is not to imply or argue that it makes no difference which order one chooses for the chapters. Clearly it will make a difference, clearly different meanings and perceptions will follow. It is to argue, rather, that one positively wants those differences: that one wants two roads diverging in the yellow wood, and that one wants to travel along each one separately and also to travel along both together. One wants to have two cakes and eat them too.

Whether James himself was reading his book in that multiple way, we now can, and do. I am reading it that way now. This way of following the text, however, means that we are reading "a novel" as if it were "a scene of writing." We are no longer following the conventions of the traditional novel, where linear narrative and plot sequence are essential. We are reading James's

The Ambassadors as if it were the work of Jorge Luis Borges, or Julio Cortazar, or — well, you name them.

— But of course we do that all the time, there's no problem with appropriating past texts to present imaginations.

— But it is not we who are appropriating this past literary work to our imagination, it is that work which seems to have prophesied our ways of thinking and reading without the author or anyone else ever "intending" to do so. *The Ambassadors* lies open to two different linear sequences simultaneously, and it has generated these two sequences "without authority" — as if by some weird accident (or fate, or deliberation) of the text. More strangely still, fortuitous circumstances collaborated with this work by putting both sequences into printed form immediately. Most astonishing of all — perhaps James's word, "fearful," is the best one — the two narrative sequences remain seamlessly "correct" no matter which of their two material forms they take.

The question is: just how deeply are these orders of Chaos grounded? Does the strange case of Dr. Methuen and Mr. Harper expose a textual freak, an accident and exception that proves the rule of normal orders of conscious control? Or is it a dramatic instance of just how strongly, and in the end vainly, we resist the presence of aleatory and random orders? In this case we observe the resistance in all the principal players: in James, in Young, in Edel, in ourselves who are surprised by all this sin.

When we think with a post-Heisenbergian imagination (or, alternatively, with a pre-Socratic one) we have no difficulty grasping the random order of things. We are not surprised by sin, by the operations of fate, by Lucretian swerves, by Mandelbrot sets. Seen through a text like the Bible these things may be taken to reveal the necessity of a willful refusal of necessity. Seen through the text of *De rerum natura* they declare the material presence of the orders of Love — Aphrodite, *alma Venus genetrix* — at the foundation of the world. We have also developed distinctive twentieth-century literary and artistic methods for expressing analogous forms of order. Yet in our scholarship and criticism we still often behave as if randomness and contradiction are not essential to the order of things — except as villainies to be normalized. In this behavior we perhaps merely execute our own habits of contradiction.

However that may be, I shall close this discussion with a pair of general and related reflections on critical theory and method. The first concerns historical criticism in general, the second textual criticism and editing, the key subdisciplines of every historicist program.

The case of *The Ambassadors* is theoretically important because no amount of nonhistoricized analysis could have exposed what is going on in that work. Historicized analysis shows the objective — the positive existence — of the work's contradictions. The analysis, that is to say, exposes, through an act of critical reciprocation, a complex prior eventuality. In rough terms, the case of *The Ambassadors* argues that facticity stands logically prior to the concept of facticity. That logical priority assumes a concrete material form. We experience and define it as a historical priority. For all its historical character, the priority is a philosophical condition.

These theoretical matters have to be emphasized if we are to appreciate the interpretive relevance of historical method, and the relative poverty of more formally conceptual models of hermeneutics. *The Ambassadors* needs to be grasped theoretically as a complex (and evolving) set of material and sociohistorical events. If it isn't, our encounter with the work will not be able to reach any deeper level than that of formal semantics. We will be limited to either structural analysis or thematized reading. While both of these critical procedures are important, they require, I believe, a historical dialectics to supply them with real critical and reflexive power. Criticism needs this vantage because the works it investigates are themselves eventual and interactive.

Eventual: While criticism wants to know what literary works are saying, even more it needs to know what they are doing in saying what they say.

Interactive: Literary work comprises a ceaseless dialogue of many agents. By their fruits we shall know them . . .

— and they us.

—What do you mean, "and they us"?

— I mean that our habitual ways of approaching literature typically fail because of our pursuit of scholastic normalizations. And we often engage these pursuits in the teeth of our own experience of the nonnormal normalities of literary works.

Critical editors condescend to modernizing editors, but both work to impose authoritative order on their texts. This happens because "intentionality" is embraced as the critical point of departure — the ultimate ground to which editors, when pressed, will generally find themselves driven. To edit "correctly," to read "accurately"; we seek to approximate what we hypothesize as a particular form of conscious purpose in the work, a form we name "the author." And we do this knowing full well that while such intentionality can be more or less sharply approximated, it (he, she) never has and never could become master of the production of text. Mastering textuality is not finally the point of entering the textual condition.

We read in the same spirit that the author writ, or at least we try to; and then — there and then — we also read not in that spirit — we read in different spirits. We are right to do these contradictory things because the texts themselves are, ab initio — and as the poet (Byron) said — "antithetically mixed" themselves.

If we looked squarely at our scholarly editions we would see that we do not practice what we often preach. Eclectic editions, diplomatic editions, facsimile editions, modernized editions: none reflects "what the author originally intended." We are deceived if we think that they do or that they could. Editors (and readers) ought to have an altogether different object in view than the approximation of an "authoritative" text. If we think about those several types of editions I mentioned, for example, we might see that each involves a formal choice about how to correspond with the texts that are coming down to us. If we want to operate critically with the metaphor of "reflection," then we might do better to think this way: what texts "reflect" is a complex dialogue with the past, or with other ways of being in the present; they reflect an effort to maintain and extend those dialogues.

In an important sense there is no such thing as a "bad text." Different texts serve different times, places, circumstances. Texts are "bad" in relation to other texts, which is to say in relation to other ways of establishing correspondences. (This is the case even for manifestly "corrupt" texts, as any scholar — perhaps especially medieval and classical scholars — understands.) The so-called Bad Quartos of Shakespeare are invaluable as guides for understanding Shakespeare and his audience. All the texts talk to us in their particular ways. Besides, if we judge some texts to be better than others, these judgments inevitably shift and change, as the recent shift in our views about the texts of *King Lear* has shown. Which text is "better," the first edition of *Sister Carrie* or the "unexpurgated" edition published decades later by Penn State University Press? People will argue the point, as they should; nonetheless, the point is undecidable. Different views will dominate at different times.

—Well then, what do you think? Which text is better? Or are you like Tennyson's speaker in "The Palace of Art"?

> I sit as God holding no form of creed,
> But contemplating all.

—I think both texts are better.

—Better than what?

—Better than themselves. And better because they are each so completely themselves, so wholly particular. All the texts are "good" because they are all "bad" too. This is why I say they are "better," because those categories "good" and "bad" tend to obscure the textual condition. One is pleased to have the Todd and Higginson edition of Dickinson's poetry, and pleased again by Franklin's recent attempt to reconstruct Dickinson's manuscript fascicles. Each of these editions has its special strengths and weaknesses, each has its special aims, meanings, achievements — and limits.

Perhaps we ought to think each is best of all just because each is so deeply involved with all the others. Johnson's edition has never seemed more important or useful than now, when its weaknesses have been exposed because of Franklin's texts. Johnson's edition made several generations think rather badly of Todd and Higginson's work, made them think Dickinson's poetry had suffered a benevolent crucifixion at Victorian hands. And of course it had (though that is not all we may see in the work of Dickinson's first editors). But Johnson hid the limits of his own work behind the limits of his forebears. These limits are now much more clear to us. We can see more texts in Johnson's edition than he knew about, more than he ever intended.

In this respect the situation of Dickinson's texts is not all that different from the case of *The Ambassadors*. And the case of *The Ambassadors*, strange as it may seem, is far from representing a textual condition.

— What does it mean?

— That by living in language we live in a material world — a world we never made, a world no one can presume to govern or control. The scholarly experience of this world recuperates the artistic experience: that it will not submit to mastering intentions. Like Frankenstein, artists raise up their creations only to find they have generated a monstrous progeny — "stubborn structures" that resist their ap(parent)ly original authority.

That experience of an active agency in created works — in creative works — passes on from generation to generation. The scholars' experience recapitulates the artists'. We scrutinize literary work with imaginations as active, in their way, as the imaginations of the poets. At no time have these critical pretensions been clearer than in our epoch, this (in)famous age of criticism. We descend on the texts with shocking eagerness, teasing or tearing out meanings their makers (and remakers) might or might not have wanted anything to do with. We are, like the poets, seeking to master these works, and we imagine theories of artistic creativity as precursive models for our second-order acts of critical pretension.

Socrates once praised dialectic at the expense of poetry because, he said, the works of the poets can't talk back. They are dumb, speechless — corpsed forms in dead documents. Gazing on the ruins of the Colosseum, Manfred saw something very different in the silent fragments of past endeavor. A "rugged desolation . . . fill'd up, / As 'twere, anew, the gaps of centuries." Spirit lives on because the material remains resist its passage into nonexistence. Manfred honors what he calls "the great of old"; honors what he calls

> The dead, but sceptred sovereigns, who still rule
> Our spirits from their urns.
>
> (*Manfred* 3.4.39-40)

That sovereignty, in which we share, is historical and material. It supervenes its representatives — in literature, that is, it supervenes the artists and their critics, the sorcerers and their apprentices. *The Ambassadors* locates a textual condition in which we all participate, and which we shall not master. The anomaly of its text is an emblem of textuality as such, where endless meaning seems to pour forth from dead letters. We glimpse such endlessness, however, not in the power of spiritual imagination, but in the deathlessness of the material scripts, in the "spirit" of their facticity — in that "positive existence" that Paul de Man, wrongly, thought literary works could never have.

De Man's sensitivity to the incommensurable in literature was very great. He saw its truth, but he saw it upside down. Keats saw it rightly when he (famously) opened his last failed project, "The Fall of Hyperion," by drawing a distinction between poetry as imagination and poetry as material script:

> Fanatics have their dreams, wherewith they weave
> A paradise for a sect; the savage too
> From forth the loftiest fashion of his sleep
> Guesses at heaven: pity these have not
> Trac'd upon vellum or wild Indian leaf
> The shadows of melodious utterance,
> But bare of laurel they live, dream, and die;
> For Poesy alone can tell her dreams,
> With the fine spell of words alone can save
> Imagination from the sable charm
> And dumb enchantment.
>
> ("The Fall of Hyperion: A Dream" 1–11)

Byron had little in common with Keats, but both came to share this view of the textual condition. The noble lord's version of Keats's idea comes in *Don Juan*, canto 8:

> But then the fact's a fact — and 'tis the part
> Of a true poet to escape from fiction.
>
> (stanza 86)

That's what happened to Henry James in *The Ambassadors*. He escaped from fiction.

PART THREE

Interpretation in a New Key

CHAPTER 8

Interpretation as a Game That Must Be Lost

In *The Need for Roots,* Simone Weil criticizes historical thinking and its search for documentary foundations. "There are holes in documents," Weil points out, so that when we read them we want to ensure that "unfounded hypotheses be present to the mind." Reading documents requires "reading between the lines, to transport oneself fully, with complete self-forgetfulness, into the events evoked there. . . . The so-called historical mind does not pass through the paper to flesh and blood; it consists of a subordination of thought to the document" (283–84).

This passage interests me for several reasons. First, it sets the idea of interpretation in a serious context. Weil always felt reading, like all forms of human action, as a spiritual emergency. Second, her critique of historicist method involves an insistence on the reader's share in any textual engagement. This insistence became such a critical commonplace during the past half-century, however, that it was far more often followed in the letter than the spirit. Readings which "pass through the paper to flesh and blood" are rare events — readings like, for instance, Weil's reading of *The Iliad,* Lautréamont's of Gothic fiction, or Acker's outrageous travesty of *The Scarlet Letter* and other classic nineteenth-century novels. The reading that Weil proposes involves what she sees as a transport and self-extinction, a passage to a human encounter "that is not me in any sense," as D. H. Lawrence once put the matter.

That way of reading leads me to my third reason for beginning with this passage from Weil, which takes off from Joan Dargan's "readerly" interpretation of the Weil passage: "it is the reader who determines where to travel in the space between the lines, which details are significant, and where their

complete meaning lies. For Weil, the discernment of the reader takes prece-
dence over the dictates of the document" (Dargan 6). That view of Weil's
reading proposal seems to me inadequate in several important respects. The
idea that an active reader can by determined effort discover a document's
significant details and track them to their "complete meaning" is not just mistaken, it is a mistaken reading of Weil. In the first place, the illusory concept
of a "complete meaning" was foreign to Weil's thinking. Furthermore, when
Weil speaks of the holes in documents, her words are figural, not literal. Do
we think she is speaking of holes in paper or vellum? No, Weil is reading the
readers of documents, and her critique applies as much to presentist historians who settle on the authority of a current reader, as it does to traditional
historicists who think the documents speak for themselves as incarnations of
a known past. Weil's documents do not contain possessable meanings, they
are full of wholes, they leak with meaning. The past is no more *given* or
unified than the present (or the future). Documents offer the possibility — as
endless as living — of an encounter with the human unknown.

"To find flesh and blood" is the ultimate purpose of reading and its sophisticated partner, interpretation. To achieve that engagement, it helps, I believe, to begin with Weil and her documents, rather than with that immate-
rial reading matter called "texts." For unlike texts, documents often do have
real holes in them, or are otherwise marked by their actual historical passage. The physical object — the specific manuscript, the particular edition or
printed object we read (like this very object you are reading now)— is coded
and scored with human activity. An awareness of this is the premise for interpreting material culture, and the awareness is particularly imperative for literary interpretation, where the linguistic "message" regularly invisibilizes the
codependent and equally meaningful "medium" that codes all messages.

The power of D. F. McKenzie's "sociology of texts" project rests in the
thoroughness of his understanding of "the primacy of the physical artifact
(and the evidence it bears of its own making)" (*Making Meaning* 267–68). As
the literary work passes on through time and other hands, to other readers
besides ourselves, it bears along with and *as* itself the gathered history of
all its engagements. Sometimes some of these codes appear explicitly in
the documents — as inscriptions, for instance, or marginalia, or bookplates or
labels or other physical transformations, like book damage or ornamental
additions. Secret and multiplying histories lie concealed in those tracings. Often, perhaps even more often, those multiplying histories have to be pursued
in other, less direct ways: who were its readers, when was it read, when wasn't
it read, where is/was it located, how was it produced, why and how has it
survived?

Those flesh and blood questions need flesh and blood answers. Why? Because interpretation is a social act — a specific deed of critical reflection made in a concert of related moves and frames of reference (social, political, institutional) that constitute the present as an interpreted inheritance from a past that has been fashioned by other interpreting agents. All these multiple agencies leave the documents marked with their diverse intentions and purposes, many of which were unapparent even to those who executed those purposes. Those three governing temporalities (past, present, future) are subject to an unlimited number of redeterminations, and every interpretational move is an instance of such a redetermination (itself subject to interpretation within what has been called "the hermeneutic circle"). Herself embedded within the circle (at "an inner standing-point," as D. G. Rossetti called it), the interpreting agent can be at most partially aware of this impinging and dynamic concert of reflection. The ideal interpreting agent can know the presence of the whole but never the sum of the parts.

I. Performative Interpretation

Within that general field of dynamic reflection we may usefully distinguish two kinds of interpretive action: a mode oriented in performative models, of which translation and parody are perhaps the master types; and a mode oriented in scholarship, which is our customary exemplar of interpretation. Although this essay will focus chiefly on scholarly interpretive models, we shall want to give close attention to performative models for a couple of important reasons.

Scholarly models regularly operate under a horizon of truth and the idea of its accessibility. This truth may be either normative (like Aristotle's rules) or positive ("scientific method" for determining facts) or some combination of both. The most advanced forms of interpretive scholarship — the production of scholarly editions — exhibit this hankering for truth in their common attachment to the idea of what has been called the "definitive edition": the edition that, if properly done, would obviate the need for further scholarly editions. When we speak of "the meaning" of a work (*the* meaning!) we are invoking the same fundamental ideological commitment. The spell of that (literally charming) ideal gets broken when one realizes (a) that scholarship is itself a historical performance executed within the framework of a certain limited (and limiting) sets of protocols; and (b) that the scholar's interpretive intervention alters the object of interpretation and the fields that organize those objects. Scholarship, in short, is itself performative. Like science, its basic commitment is not to "Truth" but to rigor (as to method), thoroughness (as to empirical evidence), and accuracy (in the treatment of its facts and data).

Scholarship and interpretation, therefore, are too narrowly conceived when they are imagined as being *about* something — as one might say that this essay is "about interpretation," or that one over there is about *Don Juan*. Rather, scholarship and interpretation are procedures that *do something about something*. The significance of that fact may become more clear if we shift our attention briefly to performative modes of interpretation per se.

In the nineteenth century, for example, the appreciation and study of literature began as recitation. "Readers" (like the famous McGuffey series of schoolbooks) compiled prose and poem texts for training people in oral performance and articulation. This ancient interpretive model lost nearly all of its authority during the last century, an unfortunate cultural lapse (we can now see). More rationalist procedures, thematically focused, worked to unhinge us from the physique of the literary experience that comes through so much more clearly in performative recitation.

Literary works can be, have been, "performed" in a variety of interpretive ways. "Did you ever read one of her Poems backwards. . . ? A something overtakes the Mind." That is Emily Dickinson's remarkable proposal for a recitation-based method of radical reinterpretation. William Morris's Kelmscott Press editions — for example of Chaucer, Keats, Rossetti, and of his own works, perhaps especially *The Earthly Paradise* — are acts of reinterpretation executed as bibliographical performances. Johanna Drucker's analysis of the different types of white space that function on a single page of the Kelmscott Chaucer — she distinguishes some twenty kinds — is a dramatic demonstration of the critical/interpretive potentials of bibliographical coding.

Such work bears a close functional resemblance to the interpretive performance of linguistic translation as such. In each case a target work is recast into another medium. If literary works were fundamentally data and information corpora, translation — bibliographical or linguistic — would aspire to as much literal transparency as possible. This is the working assumption guiding the practice of most information-technology approaches to literary works, such as TEI (the Text Encoding Initiative). But literary works covet a precision of differentials: they are machines that aspire to the multiplication of particular meaning, and adequate translations are obliged to reflect that quality.

One of the great acts of English language translation, Sir Thomas Urquhart's 1653 *The Works of Mr. Francis Rabelais*, perfectly illustrates what is called for. Rabelais is "now faithfully translated into English," we are informed on Urquhart's title page. But to be faithful in such a case is not to be literal, and if one compares Urquhart's work with his Rabelais original, one is struck by the astonishing freedom of his translation considered in a literal sense. Indeed, Urquhart's work often resembles a jazz performance in the riffs it plays off the Rabelaisian riffs it is responding to. Swinburne's translations of the "Dies Irae" or of Villon, like Rossetti's of Dante's *Vita Nuova*, are great translations because they exhibit the quality of "original works." All are also "critical" and interpretive acts, as we see, for example, in T. S. Eliot's recoil from Rossetti's work, which approaches Dante in a spirit utterly inimical to Eliot's twentieth-century Anglo-Catholicism.

Like Swinburne, Rossetti was well aware of the critical function his work was undertaking: "a translation," he observes in his preface to *The Early Italian Poets* (1861), "involving as it does the necessity of settling many points [of interpretation] without discussion . . . , remains perhaps the most direct form of commentary." We would add only that bibliographical design and recitation are equally "direct forms of commentary," as are pastiche, hoax, and parody. Brilliant examples of the critical use of such forms are plentiful from Poe and Wilde through Jarry and Borges. So far as scholarly interpretation is concerned, we have good recent examples of the critical potential of such models. The vigorous discussion that followed the hoax essay published in 1998 by Alan Sokal in *Social Text* is a succinct illustration of the critical power of the hoax form, as are the two books of Pooh parodies issued by Frederick Crews (in 1963 and 2001).

Those kinds of critical acts are humane and unnatural, which is why they are so common in the humanities, and so rare in the objective sciences, where the focus is trained on what is normative and what is natural (natural: that is to say "nonhuman," including the nonhuman aspects of human being). Acts of interpretation get invested with ludic elements in order to raise their level of self-critical awareness, on one hand, and on the other to dramatize the fact that meanings are *made* and are made for particular reasons. Philology's nineteenth-century turn to science for procedural models often obscures the subjectivity that is essential for literary and aesthetic interpretation. In science per se, objective norms are functional requirements. This is not the case in the arena of aesthetic inquiry. For us, even normative modes of interpretation — let us say, for instance, Dr. Johnson's — are proposed and argued, and are therefore always in question and at issue. Johnson would have thought Blake's interpretation of Milton and *Paradise Lost* reprehensible, perhaps even mad, and certainly not *true*. We may read Johnson with a similar critical freedom and construct (let us say) a Pooh parody of Johnson. That could be a useful interpretive act. It could not be done well, however, without bringing into play a fair amount of scholarly expertise, both procedural and informational.

II. Scholarly Interpretation

We commonly associate the interpretation of literature and culture with institutional apparatuses that develop and maintain certain rules and standards — the churches, the universities and their educational affiliates, professional organizations that monitor the literary law (that is to say, the arts and procedures for the accurate preservation of the works of culture). Within those institutional orbits — where this book, myself, and yourself are located — a host of "interpretational" activities are sanctioned and executed, and in recent years have proliferated at a rate that many find alarming. These procedures are most familiar when they coalesce under specialized headings that stand for methods of reading and critical exegesis: New Criticism, hermeneutics (various kinds), historicism (again, in various forms), theory (which develops in many meta-theoretical and interpretive subspecies like feminist, narrative, queer, psycho-analytic, etc.), narratology, cognitive poetics, Marxist criticism, literary pragmatics, and so forth. Observed from within a professional frame of reference, these activities fairly represent, so to speak, the varieties of interpretational experience. The phenomena of interpretation, that's to say.

In the heavens of interpretation are many mansions. Because all of those superstructures are "of the earth, earthy," we pursue their readerly devotions on the common ground they share with each other: the sociohistorical environment that licenses and shapes their interpretive possibilities.

So the scholar urges his friend the reader to begin the quest of interpretation "in the foul rag and bone shop of the heart." Yeats's famous line reminds us that all of literature's ladders start with the materials, means, and modes of textual production. If you are after flesh and blood in interpretation, if you mean to be serious, you begin with what the scholar calls "the history of a work's production" on one hand, and "the history of a work's reception" on the other. Those two historical strands together comprise the double helix from which the many forms of culture develop. Acts of interpretation, themselves coded by this double helix, typically select a particular aspect or view of our cultural inheritance for investigation. Whatever our governing interpretive specialization, we necessarily pursue our studies under the horizon of this double and codependent set of sociohistorical determinations. The works we examine have all been shaped by that double helix, and so have all our critical reflections on those works.

One caveat should be kept in mind, however. Certain interpreters focus their work on such technical issues — metrical and prosodic studies, for instance, or analytic and descriptive bibliography — that they often set aside as much as possible a consideration of their foundational interpretive frames of reference and agencies. Interpretation always negotiates a compromise between the demands of procedural rigor and the call for critical reflection. These kinds of technical studies remind us that an engineer and a theologian live and work inside even the most nuanced reflexive interpreter — Roland Barthes, say, or Umberto Eco. There is a foul rag and bone shop of the brain too, after all. To the degree that an interpretive procedure makes an ideological engagement with its subject, however, to that degree it will be forced to engage with the codependent pair of historical determinants (production history and reception history) and to reflect critically on its own place within those histories.

Given those general considerations, we can construct a general model for works of cultural interpretation. This model, given just below, is an analytic outline of interpretation's essential subjects and topics, whether we view interpretation as a program of work or as a practical event. The specific subjects and topics placed under each of the categorical headings call us to clarify their circumstantial character, that is, call us to a sociohistorical analysis of each element in the heading. These specific analyses, related together, constitute an analytic presentation of the category, and the adequacy of any interpretive act within that category will be a function of the range of discourse materials which are brought out for critical examination.

An interpretive investigation ranged under categories A and B comprises a theoretically finished sociohistorical program. Such a program gains a properly critical character when the material ranged under category C is incorporated into the analysis.

A. The Originary Discursive Moment

1. Author;
2. Other persons, groups, and agents invested in the initial process of cultural production;
3. The institutional frameworks of cultural production (ideological and material);
4. The material and cultural inheritances that can be shown to shape, positively or otherwise, these three factors;
5. The temporal phases that supply a coherent expository organization for analyzing each of those four factors.

B. Secondary Moments of Discursive Production and Reproduction (Individual and Related Sequences)

Discursive fields (or any portion of those fields) are dynamic and pass through processes of transformation engineered by the agencies that act within and upon those fields. These fields are what Humberto Maturana and Francesco Varela have called "autopoietic systems," that is, systems devoted to self-maintenance through processes of self-transformation. So the five dimensions comprising the "Originary Discursive Moment" all undergo a continual process of dynamic transformation and reconstruction. An "author," for example, will get re-viewed and reshaped over time by different people operating in the framework, material as well as ideological, of different classes, institutions, and groups. The number of Byron biographies illustrates the point, as it also shows that different cultural materials exert different levels of influence. Those reconstructive agencies themselves have to be studied and analyzed in terms of the five dimensions that characterize the originary discursive moment.

Discourse fields comprise specifiable works that emerge in certain concrete and specific forms along a series of equally concrete and particular avenues. Specifying the dynamic interplay of the field elements comprises the interpretational event.

The example of documentary transmission illustrates the general dynamical character of discourse fields. Literary documents bear within themselves the evidence of their own making, as McKenzie and others have shown, and those evidentiary marks solicit an interpretation of their meaning and significance. Historical patterns are literalized in the interpretation of a transmission history's documentary record.

Categories A and B are to be studied under interpretation's milder (and preliminary) rubric: "What does this mean?" Value judgments — political, ethical, aesthetic — remain after such a question is posed. Indeed, the question of the meaning of some feature of a discursive field must itself be ready for judgment, for the significance of an interpreter's questions cannot be taken for granted.

C. The Immediate Moment of Interpretation

This category proposes an analysis of the interpreter's own critical purposes. This is probably the most demanding of all interpretive tasks since it involves a critical reflection on acts of interpretation that remain in process of development.

This moment appears as a specific interpretive action that may get located in a particular essay or book, imaginative or otherwise, or in a particular constellation of such works. What is important to realize is that an interpreter may approach his subject matter critically (categories A and B) without ever subjecting his own critical work to interpretive reflection. The heuristic model for such an event (i.e., for reflection only at levels A and B) would be, for example, the production of a scholarly edition by a technically skilled editor as a set task; or the production of an interpretive essay or book from a standing-point assumed to be objective or in some fashion privileged with "enlightenment." Paul de Man's importance in the recent history of literary studies was a function of his acute critical sympathy with the blindness that accompanies the insight of most critical and interpretive acts.

Models for an interpretive action that positively seeks to approach a task from an inner standing-point — that is, models that solicit level C — would be either Thucydides' *History of the Peloponnesian War* or Trotsky's *History of the Russian Revolution*. Models from current literary studies would be Susan Howe's *My Emily Dickinson* or Charles Bernstein's *My Way*, in particular (say) his remarkable essay "The Revenge of the Poet-Critic; or, The Parts Are Greater Than the Sum of the Whole."

Works that exhibit a high degree of expertise in this third world of interpretation will almost inevitably assume a controversial position. Such works will also exhibit — probably by necessity — more or less serious deficiencies in their interpretive grasp of their given subjects (categories A and B). This interpretive *felix culpa* follows from the decision to lay the act of interpretation open to question as the act is going on. Such interpretations succeed by exposing their own interpretive limits.

Professional interpretive essays customarily organize their evidence in order to make a case for the interpretations they advance. They wait on other acts of interpretation for quality control. To that extent, such works can never themselves seriously address questions of value: is this interpretive understanding good or bad, is it right or wrong?

III. Interpretation by Indirection

Those are the questions that Simone Weil regarded as essential, and they haunt every interpretive act whether the act deliberately seeks to raise those questions or not. They are questions that can only be addressed (and readdressed), for they are open questions, they do not have "answers." The touchstone of critical and interpretive adequacy, then, follows from this question: how much has the subject or problem been opened out by the critic's intervention?

Such a question can't be usefully engaged — it too can never be closed — if the scholar or critic does not begin with a clear understanding that *every* interpretation is an abstract reduction drawn out of the original work. Scholars murder to dissect when their interpretations come to occupy the center of attention, rather than the works they are seeking out. Every critical performance is in this sense a *deformance:* but a useful deformance if self-consciously undertaken.

The great Italian scholar Galvano della Volpe developed a lucid explanation of how this critical procedure functions. His *Critique of Taste* (1960) develops what he calls a "realist" view of interpretation. Like Dante, and in contrast to, say, Coleridge or Schlegel, della Volpe sees imaginative literature as a type of "discourse" whose rationality — *ragionamento* — consists in its exploitation of the "polysemous" dimensions of language, whose structures are no more (and no less) difficult or even "mysterious" than processes of logical deduction and induction. For della Volpe, "intelligibility" is as much a feature of *poiesis* as of *scientia.*

Interpretation is the application of *scientia* to *poiesis,* or the effort to elucidate one discourse form in terms of another. Furthermore, the effort is not directed toward establishing general rules or laws but toward explaining a unitary, indeed a unique, phenomenon. A doubled gap thus emerges through the interpretive process itself, and it is the necessary presence of this gap that shapes della Volpe's critical thought. We may usefully recall here that when poets and artists use imaginative forms to interpret other such forms, they pay homage to this gap by throwing it into relief. Rossetti's famous sonnets for pictures, like all such works, from Cavalcanti to John Ashbery, do not so much translate the originary works as construct imaginative paraphrases. Rossetti's theory of translation, as we see in *The Early Italian Poets* (1861), follows a similar paraphrastic procedure.

Della Volpe's theory of interpretation runs along the same intellectual salient. When he argued that "critical paraphrase" should ground interpretive method, he was consciously installing a non-Hegelian form of dialectical criticism. In place of "a *circular* movement of negation and conservation of an original meta-historical unity of opposites," della Volpe offers what he calls "a dialectic of expressive facts" — the facts of the discrete poem and its discrete paraphrase — in which "neither of the elements of the relation can be reduced absolutely to the other . . . for . . . they . . . circulate only *relatively* within each other, in the *diversified unity of an historical movement*" (200). Interpretation for della Volpe, whatever its pretensions, always displays a gap between the work being examined and the student. But this gap does not represent a failure of criticism, or even a mysticism of *poiesis.* It locates the source and end and test of the art being examined. Della Volpe calls the gap a "quid," which comes into play as soon as the critic develops some "philosophical or sociological or historical equivalent of the poetic text," that is to say the "paraphrase . . . of the poetic thought or . . . content." Because this paraphrase will necessarily constitute "a reduction" of the original, "a comparison will necessarily be instituted between this paraphrase and the poetic thought or 'content' which it paraphrases" (*Critique of Taste* 193).

Critical interpretation develops out of an initial moment of the originary work's "degradation" via "uncritical paraphrase": "for in the case of the poetic, polysemic text, paraphrase — the *regression* to current linguistic use . . . constitutes the premise of an internal *progression* of thought . . . , an internal variation and development of meanings, which is disclosed . . . in a . . . philological comparison . . . of the paraphrase with that which is paraphrased" (*Critique of Taste* 133). Interpretation, then, is a constellation of paraphrases that evolve dialectically from an uncritical to a critical moment, from "regression" to "progression." The interpretive constellation develops as the "uncritical" features of each critical turn get exposed — as new turns are taken, as the paraphrase is successively rephrased. One moves so to speak from "degradation" to "degradation," or, as we would say, from deformance to deformance. Thus paraphrastics becomes "the *beginning* and *end* of a whole process" of comparative explorations that get executed across the "quid" or gap that a process of interpretation brings into being. Again, the process is open-ended not because the "poem itself" possesses some mysterious, inexhaustible "meaning" but because its originary semiotic determinations must repeatedly be discovered within the historical space defined by the della Volpian "quid," where distantiation licenses "the method . . . of experimental analysis" (*Critique of Taste* 199).

Della Volpe carefully separates his theory of interpretation from the dialectics we associate with Hegel and especially Heidegger. The latter involves a process of thought refinement: through conversation or internal dialogue, we clarify our ideas to ourselves. We come to realize what we didn't know we knew. This kind of reflection traces itself back to the idea of Platonic anamnesis. Della Volpe, by contrast, follows an Aristotelian line of thought, a "method . . . of experimental analysis." This method develops a process of non-Hegelian historical reflection. Interpretive moments stand in nonuniform relations with each other so that the interpretation unfolds in fractal patterns of continuities and discontinuities. Besides realizing, perhaps, what we didn't know we knew, we are also led into imaginations of what we hadn't known at all.

Being a philologist, della Volpe pursues this kind of analysis through a series of searching historicist paraphrases of the texts he chooses to consider. To attempt a sociohistorical paraphrase is to experiment with the poetical work, to subject it to a hypothesis of its meanings. As in any scientific experiment with natural phenomena, the engagement with the originary phenomenon inevitably exposes the limits of the hypothesis, and ultimately returns us to an even more acute sense of the phenomena we desire to understand. So it is with della Volpe's paraphrases. By contrast, our "experimental analyses" place primary emphasis on the preconceptual elements of text. We do this because social and historical formations seem to us far less determinate, far more open to arbitrary and imaginative construction, than they appear in della Volpe's Marxist frame of reference.

If we follow della Volpe's method, then, we feel ourselves closer in spirit to the thought of, say, Blake when he remarks on the difference between the intelligence of art and the intelligence of philosophy: "Cunning & Morality are not Poetry but Philosophy the Poet is Independent & Wicked the Philosopher is Dependent & Good" (Blake 634). Our deformations do not flee from the question, or the generation, of "meaning." Rather, they try to demonstrate — the way one demonstrates how to make something, or do something — what Blake here assertively proposes: that "meaning" in imaginative work is a secondary phenomenon, a kind of metadata, what Blake called a form of worship "Dependent" on some primary poetical tale. This point of view explains why, in our deformative maneuvers, interpretation represents a thought experiment we played with the primary materials. In the experiment of interpretation, "Meaning" is initially important as a catalyst in the investigative action. When the experiment has (for the nonce) finished, Meaning reappears in a new form, as the residues left behind for study and analysis. Meanings emerge then not as explanations of the poem but as evidence for judging the effectiveness of the experiment we undertook.

One could do worse than to recall, even in this special aesthetic frame of reference, Marx's last thesis on Feuerbach. Only philosophers try to understand art. The point is to change it. (Editorial efforts to preserve our cultural inheritance are themselves types, perhaps arch-types, of the changes we make when we try to preserve that inheritance). Our actions on these works, our deformations, help us to understand our thinking about them. To essay a more direct application of "interpretation" to imaginative work runs the risk of suggesting that interpretation can be adequate to *poiesis*. It cannot; it can only run a thematic experiment with the work, enlightening it by inadequacy and indirection. Like the art works it explores, interpretation is what Ford Madox Ford called "a game that must be lost."

In a critical age like our own, illusions about the sufficiency of interpretative meaning before the work of art are especially strong. At such a historical moment one might rather look for interpretations that flaunt their subjectivity and arbitrariness, interpretations that increase their value by offering themselves at a clear discount.

To deliberately accept the inevitable failure of interpretive "adequacy" is to work toward discovering new interpretive virtues, somewhat as Lyn Hejinian claims that the supposed "inadequacy" of language "is merely a disguise for other virtues." Interpretive works that parody or ironize themselves are especially useful — works like Derrida's *The Post Card* or Laura Riding's remarkable *Anarchism Is Not Enough*. Riding's attitude toward the process of critical thinking is helpful: "our minds are still moving, and *backward* as well as *forward;* the nearest we get to truth at any given moment is, perhaps, only an idea — a dash of truth somewhat flavouring the indeterminate substance of our minds" (*Progress* 10). This thought calls for a critical method intent on baring its own devices. We take it seriously because it makes sure that we do not take it too seriously. Examples of such critical approaches are legion: we just need to remember to look for them, and perhaps how to look for them.

CHAPTER 9

Visible Language, Interface, IVANHOE

I. Enlightenment, Through a Glass Darkly

The online game space IVANHOE was conceived, designed, and finally built as a means to expose and explain the field of interpretation at a general level. For the project to have a significant outcome, the interpretive act, the object of interpretation, and the relation between them would have to be imagined comprehensively. That traditional three-part distinction in software programming — conception, design, development — indexes the level of generality we are after.

The normative cultural object for the work, in this initial development stage, was taken to be textual (rather than graphical or auditional). It was also determined to be an aesthetic object (a poem or an imaginative fiction) rather than an informational one (an almanac or an expository essay) on the grounds that the former stands in a clear dynamic relation to the act of interpretation. Unlike informational materials, poems are not well conceived as if they were in possession of a meaning asking to be located, extracted, or put to some use; and that, once these instrumental operations are carried out, the meaning circuit will be closed. Poems are the leveraging devices in autopoietic fields which maintain themselves by making possible many meanings and many kinds of meaning.

Nonetheless, we also know that the poetic field cannot be negotiated without locating, extracting, and making use of what we take to be significant informational features of the field. In this respect the poem as a field of meaning comprehends — includes as part of its operating system — fields of meaning that are proper to informational works.

The famous, or infamous, "uselessness" of aesthetic works needs to be re-called here. A poetical work is useless only in a very specific sense. We some-times say that poems aren't made to make something happen, or that — whatever the writer's initial intentions — *in fact* they "make nothing happen," as a famous poet famously said. But of course we know that neither of those commonplaces is entirely true. Satirists regularly write to make something happen, and many writers by their writings create very specific real-world happenings, sometimes deliberately (as in the case of Swinburne's *Poems and Ballads* [1866], which generated just the kind of controversy he anticipated), sometimes inadvertently (as in the case of the lawsuits that followed the pub-lication of *Don Juan* and *Ulysses*).

Still, the idea that poetry is useless is useful. It reminds us that we cannot measure the poetic outcome in terms of a set of specific intentions, whether conscious or otherwise, whether author's or readers'. Intentionality pervades the poetic space, but its specific character or status waits on the reader's share in the interpretive exchange. You cannot have meaning without an intention for meaning. The self-subsistent "poem itself," so cultivated in the twentieth century, is riven with autotelic purpose and intentionality. A poem's useful-ness is therefore traditionally measured by its reception histories, which record the mutations it has undertaken and undergone over time.

No poem is an island. Its transformations emerge not just over time, but in spaces occupied by many people, each one altering that space — the poetic inheritance — in the use that each makes of it. In autopoetic systems like po-etry, these changes not only do not alter the basic identity of the poem, they constitute the only means by which that persisting identity can be sustained. Understanding this, a poet will say (in a poem called "The Cloud") that "I change, but I cannot die," and he will simultaneously mean us to understand that this dynamic fact about the hydrogen cycle is a metaphor for explaining the dynamics of the poem. Shelley casts his poem in the first person as a rhe-torical device for making that precise point and transformational relation. But the poem has to be read, and in that event — however it gets executed — the poem moves into a third-person rhetoric, which becomes, simultaneously, the first-person syntax of the reader. We readers understand what the poet is saying and doing because, in the field of poetry, everyone in a poetical space occupies an inner standing-point.

II. Criticism as an Artifact of Absorption

Can you locate the inner standing-point in the six paragraphs that open this chapter? Critical inquiry poses that question to every object it studies, but rarely does the question get turned reflexively back on the act of criticism itself (or its agent). For the presumption of knowledge is one of the great legacies of Enlightenment. The rhetorical position of those six paragraphs is that they know what they're talking about (so to say) and that a reader can extract that content.

That kind of expository writing comes with a set of interface conventions (printing conventions) designed to control the critical act so that its questions do not fly off in unexpected ways or — even worse — turn against the critical act itself. The normalization of spelling, typography (elements, forms, and general design rules), and archiving procedures set a precise framework for the practice of a criticism determined to authorize itself on models drawn from Enlightenment science.

All this is well known — indeed, it has been the mantra of cultural studies for almost fifty years, authorizing a variety of deconstructive procedures — social, psychoanalytic, formal, linguistic. Despite these thematic trends in the recent history of criticism, the typographical stability of the scholarly book or essay remains, nor has it much changed since Dr. Johnson's day. The contrast with the critical and scholarly inheritance that descends to us from earlier periods is notable, as the examples of Ramon Lull, Athanasius Kircher, Sir Thomas Browne, and even Leibniz show. Coleridge apologizes for the fractured, wayward, and incomplete state of the *Biographia Literaria,* yet we now understand that these incoherences are what make the work the masterpiece that it is. We appreciate and study to understand the visible experiments with language and typography that have transformed poetic practice since the mid-nineteenth century. The correspondent breeze from academic scholarship and criticism has been faint by comparison. And yet we have notable examples, ancient as well as modern, to study, imitate, and revise.

Herbert Horne was a critic who used poetry to illustrate and explain the power of typographical interface. But Horne was a scholar working in an environment that was not dominated by the conventions of academicism, as our critical space is dominated. Horne's scholarly traditions go back to people like Lull, Montaigne, Erasmus, and Browne, and they can be tracked forward in the work of Pound, Reznikoff, Riding, Graves and thence into our own period, as Susan Howe's work illustrates. But so attenuated has our practice of a *scholar's art* grown that we have difficulty seeing and understanding the scholarly value in this kind of work, the relation between scholarship and art. To this day academic critics regard the great editions of Emily Dickinson produced in the 1890s by Todd and Higginson as "corrupt," or as examples of a practice with "historical interest." Both are Enlightenment views — the one critical, the other sympathetic, but neither prepared to grasp the scholarly power of what Todd and Higginson accomplished.

We do not require a new set of expressive or typographical tools. But we do need a much greater attention to these embodiments of our studies. Like Pound's *ABC of Reading*, Howe's collage procedures in *My Emily Dickinson* use a minimal set of book design features to score her scholarly work for our later practice. Readers have difficulty with the book, if they do, because they have internalized the transparencies of the academic monograph and essay. We get unused to thinking about, or thinking in and through, the message's medium. But the medium *is* the message in the sense that a person is an embodied soul.

Charles Bernstein's critical essay "The Revenge of the Poet-Critic" is instructive here. To demonstrate how it works I quote at length from an especially salient passage:

> often it is a breaking down of the chain of sense that lets me find my way. A way away from the scanning over and over what went wrong — the failure of community that may, in flits and faults, give way to conversation. I start with the senselessness of the world and try to make some sense with it, as if words were visceral and thoughts could be tolls. It's the loss, I want to say, I don't know *of what* — but not to find either (neither voice nor truth: voicings, trusts).
>
> DON'T BE SO SURE (DON'T BE SAUSSURE)
>
> My cup is my cap
> & my cap is my cup
> When the coffee is hot
> It ruins my hat
> We clap and we slap
> Have sup with our pap
> But won't someone please
> Get me a drink

What is a poet-critic, or critic-poet, or professor-poet-critic?; which comes first and how can you tell?; do the administrative and adjudicative roles of a professor mark the sell-out of the poet?; does critical thinking mar creativity, as so many of the articles in the Associated Writing Program newsletter insist? Can poets and scholars share responsibilities for teaching literature and cultural studies or must poets continue to be relegated to, or is it protected by, creative writing workshops, where, alone in the postmodern university, the expressive self survives?

Of course I must agree, I confide to the prize-winning poet, all this stuff about poetry groups and movements is a publicity stunt for poets without the imaginative capacity to assert their unique individuality in forms and voices utterly indistinguishable from the other prize-winning poets who vote these awards to each other on panels and juries that systematically rule out any trace of individuality expressed by particularity of tone, diction, syntax, or form. Indeed, you force me to concede the point, I tell the politically committed academic, this poetry excludes most of the people in the world (who haven't yet learned English!); it's turned its back on the ordinary reader by making no effort to reach out to him or her. And, yes, indeed, Professor, I also must admit, even though it seems to go against your last point, that all this poetics stuff is just an attempt to attract readers, making the work just one more commodity being peddled. Of course you're right, I tell the few friends I have left, now that I am poet-professor at the University at Buffalo, I have retreated to an Ivory Tower, removed from the daily contact I used to have, as a poet-office worker in Manhattan, with the broad masses of the American people . . . the ones that I used to meet at downtown poetry readings and art openings.

And surely it is a scandal, I tell my students, how Americans are afflicted with attention-deficit disorder, just like they say in *Time* magazine, which after all should know, being one of the major sites of infection for the disease it laments, with its "you can never simplify too much" approach to prose and its relentless promotion of exclusively predigested cultural product. And since we all know students can't follow a linear and symbolic argument of a conventional poem, how can you possibly expect them to read the even-more-difficult poems you seem bent on promoting, interjects a concerned younger member of the faculty, eager, in his own classes, to present the ideological cracks in the surface of popular culture? You want to take things that appear accessible and linear, I reply, and show how they are complex and inaccessibly nonlinear; I want to take things that appear complex and nonlinear and show how this complexity is what makes them accessible in the sense of audible (auditable). And, I continue, waving my

arms and upping the tempo as my colleague's eyes begin to spin in orbits, isn't the nonlinearity of much so-called disjunctive poetry indeed
a point of contact with the everyday cultural experiences of most
North Americans, where overlays of competing discourses is [*sic*] an
inevitable product of the radio dial, cable television, the telephone, advertising, or indeed, at a different level of spatialization, cities? But isn't
advertising and the commercialization of culture a bad thing, inter-
rupts the future public intellectual, isn't that what poetry should be
trying to resist; and isn't the sort of poetry you promote just a capitu-
lation to the alienated, fragmented discourse of postmodern capitalism? If you say so, I reply in the manner of Eeyore, as if I had found myself caught in a Gap ad (Robert Frost Wore Khakis: "the gaps I mean").
But you can't quite have it both ways: the form of much of the most in-
novative modernist and postwar poetry may not be the obstacle you
imagine it to be, so don't use that fact as a way of dismissing the activity
as esoteric. Neither hypotaxis nor parataxis has an intrinsic relation to
poetry, cultural resistance, or accessibility: the mistake is to demonize
radically paratactic approaches as both the unreflected product of the
worst of the culture and at the same time as esoteric, though I would
suggest this particular double bind is a very effective tool for the strin-
gent enforcement of cultural hegemony within a multicultural environment. And do beware the role of Public intellectual, my friend, for
when the *New York Times* starts talking about either the death or rebirth
of public intellectuals, it can only remind us that intellectuality as a form
of linguistically investigative activity has been banned for a long time.

A more thorough act of critical reflection is hard to imagine since Bernstein's
commentary ranges abroad only to keep turning back on itself. At once deadpan and ludic, the passage does not clearly signal its intentions until the itali-
cized *"of what"* introduces a clearly marked gesture of self-reflection. This
gesture might be read "seriously," as in a style of self-address we know and admire from Montaigne's *Essais* or Wittgenstein's *Philosophical Investigations*.
But that option gets overthrown — dare we say "problematized"? — when
Bernstein introduces his witty doggerel poem. From that point forward a
faux-naive conversational style modulates with a high academic jargon to produce an act of critical inquiry that takes no prisoners.

   Notice in particular the economy of Bernstein's typographical means. Unlike Howe's *My Emily Dickinson*, this passage never deviates at all from the text-
design proprieties we practice and expect in our academic discourse. The
satiric thought requires this appearance of strict formal regularity at the level

of the signifier (the typographical design). Bernstein's doggerel poem turns out to be a signal that we have entered unaware into the poem's codependent other: here, a fully articulated doggerel academic prose. The critical trenchancy of the passage depends on the thoroughness and purity of its ludic posture.

Elsewhere Bernstein calls this writing procedure an "Artifice of Absorption." Its antecedents are Brecht's practice of "epic theater" and, less well-known, Rossetti's ideas about writing at "an inner standing-point." In each case the privilege of critical enlightenment is drawn into the scene of study and reflection. What I want to stress in this case, however, is the relevance of the expressive medium to the critical artifice. The critical practices of Howe and Bernstein exemplify a tendency, already evident in certain modernist writers (Stein, Williams, and Riding are notable instances), to break the spell of expository prose typography. More recently, we have the example of Frederick Crews's Pooh project, and dialogue has begun to reappear in the academic scene in a regular way. Or take Bruce Andrews's reading of Ashbery's *The Tennis Court Oath*, a superb instance of a deliberately fashioned underprivileged style.

MISREPRESENTATION

A TEXT FOR *THE TENNIS COURT OATH* OF JOHN ASHBERY

> Thus, when the universal sun has set, does the moth seek the lamp-light of privacy.
>
> (Karl Marx)

1. "Uh huh." "Huh." "Heh? Eh?" What *had* you been thinking about? Since, from the very start, this outward-looking topic or conjuncture of words is *convulsed*, "the face studiously bloodied" by all that combs the text. "Hush!"
   But — the conjunction — registers the tone. "but what testimony buried under colored sorrow". So this is not evidence for some theory but a gloss on loss, regret, confusion, clarity, the net of hope unraveling both night & day. And our reading *registers* this dizzying parade — of eroded representations and wreckage. Are they what we want? "When through the night. . . . Pure sobs denote the presence. . . . Of supernatural yearning".

   (from *In the American Tree*, 520)

Arranged in twenty numbered sections, Andrews's commentary references the design format of Wittgenstein's *Philosophical Investigations*, perhaps the defining example in the past century of an artifactual presentation of critical thinking. Like Wittgenstein, Andrews constructs his remarks as a theater of a mind (and sensibility) in action. Andrews is thinking and feeling his way through a text (Ashbery) that has constructed itself out of a series of "misrepresentations," to which Andrews's commentary adds its own series of further, self-reflective deformations.

The critical writings of Howe, Bernstein, and Andrews that we've examined are unusual only because they lay bare the devices of any critical artifacture. The simple but often forgotten truth about textual embodiments — scriptures, typographies, oralities — is that they let us perceive the action of our thinking and feeling. Another simple but forgotten truth is that we commonly deploy these embodiments with such undeliberateness that they come forth as mere dead letters, concealing and even killing the thinking and feeling they were meant to activate.

III. At the Interface of Text and Interface

We know how to practice many kinds of scholarly artifacture in the book medium. The opportunities are specific to that medium, however, as one immediately sees when trying to undertake traditional critical acts in a different medium altogether. Digital presentation does not take naturally to the long essay, and least of all to the interpretive action carried out in a scholarly monograph. Putting novels online shows that while the technology is an excellent medium for storage, dissemination, and data analysis, it is not a good environment for extensive acts of human reading. On the other hand, what is perhaps the greatest device ever invented by the scholarly imagination, the critical edition, lends itself very well to translation into digital media.

Executing that translation has forced us to a rigorous critical reflection on the operational capacities of both media. Trying to move our inherited cultural archive into digital forms — simply to store and make accessible digitized simulations of the things we have preserved in museums and libraries — requires a fundamental rethinking, and reimagining, of the ontologies that are embedded in those archival things. To consider just the case of textual things, we now can see very clearly, which is to say in the most practical way, that "all text is marked text" — that our documentary records are not raw data but highly interpreted and structured data. When we try to translate them into digital form, we have to sort and classify in the most precise way the complex ontological structures that pervade these "things," which can appear so simple, self-identical, and transparent.

The intersection of print and digital media has thus been a great benefit to our understanding of both. An enthusiasm for the powers of digitization drives AI (Artificial Intelligence) research in its quest to map human intelligence in digital forms. Setting aside the question of the reliability of such projects, we can say that much is to be gained from a different approach. Rather than think of the computer as a kind of brain, think of it as a kind of book. Scriptural, graphical, and bibliographical technology are parts — integratable parts — of a machinery we use to simulate and visualize the activity of human intelligence. We want to think of digital machinery in an analogy with book machinery — that is to say, as what Coleridge called "aids to reflection."

Books are clearly second-order mechanisms that enhance our capacities to recall, aggregate, visualize, and reflect on human experience, perceptual as well as conceptual. We regularly — too regularly — conceive the content and form of texts and textuality in narrow linguistic analogies. But the book is a semiotic not a linguistic machine. It is not composed of words (drawn from a dictionary) and rules for their use (syntax algorithms). It is a machine for processing a variety of symbolic forms organized in looping autopoetic structures. It is a database that stores many kinds of symbolic tokens (not just words) which its flexible interface can transform and visualize for human use and reflection.

Those are the same operations that digital tools perform. But a great opportunity comes with these new machines, as we see when we try to use them to simulate those antecedent second-order machines for knowledge transmission, books.

Philologists in the nineteenth century defined their discipline as "the knowledge of what is known," making explicit the distinctive feature of that most human of the human sciences: systematic reflection. Philosophy can be practiced, perhaps indeed is best practiced (as Plato thought), without the machinery of the book. Without the apparatus of a complexly integrated and dispersed archival system (let us call it the World Library), philology is what used to be called "antiquarian study." It becomes Philology with the coming of the order of the book. With the emergence of a digital order, Peirce's Semiotics becomes Semiology.

The logical forms appropriate to the pursuit of this human science have been an intense cultural and academic preoccupation for more than a hundred years, and the achievements have been remarkable. As we put in place machines that can make practical application of these logics — an event largely of the past quarter century — the problem of interface has emerged in stark and challenging form, as we see every day in our visits to the Internet. Digital instruments are only as good as the interfaces by which we think through them. Recall Keats's trenchant observation that "the poet and the dreamer are distinct" (*The Fall of Hyperion* 1.199):

> Fanatics have their dreams, wherewith they weave
> A paradise for a sect; the savage too
> From forth the loftiest fashion of his sleep
> Guesses at Heaven; pity these have not
> Trac'd upon vellum or wild Indian leaf
> The shadows of melodious utterance.
> But bare of laurel they live, dream, and die;
> For Poesy alone can tell her dreams,
> With the fine spell of words alone can save
> Imagination from the sable charm
> And dumb enchantment.
> (*The Fall of Hyperion* 1.1–11)

Without sophisticated techniques for knowledge re-presentation, digital programs are just so much dreaming in code. Nor do we want a class of middlemen who are the self-licensed interpreters of that field of dreams. We want the fine spells of interface to write and read them ourselves.

IV. IVANHOE: An Interface for Interpretation

Described in the metaphors of digital technology, IVANHOE is a second-order interface for enhancing our ability to transact the first-order interfaces of cultural materials. Do those figurations alienate? Book and digital scholars alike need an estrangement from our habits of thinking about the machines of representation that we think we know so well.

An essay on John Cowper Powys's *A Glastonbury Romance* is no substitute for an experience of that remarkable work, which we begin to know by an act of reading an actual book, the interface that first represents its codes for us. As Wittgenstein would say, "the meaning [of that book] is in the use" we make of it (*Philosophical Investigations* sec. 43). Uses range from a personal reading engagement with Powys's original fiction to multiple secondary acts of engagement, as in this very paragraph you are reading. We learn how to read, how to use, all of these machineries.

Playing IVANHOE is more like reading *A Glastonbury Romance* than like reading a commentary on that work. A generalized artifacture of absorption, IVANHOE installs an environment that promotes interpretation and critical reflection at an inner standing-point. As a piece of software, IVANHOE can only be learned by putting it to use. You don't want to read about playing games of interpretation with IVANHOE, you want actually to play the games (*if* you want anything to do with IVANHOE in the first place).

Nonetheless, a book space like this one has, like Ahab, its humanities. It can help to clarify the conceptual and design foundations of IVANHOE and hence to think about and assess those foundations. IVANHOE is more than a device for "Interpretation in a New Key," it is a project for investigating the interface mechanisms that are needed to promote and execute those interpretive functions.

First of all, it's important to know that IVANHOE can be played, has been played, on paper. Indeed, its historical roots are as ancient as any of our inherited cultural works. Genesis translates and transforms earlier creation stories, and Homer's epics are each carefully tailored selections drawn from a large corpus of heroic legend and history. The *Iliad* is what Rob Pope would call a "textual intervention" in the Matter of Troy.

These examples represent alterations of the form and content of inherited materials. Digital IVANHOE installs as well a procedural intervention that forces one to reimagine the notions of "textuality" and "intervention." If it is true — and I think it is — that "the best way to understand how a text works . . . is to change it" (Pope 1), the best way to understand how that changing action works is to change *it*. In this case, to recast the intervention machinery from textual into digital form. Into the IVANHOE application.

To imagine such an application you start by imagining what it looks like to play or implement a session of IVANHOE, with or without a digital environment. A group of people, two at a minimum, agree to collaborate in thinking about how to reimagine a particular work, say *Ivanhoe*. The agreement is that each person will try to reshape the given work so that it is understood or seen in a new way. The reshaping process in IVANHOE is immediate, practical, and performative. That's to say, the interpreters intervene in the textual field and alter the document(s) by adding, reordering, or deleting text, and by marking patterns of relation that these interventions generate. The interpretive moves are meant to expose meaningful features of the textual field that were unapparent in its original documentary state. Interpreters will also look for ways that their interventions might use or fold in with the interpretive moves of others working the collaborative session of IVANHOE.

Some analogies may be helpful. IVANHOE's interpreting agents approach their work much as performers or conductors approach a piece of music, or the way a director approaches a play. The performance in these cases fashions an interpretation of the original work, and the result is what Gertrude Stein, in a slightly different sense, called "Composition as Explanation." Performative interpretations of all kinds — translation, for example — have much in common with IVANHOE. Book artists and illustrators work along similar interpretive lines, and we have many cases where authors themselves illustrate or design the embodiments of their own textual works, thereby glossing them with intervening sets of interpretive signs. Some notable figures integrate text and visualization into a composite or double work — in England one thinks immediately of Blake, Dante Gabriel Rossetti, Edward Lear, Lewis Carroll. Or consider how the "Matter of Troy" and the "Matter of Arthur" are conceived and elaborated. A set of legends centering on the Trojan war and on King Arthur multiply as versions and variants that expose fresh ranges of meaning resting latently in the materials. The interpretive transformations that unfold in a session of IVANHOE seek to exploit a logic of interpretation of those kinds.

IVANHOE is not like a "creative writing workshop," however. Its textual transformations get executed in a frame of reference focused on the significance of the changes *in relation to the originary textual field and the changes that one's collaborating agents make to that field*. The presence of the initial state of the text(s) is always preserved because the point of IVANHOE is to study that field of relations as it provokes or licenses its readers to reimagine its implications and textual possibilities. Interpreters are expected to keep a journal in which their interpretive moves are justified and explained in relation to the originary work and/or the moves made by the other agents.

Though they have much in common with Oulipian exercises, IVANHOE's textual transformations promote what Coleridge called "Aids to Reflection." If it should be seen as "A User's Manual," as I think it should, the users have been imagined from the outset as students and scholars.

IVANHOE is thus a proposal for reading and thinking critically about textual fields, especially traditional works of literature and culture, in the historical context of the late twentieth century, when such works found themselves in a collision with born-digital textualities. The volatile convergence of these two semiotic machineries has made possible a new set of parameters for studying and using expressive forms, paper-based as well as digital. IVANHOE is not, however, a new "theory" of textuality. It is a practical mechanism — a kind of laboratory — for experimenting with these ideas and refining our understanding of them, and of their relevance to the general inquiry they have set us on.

IVANHOE emerged from seven regulatory conceptions, or "Theses on Textuality," which were tested against a single but rigorous measure: could the theses be practically realized in a working software application? Could the conception of IVANHOE be designed and built?

Here is the set of IVANHOE's regulatory ideas. I will take up each in turn and gloss its pertinence to the work of the project.

1. The textual field is a Bakhtinian space (heteroglossia).
2. In textual space, a equals a if and only if a does not equal a.
3. Textual fields arise codependently with interpretative action.
4. Textual forms are generated by algorithmic and autopoietic devices.
5. Interpretive action is always performative/deformative.
6. Interpretation of a textual field proceeds at an inner standing-point.
7. Textual fields are n-dimensional.

Each of these ideas is heavily invested in the others, and we do not want to think of them as forming a serial or hierarchical set. They are in a sense redundant expressions of a single proposal for thinking about textuality and fields of discourse. I have arranged them in this particular sequence strictly for rhetorical purposes, to help clarify the experimental domain that IVAN-HOE marks out for itself.

The textual field is a Bakhtinian space (heteroglossia). We begin here because Bakhtin's critical revision of formal and structuralist models of textuality is well known and broadly dispersed in literary and cultural studies. Focusing on the sociolinguistic dimension of textuality, Bakhtin demonstrated how texts are immersed in a complex "discourse field" of conflicting, competing, and overlapping "languages." Critical analysis can show how any given text folds multiple expressive forms into an organized set of dominant and indominant features. Language users inherit linguistic codes of many kinds from different sources, and while certain of these exert primary control in the organizing of meaning, latent and recessive linguistic forms are deeply embedded in the discourse field. Bakhtin's method is to show the structure of these heteroglossial forms in particular works and to demonstrate from his case studies some general principles about discourse fields and their dialectical dynamics.

Because Bakhtin's method is fundamentally oriented toward classical philology, his work does not factor into its analysis any critical reflection on the phenomenology of his own criticism. While his own critical "method" is thus more flexible than the nonhistoricist "formal methods" he opposes, it too, like the latter, does not incorporate a "critique of enlightenment" into its procedures. Like classical science, Bakhtin's method proposes that, given ideal conditions, it could expose the entire linguistic truth of any text.

In textual space, a equals a if and only if a does not equal a. Bakhtin's work prepared the ground for a more fundamental reassessment of textuality. Any given natural language text (so-called) will be marked by the presence of different language games. Imaginative texts work by exploiting these multiple expressive agencies while expository texts, which pursue an informational goal, seek to minimize ambiguity. The most extreme cases of the latter would be the formal languages written for computers. The latter propose to construct sign systems that close coherently upon themselves. They are systems where $a = a$. But in any mother tongue, while the value of a (syntagmatic or semantical) always has a known range of normalcy, it remains open to random change and is thus strictly unpredictable. This is the message that Humpty Dumpty gives to Alice, who was raised to think and speak in normal Victorian ways. Of course Victorian Alice, being both a child and a girl, has the curiosity of a subaltern person. That curiosity — Peirce called it "abduction" — sends her through the looking glass where she can begin to reimagine the world.

Formal languages are created as a function of natural language — a far richer and more powerful sign system than digital signs precisely because, in fact, a does not equal a, as any glance at a dictionary will immediately reveal. Indeed, the two most ambiguous and meaning-flexible words in the English language are the simplest, the articles "a" and "the." Textuality is, like light, fundamentally incoherent. To bring coherence to either text or to light requires great effort and ingenuity, and in neither case can the goal of perfect coherence be attained.

The paradox involved in this principle is, like all paradoxes, only apparent and logical. It arrests our attention simply because the principle of identity is taken as axiomatic in every discipline of knowledge we employ. It can be shown logically that the principle of noncontradiction is self-contradictory — a demonstration that was apparently first made by Nagarjuna in the fifth century. Far from a being equal to a, we know on the contrary the truth of the following conventional idea: that "nothing is what it appears to be."

In order to know anything, however, we have to propose the useful fiction that $a = a$. From this conscious intellectual move we can proceed to execute the primary critical act: we can draw a distinction, from which further sets of distinctions can then be generated.

The non-self-identity of objects in a discourse field is not, however, primarily a logical function — or at any rate does not immediately (phenomenologically) strike us as such. Semiotic and linguistic forms are incoherent because they have to be marked in order to be perceived at all. The marks are acoustic, calligraphic, typographic, digital; they are phonological, ideographical, alphabetical; they are semantic and syntactic. Each of these forms of distinction cuts the textual field and divides it from itself according to some assumed point of view and set of protocols. The textual fields that we know are fields that have been marked for knowing in particular ways. D. G. Rossetti wanted to represent this phenomenon in a pictorial image. He called the work—which he never carried beyond an initial sketch—"Venus Surrounded by Mirrors, Reflecting Her in Different Views."

The elementary forms of textual markup listed above are commonly deployed in instrumental ways so that we use them without thinking about them, or even being aware of their presence. This functional transparency promotes the (useful) illusion of seamlessness and coherence in textual fields, and of the ultimate illusion that objects in the field are self-identical—indeed, that they *are* "objects." Poets and book artists, on the other hand, regularly introduce second-order markup in order to expose the dynamic complexity of the textual space—to strip away the text's "veil of familiarity," as Shelley called it, and reveal it as a "dome of many-coloured glass."

These kinds of moves disrupt the self-transparency of the first-order markings and drive the textual field toward its natural state of incoherence. Or, to put the matter more accurately, they construct second-order illusions that expose the functioning presence of the first-order illusions. (An analogous process occurs when quantum physicists mark their field measurements for "renormalization.") Text illustration or—as in Mallarmé's *Un coup de dès*—deliberated typographical form introduces this second, nontransparent sign system into what would otherwise be read as a purely linguistic field. The resulting composite or doubled work gains a marked increase in self-reflexive form, creating a textual field that is able to comment on itself. Certain of D. G. Rossetti's double works—most particularly his arrangement of sonnets and painting known as *The Girlhood of Mary*—comprise an explicit manifesto for this kind of self-reflexive semiotic field.

Textual fields arise codependently with interpretative action. Speaking of the existential graph exhibited on what we now call MS 514, Charles Saunders Peirce remarked that its highly articulated structure required only one premise: that there be a space, a blank sheet, where the structure could emerge. But the graphical demonstration of MS 514 required something else: a mark to call the space into action. G. Spencer Brown would put the issue succinctly a half-century later: all laws of form extrude themselves from the assertion that "a distinction is drawn" (*Laws of Form* 1). What is involved here is not an abstract, but an embodied and executed, idea. The statement "a distinction is drawn" is an index of the demonstration which it initiates in the book titled *Laws of Form*.

Here is a simple example to illustrate Brown's point. A mark made randomly—for instance, from a meteor striking the earth—draws no distinction. Indeed, the gash in the earth is not a mark at all. Only when the gash has been marked as a sign do we see the emergence of a mark. To give any "cause" for the gash — to say, for instance, that it was made by a meteor — is already to have marked it with meaning. The marked field thus arises as a codependent function of some agency that makes a distinction.

Like biological forms and all living systems, not least of all language itself, textuality is a condition that codes (or simulates) what are known as autopoietic systems. These systems are classically described in the following terms:

> If one says that there is a machine M in which there is a feedback loop through the environment so that the effects of its output affect its input, one is in fact talking about a larger machine M^1 which includes the environment and the feedback loop in its defining organization. (Maturana and Varela 78)

Such a system constitutes a closed topological space that "continuously generates and specifies its own organization through its operation as a system of production of its own components, and does this in an endless turnover of components" (Maturana and Varela 79). Autopoietic systems are thus distinguished from allopoietic systems, which are Cartesian and which "have as the product of their functioning something different from themselves" (Maturana and Varela 80).

In this context, all coding systems appear to occupy a peculiar position. Because "coding . . . represents the interactions of [an] observer" with a given system, the mapping stands apart from "the observed domain" (Maturana and Varela 135). Coding is a function of "the space of human design" operations, or what is classically called "heteropoietic" space. Positioned thus, coding and markup appear allopoietic.

As machines of simulation, however, coding and markup (print or electronic) are not like most allopoietic systems (cars, flashlights, a road network, economics). Coding functions emerge *as code* only within an autopoietic system that has evolved those functions as essential to the maintenance of its life (its dynamic operations). Language and print technology (and electronic technology) are second- and third-order autopoietic systems — what McLuhan famously, expressively, if also somewhat misleadingly, called "extensions of man." Coding mechanisms — proteins, print technology — are generative components of the topological space they serve to maintain. They are folded within the autopoietic system like membranes in living organisms, where distinct components realize and execute their extensions of themselves.

This general frame of reference is what makes Maturana and Varela equate the "origin" of such systems with their "constitution" (Maturana and Varela 95). This equation means that codependency pervades an autopoietic structure of relations. All components of the system arise (so to speak) simultaneously and they perform integrated functions. The system's life is a morphogenetic passage characterized by various dynamic mutations and transformations of the local system components. The purpose or goal of these processes is autopoietic — self-transformation and self-maintenance — and their basic element is not a system component but the relation (codependence) that holds the mutating components in varying states of dynamic stability. The states generate measurable codependency functions both in their periods (or basins) of stability and in their unique moments of catastrophic change.

In the horizon of textuality, autopoiesis measures the codependency of those entities conventionally named "the work" and "the reader." Barthes's injunction "From Work to Text" was an initial move to break the positivist analysis of the textual condition by marking the object of interpretation not as an empirical object but as a sign system. The legacy of such a view is concretely realized in the discipline of cultural studies, where the distinction between an empirical object and its interpretation is not a procedural assumption but a central problem and focus of attention.

Textual forms are generated by algorithmic and autopoietic devices. An algorithm is a step-by-step procedure to bring about some intended result or function. Cookbooks and instruction manuals exhibit algorithmic forms in natural language. Like computer algorithms, their immediate horizon is allopoietic. But to observe this is immediately to see that when any given allopoietic function is resituated in a larger systemic context, its autopoietic character begins to emerge. Cookbooks and instruction manuals are autopoietic maintenance functions within higher-order cultural formations. Thus we see that the distinction between allopoiesis and autopoiesis is functional, that the two processes themselves stand in a relation of codependency.

Literary works emerge from and feed back into the agencies that name and preserve them as such. The works and the agencies are codependent — a relation signaled in the following famous lines: implicitly at the linguistic level, explicitly at the documentary.

> Not marble, nor the guilded monuments
> Of princes, shall outlive this powerful rhyme.
> (Shakespeare, Sonnet 55)

Shakespeare's is merely one of countless declarations about the autopoietic character of poetry and artistic work. The lines are themselves, moreover, a procedural move in a complex code that maintains itself by having itself continuously modified and rewritten. A host of commentators, exegetes, and instructors attend on these lines, including ourselves at this moment, refusing their extinction, executing Shakespeare's code, and pointing out that these scripts recode an instructional line whose origin is dateless, whose recodings are perpetual. The most celebrated precursor texts in Ovid and Horace are themselves at once signs and agents of the process.

In this sense we must be ready always to move "From Text to Work" since the sign system of any phenomenon is so widely dispersed: by no means to be identified with some particular text we see on some particular page. That text locates only an instantiated moment — itself highly volatile — of an autopoietic "work" generated from the double helix of its production history and its reception history.

Unlike cookbooks and instruction manuals, poetry and other forms of imaginative textuality comprise high-order signal codes. Poetry's autopoietic character is a commonplace among its commentators: "poetry makes nothing happen," it affirms nothing and denies nothing, or (perhaps) it builds *airy* nothings and creates virtual, self-subsistent worlds. In this precise sense we also say, have always said, that it holds a mirror up to life: a magical mirror, like Lewis Carroll's, or like the mirror in Cocteau's *Orphée*. For living systems are themselves autopoietic.

On the other hand, because art and poetry function in a larger (human) world, to say that they make nothing happen is plainly untrue. To expose for reflection an operating autopoietic structure is itself an allopoietic function. These functions are always in play, however, most prominently in forms of satire. Swinburne's famous *Poems and Ballads* (1866), that hornbook of aestheticism, has as its product something different from itself. Swinburne wrote the book to make a public stir, which it succeeded in doing. Even the most supreme of fictions, like the poetry of Stevens, make pledges of allegiance to a cause — Mallarmé called it *poésie pure* — that is surely directed at something other than itself. The history of the emergence of aestheticism — of any artistic movement for that matter — measures the allopoietic functions being executed in the codes of a supervening autopoietic system.

The algorithmic structure of poetical textuality is most aggressively articulated in a Byronic line of work that emerges with Poe, gains greater explicitness in nonsense writing and the outrageous experiments of Lautréamont and Jarry, and culminates in Roussel, Oulipo, and the vigorous tradition of procedural writing of the late twentieth century. We set these writers apart only because they call explicit attention to something that is universally the case: that a literary work codes a set of instructions for how it should be read. Unlike machine and program codes, however, these codes decipher to an indeterminate number of precise outcomes. They represent exactly what Jarry called "a science of exceptions."

IVANHOE is the name of this project partly because it so dramatically illustrates the operation of this kind of coding, and partly because it hasn't been a name to reckon with since the nineteenth century, when it was regarded as "the epic of its age," as Balzac remarked. When *Ivanhoe* was published it birthed a reception history that spread in endless commentaries and mutated into theater, popular and serious rewritings, music, art. It was a book with many lives hidden in its codes and waiting further realization. Nothing illustrates this fact so well as its moment of immediate reception. An instant success, the book brought as well a corps of sympathetic readers to complain that the story had come out wrong. The final marriage should have been between Rebecca, not Rowena, and Ivanhoe.

And of course it is perfectly true that this outcome is coded as an imaginable possibility in the book. The criticism exposed Scott's version of the story as one that was chosen, but that might not have been. When Johanna Drucker and I first played IVANHOE, my textual transformations were all directed to recasting the book so that, in the end, Rebecca and Bois-Guilbert end up together. This (clearly Byronic) reading of the tale responds to codings that are present, if unexploited and even resisted, in the *Ivanhoe* Scott published. Reorganizing the book so that this outcome emerges brings a critical explication to Scott's work. Many other features and elements in the book might be imagined as part of an interpretive assessment of its tensions and complexities, and the same thing is true for any aesthetically coded work.

Interpretive action is always performative/deformative. The broad practice of literary and cultural theory during the past half-century did much to restore this kind of performative approach to critical work. Barthes and his successors did not have to struggle against the empirical historicisms that so plagued Nietzsche. The service economics of nineteenth-century philology had been supplanted in the academy by a different nineteenth-century model derived from Coleridge's idea of the clerisy and subsequently modified to a more secular Arnoldian form. This creature, the famous New Criticism, was Barthes's — and Theory's — point of departure.

Between *Philosophical Investigations* and *Of Grammatology* a great shift had taken place in the concept of criticism. No longer tied to a system (Kant, Hegel) or even to a set of ideas (Arnold), criticism now seemed better pursued as a reflective or rhetorical practice: provocative strategies of thinking rather than an exemplary body of thought. This philosophical turn had an enormous impact on literary and cultural studies. Nonetheless, positivist ideas about textuality have remained strong. Nowhere is this fact more clear, or perhaps more surprising, than in the cultural study of digital media, which is regularly celebrated as the convergence of a dynamic medium with a dynamic reader — in contrast to traditional text, which is represented, by contrast, as inert. A digital environment with hyperlinks is called "active" and a Web site like amazon.com appears to talk to its customers and anticipate what they want. To the degree that any dynamic interaction between human and machine actually occurs in a digital space, however — an unlikely event at best — it differs from the interaction between a book and a reader only in the speed with which information is transacted and exchanged. Book space, like digital space, is a field of simulations, and in each case the machine — the book or the computer — is capable of connecting itself to a host of related, equally complex information networks.

In one obvious and crucial sense the book-machine may license far greater flexibility, range, and speed for a reader than digital space offers to its users, so linked to visualizations as digital tools currently are. The visual constraints of book technology have coded its space as primarily a space of imagination — in the most technical sense — whereas digital space is being coded primarily in sensational terms. Because a persistent Romantic ideology assigns a kind of transhuman value to imagination, this difference produces works like *The Gutenberg Elegies*. The IVANHOE project sees no reason to resist the resources of either machinery. Indeed, one of the project's chief aims is to build an interface where these two information technologies can be made to interact and reflect on each other.

In that frame of reference, IVANHOE proposes that Barthes's theoretical orientation to textuality be critically assimilated to the approach of another dialectician of texts who emerged in the same period: Galvano della Volpe. Although both were in debt to Marxist dialectics, Barthes's roots went to structural linguistics, while della Volpe's were philological. In della Volpe's view, the agency of the reader would always be checked and constrained by the heteroglossia of the texts under examination. The reader's part, according to della Volpe, was to produce an interpretation of a given work — he called it a "quid" — which would then be tested for its adequacy as an account of the work being interpreted. A successful interpretation would clarify salient lines of interpretive failure and thereby feed back into a new set of interpretive moves.

What joins Barthes and della Volpe is their shared understanding that interpretation makes an active move on the textual inheritance. This was a common theme in a period that saw the emergence of deconstruction, various hermeneutics of suspicion, and — not least remarkable — Harold Bloom's celebrated dictum that "all interpretation is misinterpretation." All are highly performative, not to say deformative, modes of critical engagement. With certain notable exceptions — Susan Howe, for instance, and Charles Bernstein — this critical work preserved the idea of a careful separation between the integrity of an observed object of criticism, and the integrity of the critical observer. The thinking was the clear legacy of nineteenth-century philology and the scientific models it pursued.

Certain consequences of these procedures may be remarked. First, the academy set the interpretive essay at the center of its critical agenda. This instrument reified the integrity of "the poem itself" and marked critical reading and reflection as a spectator's game. More significantly, it obscured the fact that interpretive commentary had much less in common with the procedures of science and much more with those superb imaginative flights from the word of God in midrash aggadah. The case of Freudian and psychoanalytic criticism, so central for twentieth century modernism, is exemplary here. It took the startling work of Lacan to show that psychoanalytic interpretation had more in common with astrology than with science, and that it would be most accurately read as an imaginative commentary upon elusive and imaginary materials — ultimately, on the discourse of ideology.

Because the performative character of "Theory" has been largely pursued within models inherited from the nineteeth-century academy, its transformational power has been checked. An empiricist inertia gets passed on through these models that late twentieth-century theorists struggle against, as one can see in the period's fixation with Nietzsche. Derrida stands virtually alone among that celebrated theoretical company in having produced works like *Glas* and *The Post Card*. For a period with such an academic interest in pastiche and parody, few academics availed themselves of the resources of those performative critical subgenres. Frederick Crews's remarkable *Pooh Perplex* (1963) created a noise like a tree falling in an empty forest. Perhaps his wicked reprise, *Postmodern Pooh* (2001) will wake some of his neighbors up.

The most arresting and important critical deformations of the late twentieth century would come, however, from an unusual quarter: from bibliographers and scholarly editors. For nothing strips away the veil of familiarity from an aesthetic work so much as an elaborate scholarly edition. These works help to restore the originals to a modicum of their true autopoietic range, depth, and multiplicity. They drive their readers — if those who enter such works can still be called readers — back to the foul rag and bone shops where these works made (and keep making) their grand and (dis)continuous historical passagings. Change, non-self-identity, and metamorphosis rule the field of texuality because its works are material incarnations.

Massive acts of bibliographical defamiliarization were executed on the works of key figures: Coleridge most recently, but the line reaches back to the genetic editing of Hölderlin at mid-century and has carried forward in different ways to the works of Shakespeare, Flaubert, Dickinson, Joyce, and others. Imagine trying to *read* Wordsworth in that magnificent Library of Babel, the "Cornell Wordsworth." Or Rossetti in the labyrinths of the *Rossetti Archive*. Looming over all this work in his bad and magnificent eminence is the Renaissance bibliographer Randall McLeod. At once ludic and immensely learned, McLeod's scholarship came before IVANHOE as a chastisement, a spur, and a liberation.

Interpretation of a textual field proceeds at an inner standing-point. Funding many of these forms of critical energy — these tigers of instruction — is a belief in the enlightened power of the critical mind. IVANHOE was conceived, however, to speak somewhat preposterously, as a kind of negation of that negation. IVANHOE is organized so that those working in its spaces will continually encounter themselves as part of the subjects they address and the problems they want to solve.

Some of this model comes from the Socratic tradition, but the immediate inspiration was D. G. Rossetti's idea that a critical art should execute itself at what he called "an inner standing-point." This vantage is especially important in difficult cases since they *are* difficult exactly because they define an area of volatile opinion and judgment. Rossetti developed his theory, first, when he constructed a procedure of critical pastiche for handling medieval religious materials in the radically belated and alien context of middle-class Victorianism; and, second, when trying to find a way to expose the volatile subject of Victorian prostitution and the relation between ideal and sexual desire. For its part, the great force of Plato's myth of Socrates rests in the inner standing-point from which Socrates pursued his inquiries. The *Apology* is the touchstone document for Plato since it defines all of Socrates' dialogues as life-and-death matters.

Critical measurements, whether scientific or humane, fall under the rule of a Heisenbergian uncertainty. Burns's reformulation of that rule — "To see ourselves as others see us" — has proved an especially useful guide to method in IVANHOE . The space is organized so that players are twice constrained to an inner standing-point. The first constraint comes from the impinging social nexus of the other players' subjective moves. The second is a function of a refinement made to IVANHOE after its first iteration. We realized that we could enrich the critical function of the play space if the players would be required to execute their moves *en masque*. A second level of reflection emerges when players construct their moves as if they were being made by some specific person or character. When we tested IVANHOE with the focus on *Wuthering Heights,* for example, all of my moves were made as if by the notorious book collector and forger T. J. Wise.

Thinking slows the drift toward simple exposition when thinking includes itself in the field of its attention. It is intellectually dangerous to take what one says and thinks too seriously. A ludic element therefore pervades the idea and practice of IVANHOE . Comic and playful procedures are not only imaginative resources, as we know, but useful avenues for developing critical resistance to filtered and administered thinking, not least of all one's own.

Textual fields are *n*-dimensional. This idea is foregone within the six categories just examined. But the formulation *"n*-dimensional" is important as a rhetorical move to situate IVANHOE within a context where quantum mechanics and self-organizing systems can meet the cultural tradition's commitment to the search for meaning.

We might begin from the following observation by the celebrated mathematician René Thom: "In quantum mechanics every system carries the record of every previous interaction it has experienced — in particular, that which created it — and in general it is impossible to reveal or evaluate this record" (Thom 16). A literary scholar would have no difficulty rewriting this as follows: "In poetry every work carries the record of every previous interpretation it has experienced — in particular, that which created it — and in general it is impossible to reveal or evaluate this record." It is impossible because the record is indeterminate. Every move to reveal or evaluate the record changes the entire system not just in a linear but in a recursive way, for the system — the poetical work — and any interpretation of it are part of the same codependent dynamic field. Consequently, to speak of any interpretation as "partial" is misleading, for the interpretive move reconstructs the system, the poem, as a totality. This reconstruction corresponds to what is termed in quantum mechanics the collapse of a wave-function into its eigenstate.

Note that Thom refers to an interpretation "which created" the system (as it were) in the first place. But the work of Merleau-Ponty, Maturana, and von Foerster — to name just the most prominent instances — has shown that this creating interpretation is what a positivist view would call, has called "the poem itself." For certain interpretive purposes we find it helpful to think about "Kubla Khan" as Coleridge's creation, but other ways of observing the poem are normal. Indeed, except as an indexing convenience, Coleridge's authorship scarcely enters even a majority of the work's interpretations. "Kubla Khan" is not self-identical, it is an emergent function in an autopoietic field that comprehends the interpretive agent.

To demonstrate how his "constructivist" philosophical position works, Heinz von Foerster proposed the following "Reality Game":

> First, there must be two players. . . . They create a large board with lots of objects on it which they agree to call "The World." Then they put themselves on the board and invent a set of rules for the objects. These rules they agree to call "The Laws of Nature." If, during the game, it turns out that the rules they applied in creating the objects don't jive with the rules they invented to play with the objects, they change these objects or change "The Laws of Nature."
>
> Now they can play. The goal of the game is for both to agree on how they themselves shall move on the board, even under disagreement. It is clear that A can win only when B wins and vice versa. For if B loses, A is lost too. Then reality disappears and the nightmares begin. (Segal 148)

The Reality Game has much in common with Peter Suber's rule-changing game NOMIC, which it may well have inspired. IVANHOE too is a version of von Foerster's "Reality Game." IVANHOE is a less abstract game than either von Foerster's or Suber's, however, because "The World" of IVANHOE emerges through an intervention in an already given, quantized, and interpreted world. IVANHOE permits no illusion of an ex nihilo moment of creation: you don't invent objects or rules, you choose to move and define meanings in certain ways within a field already prepared — by being understood — as n-dimensional.

PART FOUR

Humanism for the Twenty-First Century

CHAPTER 10

Impossible Fiction; or, The Importance of Being John Cowper Powys

I

Within the tradition of prose fiction, and of the novel in particular, certain books have been written not so much to be read as to explore and expose the scene of reading itself, of language as the defining state of human being. To enter any of these books is to be lost in wonder. All such works are monstrous, and their monstrousness often appears as a simple matter of length.

John Cowper Powys wrote at least two books of this kind. More to the point, his work is, like Scott's, all of a piece, a "scene of writing" (in the useful jargon of our day) that consumes the individual works, even the greatest of them, into its larger function and purpose. Besides *Porius*, the English language of our twentieth century produced at least three other monsters of this kind, Stein's *The Making of Americans*, Powys's own *Glastonbury Romance*, and (the academically approved case) Joyce's *Finnegans Wake*. (Powys would have added — did add — Dorothy Richardson's *Pilgrimage*, and most readers would also cite Beckett's trilogy.) In Powys's case, Rabelais and Cervantes are mastering spirits of the writing, and the vast cycle of Arthurian texts, a self-engendering linguistic corpus, is his other exhaustless source. In France, after the Middle Ages, there are Balzac's vulgate excesses and Proust's elegant ones; in Russia, Tolstoy and Dostoyevsky. And remember that, except for Stein and Beckett, every one of these writers and writings was for Powys what Yeats called a "sacred book." He wrote and lectured about them all, often extensively, and his studies moved his fiction (in the words of one of his late works) "Up and Out" of the conventions of the regional and the realistic novel. He never left those conventions entirely behind — how could he have, when the foundation of his work is so accretive and (in pagan rather than Christian terms) salvific? But between *Wolf Solent* (1929), his last and greatest "novel," and *A Glastonbury Romance* (1932), the first of the unique prose inventions he sometimes called "romances," Powys moved his writing, as Joyce was moving his, to a new order and level.

Powys was well aware of Joyce's post-Ulyssean adventures in language. Indeed, he studied Joyce's progress very closely and wrote about the new "Work in Progress," as he had earlier about *Ulysses,* with great perceptiveness. Not many remember that Powys was one of the three witnesses who spoke for the defense at the infamous *"Ulysses* trial" in New York in February 1921. The late essay on *Finnegans Wake,* which he wrote in 1942 just as he was beginning the seven-year task of *Porius,* is as much a forecast-commentary on *Porius* as it is a retrospective commentary on Joyce's achievement. In Joyce, Powys sees (correctly)

> the mingling of that almost ecstatic sense of word-play — word-implications, word-conjuring, word-coining, word-marrying, word-murdering, word-melting, word-apotheosizing, word-hypostatizing — which takes up the basic facts of sex and perpetually ravels them and unravels them, with passages of almost Shakespearean imagination. The mischief is that the obscurity — for the average person — of the Work in Progress retards and perplexes us in our approach to this amazing tour de force, where a superhuman and inspired scholarship is so evidently at work. (*Obstinate Cymric* 19)

Porius is unquestionably Powys's attempt to rewrite *Finnegans Wake* in a more accessible literary dialect. As much as the latter, *Porius* is dominated by what the book's in-house editor called Powys's "philological interests." Powys must have thought that his book's preservation of more traditional narrative conventions would undo the "mischief" he saw in Joyce's "obscurity," which put a barrier between the work and the English common reader. In fact, Powys's late "romance" style would prove an even greater barrier and source of obscurity for readers trained to read in the conventions of realist fiction — even, and perhaps especially, the realist fiction that was codified in the precepts and example of George Eliot and Henry James.

Nothing shows more clearly the issue at stake than the response of Powys's first reader, Norman Denny, the cultivated editor at Bodley Head, where the book was first submitted for publication. Because Denny's experience focuses the problems that *Porius* can create even to this day, to recover that early and defining moment in the reception history of *Porius* can help to clear a space for beginning all over again not only with this amazing work, but with the entire revolutionary fictional project that Powys's work represents.

Denny's letter to Powys after reading the book (December 4, 1949) is touching for its sympathy, its candor, and finally its exasperation. After speaking warmly to some of the "peculiar and unique virtues" of the book, Denny launches — reluctantly — into his critique. As Powys's response to him will observe, Denny's strictures amount to a fundamental rejection. Here is Denny as he begins to lay out his disapprovals:

> you seem to be resolved to slow up and obscure and entangle the progress and movement of your story in every conceivable way — by homilies, dissertations, diversions of all kinds ? by loading it up with non-essentials, inconsequent details, trivialities, sheer perversities by which I mean, for one thing, the constant playing with Celtic and Brythonic words, which you frequently drag in by the heels for your own pleasure and not for that of the reader, who cannot be expected to share your philological interests. There is indeed an immense amount of sheer self-indulgence in the book. You seem to be determined to reverse the old and sound precept that the secret of story-telling is to know what to leave out, and to be determined to see how much you could possibly bung in. (Quoted in Ballin, *Powys Notes* 26)

Later Denny speaks more fully and negatively about Powys's "Brythonic words" and "philological interests," which seem to him "innately meaningless" much of the time, and at certain telling junctures, simply "ludicrous." The linguistic grotesqueries have their episodic equivalents:

> But then I came to the Cewri episode. I should have to do a lot of talking, I think, to explain to you the reasons why this stuck so badly in my gullet. The purpose of the episode is clear, and if you had presented it as a kind of erotic vision — a wild wet dream! — I might have been able to accept it. But being offered it on the same level of reality as the rest of the book . . . I found it not only distasteful but utterly unconvincing. It broke the spell of the book, which until then had never quite failed, in spite of your wordiness, and it shook me badly. (Quoted in *Powys Notes* 26)

Like several early reviews of Shelley's *Prometheus Unbound* which denounce the work for its atheism and blasphemy, Denny is reading the book accurately.

He is also, however, betraying the gulf that separates his expectations about what can or ought to be done in fiction from Powys's working premises. At issue here is everything that opens the possibility of works like *Finnegans Wake,* García Márquez's *One Hundred Years of Solitude,* Vollmann's *Seven Dreams* — or *Porius.*

Toward the end of his letter, when Denny pleads with Powys "to regard the book as unfinished . . . encumbered with the redundant material that one expects to find in the first draft of any novel," the source of the problem is made explicit. Denny thinks of *Porius* as a novel, or a novel-in-the-making. Since the book deploys so many conventions of the novel, his thought and his reactions are completely understandable. But the fact is that the book is not a novel; it is — as its subtitle says — *A Romance of the Dark Ages.* More particularly and to the crucial point, it is a "romance" written in the dark age of the mid-twentieth century. Powys was learned in Arthurian romance — an important fact to remember. He knew as well that such a fictional mode was alien to the (realistic) traditions of fiction that ultimately defined "the novel," where "probability" and "verisimilitude" (of both character and action) are essential, and where "organic integrity" must be preserved in order not to "break the spell" of the story. Indeed, Powys's early schooling as a writer of fiction came through his study and imitation of a late master of the novel, Thomas Hardy.

To revive romance conventions in the period of modernism, which is what Powys definitively began to do with *A Glastonbury Romance,* was in effect to do what Eliot said Joyce had done with *Ulysses:* it was to prophesy the end of the novel as the dominant set of conventions for fiction. Powys is interested in the work of Joyce and Proust exactly because they mark a watershed in the modern history of fiction.

Of course, the romance had never been entirely displaced by the novel. The presence of Sade and Sterne at a determining epoch in the history of the rise of the novel is important to remember. But both have been anomalies, and academically useful for just that reason. It is true that Sade, like Joyce, writes in a posture of programmatic defiance of accepted cultural and aesthetic conventions. But Sade did not have the nineteenth century to defy, which was Joyce's good fortune, so his books have been handled, in the house of fiction, like prehistoric creatures. And as for Powys, who is about as undefiant a figure as one could imagine, the problem was not to overthrow or pass beyond traditions he inherited, it was to incorporate and metamorphose them. (According to Powys, the one is an Irish way, the other Welsh.)

However that may be, Powys's historic importance in the history of fiction lies in this: that he worked to incorporate the novel back into its romance origins. The move is the exact reverse of Scott's move, which was an effort to accommodate romance fiction to the novel. Scott's abandonment of the long Ariostan poems for the prose tales signals this effort, which was to have such a fateful impact on the course of European fiction for the next hundred years.

As with Scott, Powys's stylistic procedures have clear historic and even political significance. When the skeptical John Crow, in *A Glastonbury Romance,* reflects on "all the sweetsickly religious lies that had medicined the world and lulled to sleep the minds of the generations," his words recover a famous passage in *The Communist Manifesto.* The allusion is central to a book that, in its political-historical sense, studies so closely the problems of class and society at such a crucial moment. *Porius* is, as anyone knows who has thought about the matter at all, a profound meditation on the twentieth century's abiding social sicknesses, and on fascism in particular, their emblematic form.

I point these matters out not merely in passing. So much attention is paid to the mythographic features of Powys's work that one wants to remember how preoccupied he was with temporalities and "mortal strife." John Bayley's splendid efforts to keep Powys aligned with writers like Hardy and Arnold Bennett work in this direction, although of course Bayley's focus is a tight one: British, let us say, rather than international-modernist. Powys's importance lies in the odd way he marries his British to his modernist allegiances. The former are sharply focused when Powys deploys the trappings of the regional novel, as in *Weymouth Sands* and *Maiden Castle,* the latter when he experiments with the conventions of the romance, as in *A Glastonbury Romance* and *Atlantis.*

As we know, Powys often compared himself to a teller of tales. His loose narratives feed on traditions of oral fiction, from which the sophisticated and literary conventions of romance developed. The novel by contrast moves to organize its fictional elements in schemes that control the free play of the fictional materials. It pursues an ideal of "organic" or "architectonic" form. In books like *Finnegans Wake* or *Molloy,* a departure from the strict, "realist" conventions of the novel is plainly declared. That programmatic declaration never comes in Powys, though its presence is everywhere apparent. As a result, his books, and preeminently a book like *Porius,* seem to hover between a set of contradictory allegiances.

Consider the narrator of Powysian fiction. This figure, this teller of tales, occupies an oddly dislocated position in Powys's work. Although his style is formally that of an "omniscient narrator," slipping as he likes into the minds and feelings of his characters (animate as well as inanimate, human and non-human), his omniscience seems itself no more than a point of view. He recalls Hardy's damaged monotheist divinity, who is surprised to discover that his creations have somehow acquired lives and purposes on their own, and that these purposes may not only escape his divine control (or may not), they may become independent forces for good or ill.

Often a ludicrous figure even in his own eyes, Powys's omniscient narrator becomes himself a kind of character. The contrast with George Eliot's or Henry James's narrative styles could not be more complete. Because neither has a trace of either Rabelais or Sterne in their writing, their narrators always expect that we take them seriously. Powys cannot resist any opportunity to detach his narrator and his narrative from the writing that sweeps both along, as we see so clearly in the opening sentence of *A Glastonbury Romance:*

> At the striking of noon on a certain fifth of March, there occurred within a causal radius of Brandon railway-station and yet beyond the deepest pools of emptiness between the uttermost stellar systems one of those infinitesimal ripples in the creative silence of the First Cause which always occur when an exceptional stir of heightened conscious-ness agitates any living organism in this astronomical universe. (1)

That is comic style taking itself with complete and abandoned seriousness. Surrounded, as was Powys, by a supremely enlightened world, Sterne would dare a similar type of stylistic *non serviam,* though not even Sterne would go so far as Powys goes here. The outrage upon decorum is essential to the comic humanism of such writers. Consider the "Consummation" chapter of *A Glastonbury Romance,* which features an extended set-piece exposition on the difference between "the state of love" in men and women. The narrator opens his discourse with an elevated Paterian allusion ("The oldest of all fem-inine smiles crossed her face," 304) and then plunges into his anatomy of love — an exploration of the intricate "levels of feminine emotion . . . entirely and forever unknown to men" (305). That ludicrous remark passes unnoticed by the Powysian narrator, whose words are engulfed in a flood of prose that runs on for another thousand words, a signature instance of that staple Powysian rhetoric, anticlimax. Powys's narrator is not debunked by this shrewd and generous art of sinking, however. On the contrary, the effect — again as in Rabelais and Sterne — is to mortalize him.

Don't imagine that Powys is unaware of precisely what he's doing. The passage opens with the Pater allusion and closes with this recollection of Poe:

> The act of imaginative will to which I refer gives a man, in fact, the power to treat his woman, in her lifetime, *as if she were dead* . . . which

is the rarest essence of human relationship and the supreme triumph
over matter of the human spirit. (306)

Powys frames the narrator's long discourse on gender and love so as to locate
it in an exact historical frame of reference. It thereby gets marked as a fully
elaborated statement of a particular ideological set of ideas and attitudes. This
specifying move is not made under satiric signs, however, but rather in the
mode of comic sympathy. We know this because the exposition is developed
to such detailed and extravagant lengths. The prose is prepared to turn all of
its resources over to the narrator so that he can tell us everything he thinks or
might think of this subject. Defined in terms of the quasi-allegorical names
Pater and Poe, this prose spectacle of folly and candor humanizes (histori-
cizes) the narrator's well-meaning pretentiousness.

The narrator's diminishment thus merges with a discourse field that is
comic and uncertain at every level and in every point of view. His underprivileged status turns Powys's fictional "narration" into a flow of writing that,
like Byronic Time, "brings all beings to their level." The Powysian narrator
and the human conversations he records may at any moment yield to narrative and conversational interludes from astonishing, unimaginable sources.
Trees, corpses, and all manner of existent creatures think and feel and talk together, some of their interchanges and meditations extending to wondrous
length (as in the truly wondrous narratives of *Atlantis*, for example).

The effect on the reader, as Denny's comments indicate, is necessarily
catastrophic, though the catastrophe is scored in a minor, benevolent key. If
writers must gain an inner standing-point in their writing, the same is no less
true of readers, and in particular of critical readers. The hero of *Porius* dis-
dains the preposterous myth-haunted tale-teller known as the Henog, but
Porius will be lectured about the matter in this telling way:

> Thus while the Henog's hearers . . . may actually be tearing to pieces
> the tale he is telling them, they are themselves, as far as the story-teller
> is concerned, irresistibly compelled to assume the role of small and
> unimportant portions of the perfect pattern of his vision. (572)

Powysian writing levels the discourse field so drastically that the enlightened
reader, like the Flaubertian artist, gets comically reconstructed. As in Rabelais
and Sterne, the only enemy of the Powysian world is the administrative conscience, and that too gets admitted as a necessary counterspirit athwart
which — within which — the fiction can move. Few norms guard the gates
of Powys's writing and those few are easily distracted. As a consequence, the

reader — like the Powysian narrator, like the characters in the messy and meandering stories — has to be prepared for just about any kind of event of story or of style.

Powys's distinctive prose emerges from those contradictions. Nurtured in the cultural ideas of modernism through its great decades (1910–30), and an active promoter of "the tradition of the new" until he left public life in 1932, Powys never abandoned the resources of the fictions passed on to him by Scott and the Victorians. His modernity, in fact, defines itself most clearly when he is negotiating the contradictions of his own stylistic and cultural inheritance and commitments.

The contrast with William Morris is instructive. Morris's interests are more antiquarian than Powys's, his alienation more extreme. Consequently, his writings — prose and poems alike — are sustained in melancholia. Powys's work is completely different. The writing seems always energized rather than wearied by the emptiness it must transact. As the prose enters its belated and threadbare worlds, it springs to a nervous, strangely robust life, as if those worlds could never satisfy its curiosities, as if its own fascinations were themselves undiscovered countries. How many of Powys's paragraphs begin with the word "But"! The prose turns and turns again, out toward matters that seem to come from any sort of unsponsored source, or back into restless reflections and descriptions, at once sprawling and meticulous.

The passages in *Atlantis* describing "the garden" tended by the dryad Kleta emblemize this strange Powysian textuality. Not a garden at all but "simply and solely a wild strip of uncultivated woodland" (42), as ancient and as inconsequent as Kleta herself, it is tended with infinite care by this "emaciated" leftover from a more heroic time:

> What the old Nymph liked to do was to arrange every tree, every shrub, every flower, every clump of grass, every dead or living root, every wild fern, every spray if ivy, so as to make exquisite patterns and delicate arrangements, and even to design suggestions of god-like terraces, and the mystic purlieus and enchanted courts and secret vistas leading into divine sanctuaries where the smallest insects and the weakest worms could be safe at last from all those abominable injustices and cruel outrages, and all those stupid brutalities and careless mutilations that lack even the excuse of lust. (43)

Such is the sympathy of this prose that it becomes an index of its subject, a verbal instantiation, a "symbol that stands for itself." The narrator is to Kleta what this obsessed writing is to her garden. Garden and text possess a strange, disheveled vitality that seems to command the devotion of their attendant spirits, Kleta and the Powysian narrator:

> Anyone, whether human or more than human, who turns nature into a garden is liable to find an unbelievable number of very small things that have once been parts of other things but are now entities on their own such as bits of wood, bits of stalk, bits of fungus, bits of small snail-shells, bits of empty birds' eggs, bits of animals' hair, bits of birds' feathers, bits of broken sheaths of long-perished buds and shattered insect-shards, strewn remnants of withered lichen-clusters, and scattered fragments of acorns and berries and oak-apples that have survived in these lonely trails and tracks to be scurf upon the skin of one world and the chaos-stuff for the creation of another world. (44)

Notice that both of those passages run on as a single sentence each, extruding themselves out of themselves, feeding off their own vitality and exhaustion, like the driving terza rima verse of Shelley's "Ode to the West Wind."

Those characteristic features of Powysian prose style have a distinct narrative equivalent. Medieval scholars call it *entrelacement,* "the poetry of interlace" organizing the branch narratives of Powys's favorite fictional materials. Traditional plot retreats in Powys to the level of the episode as the overall design spreads out to accommodate as many persons, places, and things as possible. The consequent fictional form is resolutely acentric, anti-Aristotelian and nonorganic (in the sense given to that term by scholarship). Its signal marks are digression, polyphony, improbable events, and the studied meandering pursued so closely by so many of our most impressive recent readers and thinkers, like W. G. Sebald.

From its roots in oral narrative and chronicle history, this kind of textuality sprang to its first maturity in the thirteenth century and from that point, in the words of Eugene Vinaver, "held the whole of civilized Europe spell-bound" for over three hundred years. Its most exquisite creations, indeed, are found in its latest forms: in Rabelais, Ariosto, Spenser, Sidney, Cervantes. With the rise of the novel the form was displaced (but not forgotten — nothing so demanding could possibly be forgotten). Like Proust and Joyce, Powys's work may and should be taken as an index of the novel's twentieth-century recession, first announced, perhaps, by Lautréamont's outrageous *Chants de Maldoror.*

II

Powys never abandons entirely the basic conventions of the novel. But he preserves those features with such scrupulous excess that they regularly mutate into hybrid forms. *Porius* lacks the complexity and depth of Powys's master-works, in particular the incomparable *Glastonbury Romance*. The deliberated character of the book, however, its virtually programmatic turn against the inheritance of Flaubert and James, supplies us with especially clear examples of what makes Powys such an indispensable figure in the history of twentieth-century writing and culture.

For example, the book illustrates its eccentric textual method right away, when it seems to launch itself into immediate plot complications. *Porius* begins with "two disturbing pieces of news" just received by Porius that, we are told, "would affect, and affect catastrophically, every person connected with him."

We then travel across almost thirty closely printed pages before we learn what those two pieces of news are. But the effect on the reader is the opposite of suspenseful. The prose moves into such a thicket of unfamiliar details — we are located, after all, in Britain in the year 499 — that those two disturbing pieces of news sink from sight and attention. It is as if the prose in its self-unfoldment had fallen into a kind of highly energized trance. We focus on this or that and seem to be moving through a random series of intense immediacies. The two pieces of news and their supposed catastrophic import begin to drown in a textual flood.

When the news is finally revealed, it comes marked with the rhetoric of anticlimax. And as the entirety of Powys's text continues to thicken and coagulate chapter by chapter, these determining messages with their catastrophic import simply disappear, like Napoleon in *War and Peace*. When they are returned to our attention from time to time, they seem to have acquired the extreme clarity of meaningless facts.

The rhetoric of anticlimax is probably the most distinctive quality of Powys's narratives. It has much in common with Tolstoy's narrative style, which George Steiner has been so acute to emphasize when speaking of Powys. The style disestablishes conventional hierarchies of value and priority. Because the manner is comic, however, the disestablished values get preserved in bizarre forms, as if their power or materiality had been saved for no apparent reason. In a Powys text, salvation comes as just this kind of pure grace. If something transpires as we think it ought, that event can appear unaccountable. The half-lives of the lost may or may not return from their half-deaths to perform other functions. In the Powysian world it doesn't matter. What does matter is that they should be seen to undergo processes of change and death and still live on, whether or not they also appear to have something to live for or some function to perform.

Skirting both nonsense and its more administered fellow traveler, surrealism, Powys's writing tempts the impossible in fiction. It undertakes textual representations that disbelieve in the myth of art. The prose gives its faith to graces (they are not textual) beyond the reach of art. It is, most especially, to tempt the impossible in modern fiction. Modernism had opened possibilities like *Finnegans Wake*, the most exact kind of work "in progress" since Flaubert. *Porius*, on the other hand, is impossible. Why? Because a central myth of modernity is that one can go forward but not backward. Of course, one can return to the past, reframe it as "myth," and take it over into the works of the present. We call that anthropology. But what if one were to imagine the present being overtaken by the past, being made subject to the authority of what our historical sense declares is dead and gone — or, if "alive," then living "as myth"? With *Porius*, Powys finally (openly) proposes that we must think in just this way. And the method of medieval romance serves his purposes well. The acentric procedure allows him to organize a structure of events where anything is liable to happen at any time. So Denny's recoil and advice make perfect sense: "cut out the Cewri . . . because I don't believe anyone is going to swallow them." If they must be there, admit them "in the form of a dream."

Powys's response was a refusal, naturally:

> Nothing wd, my dear friend, induce me, or make me leave out the Cewri, or make them a dream, or tamper with them as they are here in any way. . . . To leave out Marvels & Wonders wd be to make the whole thing false, to make it ring untrue & unreal, to make it a tiresome & tedious transferring of our present pseudo-scientific & narrowly exact scientific attitude to life and the cosmos into the brains of the people of that time. (Ballin, *Powys Notes* 30)

What is important here is not that Powys himself believed in the literal truth of "Marvels and Wonders." We know that he did, and many have read what he wrote on such matters. More important is to realize that he wrote "a Book that aims at catching the actual real atmosphere — as the people of those days felt that atmosphere." Powys's moral object is to try to recover for "the particular generation" the reality of "the impossible." This reality, which is impossible in every sense (impossible to recover, impossible to represent), can be a very simple thing — Powys's books are full of the most charming, the simplest, impossibles. But great marvels and wonders, like the episode of the Cewri, are crucial from a stylistic point of view. They cannot, Powys insists, be treated in reductive modernist terms — as dreams, for example. Powys forecasts the view that will be taken a generation later by García Márquez, Thomas Pynchon, Haruki Murakami, and other salient writers.

Far more is involved here than a Coleridgean "willing suspension of disbelief." Powys's literal fictions, as Denny saw, break the spell of their own fictionality. That is the fateful stylistic demand he makes on the reader.

What happens as a consequence "broke the spell of the book," in the manner of *Ulysses,* but the consequence comes as the inverse of a modernist "baring the device." Like Joyce or Flann O'Brien or any number of twentieth-century authors, Powys regularly parades the game of his own writing. That is what storytellers do, flaunt their styles, make a theater of their tale-tellings. Unlike most modernists, however, Powys constructs these theatricalities not to celebrate realities of style, but exactly to define the limits of style.

Master celebrants like James, Proust, and Joyce reweave "the spell of the book" by breaking the spell of the novel. Accepting the judgment of history, Powys treats the novel as a primitive form — indeed, as a sign of the immanence and extent of primitive life-forms. When Powys cultivates the evacuated conventions of the realistic novel in a romance structure, he perforce breaks the spell of his own work's "style." The result is a book whose materials appear to have an independent vitality, as if they existed beyond the imagination of their "author," as if that "author" were himself not a "creative artist" but (as Powys called himself) a "Medium," a function of the materials rather than their master (and least of all their creator). To pretend to anything further — to cultivate, for example, a modernist style — would be the aesthetic equivalent of "this generation's particular passion for the verifyable & the positively scientific," with its "Research Laboratory at the end of the Tube Station that the fashion of the present generation alone allows." The antivivisectionist Powys was probably thinking of a biological research center. Academic readers would do well to realize that the "Humanities Research Center" — we have seen the rise of many — has to be, for Powys, a parallel institution.

As a stylistic event, therefore, as an act of "cultural intervention," a book like *Porius* is a root-and-branch critique of the present. It situates itself in AD 499 in order to take up a literally impossible point of view toward the contemporary world. What is perceived to be dark here is not a remote spot in ancient Wales but the "Dark Age" of this century.

I'm not saying that what Powys did was better done than what Joyce did, or Proust. Only that it was equally impressive and equally distinctive and, from a cultural-critical point of view, more pertinent to our current social dehumanization, so much more advanced than it was in the 1925 of José Ortega y Gasset. Admirers of Powys's work often follow the academic leads that have helped to explain various accredited masters when they want to explain the work of this great uncredited, or discredited, writer. So names like Heidegger and Derrida are invoked, or the mythographies of Lévi-Strauss or Geertz, or modernist and postmodernist theories of decentering (or historicist moves that invoke medieval literary analogues!). But in all this one has to proceed with great caution. Powys is a deeply alien writer, truly (as we now say) "the radically other." If we see that *Porius* is his attempt to rewrite *Finnegans Wake* and, in Blake's sense, to "correct its errors," we must recognize the outrageousness of such a project. For Powys, the error of Joyce's masterpiece is that it forbids access to anyone but those who have passes to the Research Laboratories. So he will write a *Finnegans Wake* as if he were George Eliot or Arnold Bennett or H. G. Wells. The result is that Powys becomes, in the phrase of another badly neglected inspirator, "Lost on Both Sides."

That event in twentieth-century cultural history is written — literally prophesied — in Powys's writing, of which *Porius* is an exemplary case. The fact measures the extremity of the book's self-contradiction. *Porius* does not represent (as Eliot said of Pound's *Cantos*) a hell (or a heaven) "for other people"; the book catches a clear and piteous look at its own author, who — like Riding — made such an important presence in the founding years of modernism, only to repudiate that investment — again like Riding — just as it was turning blue chip.

We see the importance of Powys with greatest clarity through the episode that finished *Porius* for Norman Denny: Porius's encounter with the Cewri culminating in their deaths in the mountain tarn (chapter 23).

In the context of the whole book, the death of these impossible monsters is the exemplary human catastrophe. (And recall that this catastrophe has absolutely nothing to do with the two "catastrophic" messages that initiated Powys's tale.) It represents the disappearance of "the Impossible." The character Porius, for whom these creatures are by no means impossibilities, registers a premonitory sense of what this catastrophe entails. Having been the immediate cause of their deaths — of these creatures who are his own being's root and center — Porius lapses into a brief state of shock.

> In his mind the river of time carried him away up the centuries, up thousands upon thousands of centuries, till he was permitted to behold in his own person the terrestrial catastrophe which caused this almost bottomless mountain-lake to be formed, and this prison of submerged rock to make captive these two corpses. (553)

The passage is clearly placed at the brink of a "modern" displacement — as if one might look on such a stark natural scene and imagine some kind of "mythical" event that would be adequate to one's feelings of wonder and estrangement. The episode's series of descriptions all work toward this end: for example, when the two giants plunge into the waters of the slate Welsh lake:

> They sank so rapidly and heavily, that when they struck this projection of splintered rock their weight forced them through an orifice between two jagged teeth of slaty stone, that had been broken at such an angle by the original upheaval that what once passed through them could never come forth again. (552)

Once again the description is premonitory. We register the premonition very easily — we know our symbolisms — so that we would say the scene and event "symbolize" the disappearance of the world's human Impossibles. The catastrophe is that these Impossibles might be, as in this very text, translated into a symbolic order, whether of nature or of imaginative writing.

Powys underscores the threat he is imagining when he makes his character Porius reflect on the event. The effect is ludic and uncanny. Thinking in 499, Porius's mind moves to twentieth-century idioms: "There *must* be a consciousness in chance. . . . If there's no consciousness," his thought went on, "in these chance events, there's something parallel to it that may work even better!" (553) The typographical sign of emphasis highlights the entrance into the text of "the Impossible." Here it is a small instance of a distinctively Powysian reflection put in the mouth of a person who could not possibly have had such a thought. Or couldn't he, this student of Pelagius? Either way, it is just the kind of moment that "broke the spell of the book" for Denny.

Fiction as a vehicle of probabilities is at a clear crisis in this scene from *Porius*. Most important, the crisis threatens the book that has raised it up, as we see in the final event of the episode, when Porius makes his obsequies over the mutilated body of Mabsant, the dead boy who had been the object of the Cewri's disastrous invasion of the Romanized world:

> "Rise to immortality and intense happiness, Mabsant, soldier of Arthur!" was what he muttered as he rose from his knees and limped off; for it had always been a friendly matter of dispute between him and Brother John whether the prayer for "eternal rest in peace" did or did not imply a secret instinctive faith in the blest relief of annihilation. (553)

The sharp change in the linguistic idiom is telling. At this point the paradoxes have been perfected as impossible contradictions, which the book (paradoxically) treats in the gentlest way, as if they were just "a friendly matter of dispute." Are the Cewri annihilated forever? Can there be marvels and wonders — "ages" of such things, as one might say — and then no more? It is possible, it is not possible. It is possible (and not) that either event could be a source of "blest relief" or otherwise.

And then there is the possibility that John Cowper Powys's *Porius* has dealt a death stroke to fiction, and most especially to Powys's most cherished ideal, the fictionality of the marvelous. That possibility arises out of Powys's daring move to allegorize the death of the marvelous in the deaths of the Cewri, and to figure his own responsibility for the event in the actions of his hero Porius. At this conceptual level, Porius entertains the one impossibility he does not want to believe. For the writer Powys, the marvelous is and must be, and not merely as a fictional possibility. And so he writes *Porius* to realize the reality of the marvelous, and at the heart of its stories he imagines the possibility that the marvelous may be finally impossible, because that is the dynamic nature of the marvelous. Denny registered this ultimate contradiction correctly when he said that Powys made no distinction between "the real" and "the marvelous." And Powys figures the contradiction in his own terms when he constructs the "impossible" story of the death of the Cewri as an allegory of the threat that writing and imagination bring to the reality of the marvelous. This is why Denny's recoil is figured in the work from the start and cannot be dispensed with. It represents the limit of what a schooled literary imagination declares to be possible, a limit the book moves to breach at all points.

CHAPTER 11

Beauty, the Irreal, and the Willing Assumption of Disbelief

> You have conquered, and I yield. Yet henceforward art thou also dead—dead to the World, to Heaven, and to Hope.
>
> —E. A. Poe, "William Wilson"

For about a hundred years there has been something called "the death of beauty." Recently people have been telling us that it's time for beauty to come back into the eye of the beholder. But how does one make that happen? As the unbeautiful (if otherwise impressive) Lenin might say: "What is to be done?"

I

The problem has been a problem of Enlightenment and the critical spirit that Enlightenment fosters. To the enlightened mind — think of Apollonius in Keats's "Lamia" — Beauty is at best just another pretty face, and at worst a snake lady. Or the *idea* of a pretty face, the *idea* of a snake lady! Maybe all those things together because of their various ideological entanglements with each other. Whatever, the simplest truth is that beauty disarms one, seduces, takes away our critical and reflective intelligence. Or so a certain kind of enlightened mind has argued. Coleridge countered that kind of skepticism with his famous theory of "poetic faith" and its different kind of enlightenment. In face of the imagination's panoply of arresting appearances Coleridge called for a "willing suspension of disbelief" — a move that would, as he was well aware, save the appearances of "the real" and the appearances of art as appearances.

A short time ago I saw and heard a different mind of enlightenment take a very different view and make a very different argument. Actually, I was confronted with two minds — Mozart's eighteenth-century mind and Zeffirelli's late-twentieth-century postmodern mind working together in *Don Giovanni*. The Met in New York had a revival of Zeffirelli's famous 1990 production of Mozart's masterpiece.

Let's recall briefly what Mozart (and Zeffirelli) were doing with that remarkable, and remarkably self-conscious, work. *Don Giovanni* is an anthology of beautiful musical set pieces, as everyone knows. It is also the story of a notorious rake, rapist, and — in Mozart's version — murderer. All that beauty gets focused on this degenerate, a character who flaunts his wickedness and even sings, at one of the opera's greatest moments, that "nobody is as talented as I am."

That is one of the most self-reflexive moments in a very self-reflexive work. At one level we know that Don Giovanni is parading his erotic prowess, but at another we understand that Mozart is using the Don as a mask for himself and the action of his music. As the whole game of artifice that *is* this opera is brought to our attention, the artifice of representation — that's to say, the illusion that the opera is an imitation of life — falls away. Don Giovanni and all his friends, enemies, acquaintances, and deeds — his rapes, his loves, his murders — all are illusions cast before our mind's eyes and ears in forms of beauty. And they are cast before us in these forms so that we will not let our minds fall into that worst of Enlightenment illusions: that the world of art and its beauties is a reflection, an imitation, of life. It is precisely an illusion that Don Giovanni is a murderer and a rapist. Murder and rape do not happen in art, they happen in life. That is, ultimately, a part of the *argument* of *Don Giovanni*. And the function of art and its clear beauties — in Mozart's and Zeffirelli's enlightened views of the matter — is to help clarify the distinction between what is real and what is illusion. And to re-celebrate the power of art's illusions. We are to leave Mozart's theater more prepared to be truly serious — that's to say, seriously ludic — in our thinking about moral questions, including the moral question, and function, of art, which is to instruct through pleasure.

Seeing *Don Giovanni* makes me remember something else: that Gerard Manley Hopkins posed and answered Lenin's question in a famous sonnet:

> What do then? how meet beauty? 'Merely meet it; own,
> Home at heart, heaven's sweet gift;' then leave, let that alone.
>   ("To What Serves Mortal Beauty")

That's just about how we want to encounter *Don Giovanni,* and the lines will set the rest of my agenda in this essay. We want to enlighten ourselves about Beauty, about how it works. And because Beauty always works by apparitions rather than by concepts, we'll take our lessons in Beauty not by instructive ideas and precepts, but by some examples that, we hope, may arrest our attention and, as Blake would say, open our doors of perception.

Let me begin with a set of questions of my own, rhetorical ones. What if our environment of vision simply became too administered so that Beauty appeared to disappear along with all its certain signs: elegance, wit, surprise, wonder? What if the dismal history of "the decay of Beauty" were a protest testimony, a long-lamenting *non serviam* uttered by souls living in a hell they never made, though a hell in which they might be cooperating and for which they must still take responsibility? What if those suppositions were, as Wittgenstein would say, "the case"?

I shall work from these hypotheses and try to prove them true. The proof will be practical and performative, as in an instruction manual. I mean to make the machine of my thinking about Beauty work.

So let me switch genres and take another example, this one from Wittgenstein — specifically, the famous opening passage of the *Philosophical Investigations.* He starts by quoting Augustine's *Confessions* to illustrate a theory of language in which "the individual words name objects [and] sentences are combinations of such names [so that] the meaning is correlated with the word [and] is the object for which the word stands." He then asks us to

> think of the following use of language: I send someone shopping. I give him a slip marked "five red apples." He takes the slip to the shopkeeper, who opens the drawer marked "apples"; then he looks up the word "red" in a table and finds a colour sample opposite it; then he says the series of cardinal numbers — I assume that he knows them by heart — up to the word "five" and for each number he takes an apple of the same colour as the sample out of the drawer. — It is in this and similar ways that one operates with words. — "But how does he know where and how he is to look up the word 'red' and what he is to do with the word 'five'?" — Well, I assume he *acts* as I have described. Explanations come to an end somewhere. — But what is the meaning of the word "five"? — No such thing was in question here, only how the word "five" was used. (*Philosophical Investigations,* 2e–3e)

This is a beautiful moment in the history of philosophical prose. I might have said "in the history of philosophy," which is *also* what I meant, because here

Wittgenstein alters its history by setting a new example for the way it might be written. Probably the beauty of the passage seems clearest to persons with some awareness of (a) the history of systematic and analytical philosophy, and (b) some recollection of the *Tractatus*, where Wittgenstein made his public commitment to cognitive precision and elegance. But even without such knowledge we can be arrested by the drama of the passage. To begin a philosophical investigation in this way! An investigation in the analytic tradition! The brilliance of the rhetorical move turns the reader around. By an act of written thinking Wittgenstein is, like Thoreau in *Walden*, waking his neighbors up.

Most important to see is this: that the passage's leading *idea* is being demonstrated as an act of linguistic pursuit. The whole of philosophy is being reconstructed here as a matter of thinking with language, rather than of thoughts or concepts. And the ground of the thinking is not abstract, it is common, conversational. (Soon afterward the professors would give it a formal academic name — "Ordinary Language Philosophy.") The idea of the passage cannot be summarized or plucked out, though one could abstract certain ideas *from* it for particular purposes. Its key thoughts pervade the passage, which is staging a little drama of a man thinking.

The passage can recall the drama of thinking that, for instance, Byron is always staging for us in his poetry. This prose drama is more striking because philosophers — professional philosophers — don't normally write or think this way. To begin reading Wittgenstein's *Investigations* is to know immediately that one is not being ushered toward a statement of premises or first principles, from which the philosophical work will proceed. So the drama comes to show — to tell by showing — that effective ideas are dynamic not abstract. By implication it also shows something that will become clear only later in the *Investigations:* that abstractions are poorly seen *as* abstract, that abstractions are tools the investigating mind uses for specific ends.

What is the reader's part in all this? As an audience receiving pleasure and instruction? Clearly not. Wittgenstein's double, the questioning addressee with whom he converses, is ourselves as much as himself. The work is a series of unfolding provocations, of which the first person's apparently confident replies are not the least provoking. If this is a kind of mental theater, its theory is closer to Brecht than it is to Aristotle.

To be brought to Brecht is to need another example. For Brecht underscores a crucial aspect of the dynamic of thinking: that its dialectics are social, involving — in a textual condition like the *Investigations* — those figures we name "author" and "reader." Not pursuing his work as a conscious *poiesis*, though the *Investigations* is very much an artistic result, Wittgenstein does not make a meticulous exposition of the reader's part in his drama. Brecht does. In this move Brecht is elaborating Poe's revolutionary transformation of the dynamics of Romanticism, which is to say the transformation of the dynamics of Beauty. *That* subject will have to wait a bit, however, because 150 years of cultural administration have made Poe's work difficult to access.

II

The access may become easier if we first make a passage through a pair of contemporary poems. I start with Charles Bernstein's "The Klupzy Girl" (*Islets/ Irritations*, 1983)—its opening thirty-two lines. The title is especially salient for our general subject. It suggests that some kind of portrait is to follow — perhaps narrativized, like Keats's "La Belle Dame Sans Merci" or Rossetti's "Jenny," perhaps more formally presented, like Williams's "Portrait of a Lady," or Stevens's "Lulu" poems. All such works are by genre-definition "muse" poems. Their subject is always Beauty.

> Poetry is like a swoon, with this difference:
> it brings you to your senses. Yet his
> parables are not singular. The smoke from
> the boat causes the men to joke. Not
> gymnastic: pyrotechnic. The continuousness
> of a smile — wry, perfume-scented. No this
> would go fruity with all these changes
> around. Sense of variety: panic. Like
> my eye takes over from the front
> yard, three pace. Idle gaze — years
> right down the window. Not clairvoyance
> predictions, deciphering — enacting. Analytically,
> i.e., thoughtlessly. Begin to push and cue
> together. Or I originate out of this
> occurrence, stoop down, bend on. The
> Protest-ant's voice within, calling for
> this to be shepherded. For moment's
> expression enthroning. Able to be
> alibied (contiguity of vacuity). Or
> telepathetically? Verena read the epistle
> with much deliberateness. If we are
> not to be phrasemongers, we must
> sit down and take the steps that will

give these policies life. I fumbled clumsily
with the others — evocations, explanations,
glossings of "reality" seemed like stretching
it to cover ground rather than make
or name or push something through.
"But the most beautiful
of all doubts is when the downtrodden
and despairing raise their heads and
stop believing in the strength of their oppressors."

(*In the American Tree,* 285)

I'm aware that many persons have been annoyed and/or baffled by poetry like this. I'm also aware, and this is important to say, that many others — myself among them — are ravished by it. Bernstein's Klupzy girl is one with Keats's Belle Dame, Swinburne's Sappho, Stein's Suzie Asado, Graves's White Goddess . . . the list is endless, their name is Legion. Bernstein knows very well that a girl named Klupzy doesn't *look* like a Blessed Damozel. Klupzy suggests "clumsy" raised to a higher power — which is why Klupzy girls are nowhere to be seen at yacht clubs and cotillions in Great Neck and Manhasset. Nor has "The Klupzy Girl" — this poem that's to say — been invited to the well-bred parties that celebrate the Beauties of our academic culture. Is she beautiful, is she ugly? Who could tell when she *dresses* so . . . well, so *oddly!* Best not to invite her at all, she'll only create problems, like a Dickinson kangaroo among the beauties.

And besides, you might well ask (like Wittgenstein's internal interlocutor): "What is the meaning of the word 'Klupzy'?" And like his other self I would want to reply: "No such thing was in question here, only how the word 'Klupzy' was used." For with a girl and a poem like Klupzy, the problem comes when we come to her with Augustinian expectations.

Let's take a different approach. Let's say "The Klupzy Girl" names the poem that we will read. And let's say that we try to see her for what she is, for what she's *doing.* Let's say (further) that all the referential features of the poem — its dictionary meanings, its allusions, the overtones and suggestions that are a function of certain linguistic usages, wordplays, and arbitrary phonic arrangements — let's say that all these reference one thing, one being, one Beauty: "The Klupzy Girl." The sequence of sentences and sentence fragments, their grammatical forms and rhetorical unfolding — these put the person of the Klupzy Girl into action so that we can follow what Marjorie Perloff calls "the dance of [her] intellect." "Fumbl[ing] clumsily with the others" — this poem is replete with "others" — we find ourselves inside the world of "The Klupzy Girl."

And it is very much a Shelleyan world of "Intellectual Beauty" we discover through this poem, where our sense derangements — isn't that what Beauty *does?*—flirt us into new derangements that are also new arrangements. And we have to be quick on our metrical feet, in our minds, for the aesthetic immediacy of the verse is extreme. Negatives, alternative conjunctions, and questions function to throw open the amazing play of the language as such: "Not / gymnastic: pyrotechnic." "Not clairvoyance, / predictions, deciphering — enacting." "Or / telepathetically?" As in each of those examples, line terminations are crucial for turning our heads: "The continuousness / of a smile — wry, perfume scented. No this / would go fruity with all these changes / around." The remarkable "Sense of variety" in such passages might well suggest, as they do briefly here, "panic." But not for long, for the text — to borrow one of its own locutions — is continually originating itself out of this, its own, occurrences. Like the human world, it can only be explained in its own terms — from what D. G. Rossetti called "an inner standing-point."

And so, like *Don Giovanni,* like the passage from Wittgenstein, this poem talks to itself. Its first person is a device, not a controlling or supreme fiction, as it would be in a Romantic poem. Or I should say its "first persons," as we see in the concluding twelve lines of the quoted passage, which comprise three different types of first-person sentences. They come together in the poem like a company of honest, unpretentious souls, a little signifying set (I will suppose) of Klupzy society characters whom we briefly catch thinking about some large ethical issues. "The Klupzy Girl," it's important to see, is not just another pretty face.

Another example, this one much more self-consciously literary: Kit Robinson's "In the American Tree" (*Down and Back* 1978). I choose it for two reasons. First, it flaunts an ironical postmodern stance — a style of address that has been taken as the very emblem of the decay of Beauty. Second, it raises the subject of Beauty in an explicit way. Ron Silliman took the poem's title for the title of his important 1986 anthology — virtually a manifesto for postmodern writing — and he used Robinson's poem to head up his book, exactly the way Yeats used Pater's "Mona Lisa" passage in his equally polemical anthology of 1935, *The Oxford Book of Modern Verse, 1892–1935.* Here is the text from Silliman's anthology.

A bitter wind taxes the will
causing dry syllables
to rise from the throat.

Flipping out wd be one alternative
simply rip the cards to pieces
amid a dense growth of raised eyebrows.

But such tempest (storm) doors
once opened, resistance fades away
and having fired all the guns you find you are left
    with a ton of butter,

Which, if it isn't eaten by some lurking rat
hiding out under the gate, may well be picked
up by the wind and spread all over

The face you're by now too chicken to admit is yours.
Wheat grows between bare toes
of a cripple barely able to hold his or her breath

And at the crack of dawn
we howl for more
beer. One of us produces

A penny from his pocket
and flips it at the startled thief
who has been spying on her from behind the flames

That crackle up from the wreck.
The freeway is empty now, moonlight
reflecting brightly off the belly of a blimp,

And as you wipe the red from your eyes
and suck on the lemon someone has given you,
you notice a curious warp in the sequence

Of events suggesting a time loop
in which bitter details repeat
themselves like the hands of a clock

Repeat their circular travels in a dreamlike medium you find impossible to pierce:
it simply spreads out before you, a field.

Now you are able to see a face
in the slope of a hill,
tall green trees

Are its hard features,
a feather floats down
not quite within grasp

And it is Spring.
The goddess herself
is really

Feeling great.
Space assumes the form of a bubble
whose limits are entirely plastic.

The poem is a deliberate reprise and parody of William Carlos Williams, as the title — recalling Williams's *In the American Grain*— signals to us. The parody is more specific, however. It is a comic and playful playback of the title poem in Williams's famous, and probably his greatest, book of poetry, *Spring and All*.

The playfulness of the work is the matter I want to focus on. But first let's briefly note how like the poem is to Bernstein's. Both poems expel realism — the conventions of that language game — from their accustomed poetic primacy. The poems work by extruding themselves out of themselves, using the resources of reference as stimuli for surprising linguistic inventions. Here that procedure is most clearly signaled in the climactic tenth and eleventh stanzas, where we enter the "time loop / in which bitter details repeat / themselves like the hands of a clock." The lines call back the opening of the poem ("A bitter wind taxes the will")— a callback repeated in the next stanza, which references stanza four.

These "circular travels in [the poem's] dream- / like medium" we "find impossible to pierce" because they aren't *meant* to be pierced. They are meant for envelopment and attention, which is why they simply "spread out before [us]" in the aesthetic "field" of the poem. When we arrive at that realization we are licensed to complete the poem, that is to say, to enter wholly into its "plastic," paradisal space.

"Spring and All," the basic point of departure, provides Robinson with the governing theme of the resurrection of Life and Beauty out of a dead world. Williams's poem is the emblem of that world, where Beauty — Persephone, let's say — seems rapt away from us. But Robinson doesn't read Williams's poem as a nature story — "dazed Spring" approaching once again from that famous wintry earth "on the road to the contagious hospital." He rereads it as a poem about art and poetry, which is what Robinson's poem is about. No more and no less.

Poems about poetry, art whose subject is art, have become emblems in our time of two related ideas: of art and poetry operating at a pitch of highest seriousness; and of art and poetry as the province of an overeducated and re-moved elite. Harold Bloom's theory of "the anxiety of influence" is only the most celebrated example of this two-handed cultural enginery. Robinson's poem, however, like Bernstein's, is *precisely* a comical reduction of those ear-nest formulas. And so Beauty makes her return at the end in a playful regis-ter: "And it is Spring. / The goddess herself / is really / Feeling great." Like the ladies in *Don Giovanni*'s palace of art, this goddess is more amazing for be-ing less transcendental. "Awesome," as we hear today in the comic vulgate of the young.

Robinson's delicacy comes clearly to view if we try rewriting the poem's last two words "feeling great" as "looking great." That would be a mistake, however, that would be Beauty from the elders' point of view, not Susannah's. But here we are not called as *spectatores ab extra*. We have been assumed into this poem, which has arranged itself, including the reading of itself (which is part of itself), at an inner standing-point. The poem's subject arises through the act of reading the poem. The happy arising of the goddess, the emblem for that action, thus appears at the climactic moment of the textual process. At that point we can see the whole of what has been happening in the poem, the completion of the act of reading, the completion of the dynamic of art. The process, the art, is at once very simple and very marvelous: like Spring.

III

Poe was the first to demonstrate a full theorization of the aesthetic we've been tracking through these poems. The theory is playful and performative, and it is developed in conscious opposition to Wordsworth's "Preface." Its most arresting expression comes in a notorious pair of texts, "The Raven" and "The Philosophy of Composition." Poe stands against Wordsworth in two key particulars: poetry for him is not the spontaneous overflow of powerful feelings, nor is poetry's linguistic norm the language "of low and rustic life." Poe's paradise is artificial, not natural, which is why he became a foundational figure for writers from Baudelaire to Rossetti to Borges.

To this day readers have difficulty deciding whether or not Poe means us to take "The Philosophy of Composition," or for that matter "The Raven," seriously. The literary hoax is a genre of choice for Poe, allowing him to set puzzles and problems for his readers. Are "The Philosophy of Furniture" and "Morning on the Wissahiccon" familiar essays or stories, and what difference does it make? What about "Diddling Considered as One of the Exact Sciences"? Essay or tale? Perhaps more important still, his hoaxes and parodies are as often as not executed in the open, like "How to Write a Blackwood's Article," its pendant piece "A Predicament," "The Balloon-Hoax," "Mystification," or "Von Kempelen and His Discovery." All are transparent hoaxes, written in and for disbelief.

Poe cultivates an aesthetic of self-awareness. When he makes a parade of his views in "The Philosophy of Composition," the reader's self-awareness becomes a central issue. The text is deliberately provocative, not to say impish and perverse. Our puzzlement at the meaning of the essay — or perhaps the essay is "really" a story? — signals the design he has laid on us, the problem he has set. The essay is a theory of poetry we would imagine written by a man like Dupin. Or by the fisherman from "A Descent into the Maelstrom."

As much as Poe rather despised Wordsworth's approach to poetry, he greatly admired Coleridge's — not only in the highly imaginative practice of works like "Kubla Khan," but in the brainy prose commentaries, especially the *Biographia Literaria*. Poe's work is a Coleridgean derivative. However, it makes a slight but crucial swerve from Coleridge in its understanding of the mechanism of poetic artifice. Coleridge speaks of his own poetry as an effort "to procure for [the] shadows of [his] imagination that willing suspension of disbelief for the moment, which constitutes poetic faith" (*Biographia Literaria* chapter 14). Coleridge assumes — and assumes that the reader assumes — the fictional status of the poem's materials. Poetry is for him an act of imitation and as such stands at one or (according to Plato and his followers) two removes from the reality it represents. In order to "constitute" belief in the reader, the poet has to construct illusions that readers "for the moment" will find believable. This is necessary because a poem raises up only "shadows of imagination," not the Imagination itself. The latter, for Coleridge, is transcendant and wholly "Ideal" (Coleridge's term): a repetition in the finite mind of the eternal act of creation in the infinite I AM.

For Poe, however, *poiesis* involves something that might better be called the willing suspension of belief rather than disbelief. Poe's fictions come in two forms, verse and prose, and he makes an interesting distinction between the two. As works of imagination, both stand opposed to what he called "the heresy of *The Didactic*." The object of the poem is to embody "the idea of the Beautiful" as such. To encounter a poem we must suspend our belief that it involves anything other than its literality, its *haecceitas* as Scotus would say.

The poem is simply "this poem written solely for the poem's sake" (*Essays and Reviews*, "The Poetic Principle" 76). It allies itself with musicality — with metrical form — in order to ensure that it will ever have "only collateral relations" "with the Intellect or with the Conscience." Prose is different, in particular the short story, of which Poe wrote that "next to . . . a poem [it] best fulfill[s] the purposes of ambitious genius." Indeed, Poe argued "that the tale has a point of superiority even over the poem": it can avail itself of a "vast variety of modes or inflections of thought and expression." For Poe, the tale is the genre of the "Intellect" (whereas the poem is the genre of the "Soul"). He thus uses his tales as vehicles for developing explanations, or what he called "ratiocinations," of the imagination's operating system. The tales' key feature is that, as part of that system, their explanations unfold as embodiments of the system, not abstractions from it.

Whether poetic or prosaic, then, Poe's fictions are not *shadows* of Imagination. They are its real and substantial forms, like *Don Giovanni*'s music. Reading Poe, what we have to suspend is our belief in them *as shadows,* for taken as such they will always haunt us with the absent presence of something Ideal and transcendent — that's to say, the illusion of something "real" like (say) the resurrection of the dead Ligeia or Don Giovanni's career as a rapist. That condition of being haunted — an experience regularly hypothesized in Poe's so-called horror stories — is the artifice constructed by Poe's lucid imagination. To recall and paraphrase Blake's "Auguries of Innocence," these stories will involve a strange and shadowy artifice "to those poor souls who dwell in night," but "to those who dwell in realms of day," they will appear simply, magnificently, as "human forms," forms of the imagination's sympathetic power. Poe writes them as machines for engaging the imaginative lucidity of his readers. Like Brecht, his idea of the imagination is dialectical. His purpose is to play its plays with the house lights turned on.

"A Descent into the Maelstrom" is a virtual allegory of Poe's aesthetic views. It is a tale within a tale, the core being the story a Norwegian fisherman tells to the narrator about his terrifying plunge into a maelstrom off the Norwegian coast. The fisherman has brought the narrator to a precipitous summit overlooking the place of the maelstrom. The narrator's fright at their situation is extreme, and he is even more amazed at the fisherman, who is utterly unfazed by the terrors of the place. "You must get over these fancies," he tells the narrator, and he unfolds his story like the ancient mariner speaking to the wedding guest. The fisherman's story is a moral lesson to the narrator, and Poe's tale — since the narrator is the reader's surrogate — is an aesthetic lesson to the reader.

The moral lesson is about the need for imaginative clarity. Unlike his brother, who is swept to destruction (that's to say, he disappears from the story!), the fisherman saves himself by cultivating a series of cool realizations about himself and his circumstances. He tells the narrator how, in the very center of the maelstrom, he grew self-aware and curious. He comes to a positive *"wish* to explore [the] depths" of the frightful maelstrom, and even cultivates what he calls *"amusement* in speculating" on its operations. The old man survives in this semiotic world as he should survive — that's to say, he survives literally. He survives because he treats his experience in the maelstrom as a decipherable system of signs.

The aesthetic lesson is completely correspondent with all this. The fisherman's maelstrom is a figure for any of Poe's tales of terror — *this* very tale, for instance, whose fictional construction we are being asked to read exactly as the fisherman learned to read the details of his experience in the maelstrom. The result will be — as the classical formula suggests — "pleasure and instruction."

Note that these effects come from focusing on the tale as such, on what Laura Riding calls "The Telling" of the tale (rather than on what the tale *suggests* through its fictive linguistic representations). If we attend to the latter we end up like the narrator, or like the fisherman's brother, immersed in fear and the paraphernalia — the real illusions — that generate fear.

IV

We require, in Poe's view, what Flaubert called a sentimental education and what Charles Bernstein calls an "artifice of absorption" — "a swoon," as "The Klupzy Girl" has it, that "brings you to your senses." The greatest of his tales — "Ligeia," "The Fall of the House of Usher" — are at once absorbing and demystifying. The opening paragraph of "Usher" is exemplary.

> During the whole of a dull, dark, and soundless day in the autumn of the year, when the clouds hung oppressively low in the heavens, I had been passing along, on horseback, through a singularly dreary tract of country, and at length found myself, as the shades of evening drew on, within view of the melancholy House of Usher. I know not how it was — but with the first glimpse of the building, a sense of insufferable gloom pervaded my spirit.

"I know not how it was"?! Perhaps the narrator knows not, but every reader can see perfectly well *how it was*. The narrator appears to know not because he is absorbed in the fiction being constructed through the language of the narrative. But readers — the readers solicited by Poe — are to be differently absorbed. We enter this scene as it is a work of art, which is why we can *see* the

signs that produce the narrator's "insufferable gloom." Like the purloined letter, the signs — the manifest Gothic language — are hidden for us in plain sight.

But we have to read the scene closely and with extreme care, like the fisherman in the maelstrom tale. We have to undertake an absorbed attention in the action, which for us is the action of the language. To do this we have to willingly suspend our belief in the referential illusions of that action. We have to read *literally*.

The next sentence is a particularly revealing invitation to get absorbed in this way: "I say insufferable," the narrator tells us, "for the feeling was unrelieved by any of that half-pleasurable, because poetic, sentiment, with which the mind usually receives even the sternest natural images of the desolate or terrible." As so often in his work, Poe is playing a wordgame with us — a game with a serious comic point. "Insufferable" is an equivocation, very like the "quaint and equivocal appellation of the 'House of Usher'" that Poe calls to our attention two paragraphs later. The narrator's own explanation of the word shows that he is using it imprecisely, as a loose general superlative. For clearly the gloom is *not* beyond his enduring or toleration. Indeed, it is a gloom he covets and cherishes, as is also perfectly clear in the way he cultivates his overwrought Gothic discourse. Consequently, the conclusion is foregone that his gloom is unrelieved by the poetical half-pleasures he mentions. The text is an algorithm coded by the narrator, an algorithm ensuring (for him, not for Poe or for us) a catastrophic outcome.

But the narrator's loss is the reader's gain, for in transacting this text we uncover the narrator's coding. In this reading event we are recoding the scripts of the tale, discovering "the pleasures of the text" exactly as the fisherman discovered amusements in the maelstrom, and as we are pleased with the wicked career of Don Giovanni. Poe writes to cultivate these readerly clarities. Later in the opening paragraph, for example, the narrator laments his inability to explain "what . . . so unnerved me in the contemplation of the House of Usher." He admits that while everyone knows that "combinations of very simple natural objects . . . have the power of thus affecting us," "the analysis of that power lies among considerations beyond our depth." All of Poe's work stands against such an idea, and one of the greatest charms of this particular tale is to watch the narrator fail to understand what his own words reveal. After he admits being "beyond [his] depth," the sentence reads:

> It was possible, I reflected, that a mere different arrangement of the particulars of the scene, of the details of the picture, would be sufficient to modify, or perhaps to annihilate its capacity for sorrowful

impression; and, acting on this idea, I reined my horse to the precipitous brink of a black and lurid tarn that lay in unruffled luster by the
dwelling and gazed down — but with a shudder even more thrilling
than before — upon the remodeled and inverted images of the gray
sedge, and the ghastly tree-stems, and the vacant and eye-like windows.

The sentence is a spectacular example of an artifice of absorption. If the narrator could inhabit his words the way we do as readers, if he could *authorize*
rather than simply *suffer* them, he would make the escape he is thinking
about. But his are a pair of eyes wide shut, as "vacant" as the windows of the
house that oppresses him — the house of his life that is the house of this text,
"the House of Usher." So, persisting in his unwise passiveness, he follows the
text through a different arrangement of its parts to a similar gloomy end: "the
precipitous brink of a black and lurid tarn."

For us, who can see what is happening, however, the passage is wonderfully comic and "poetical." As absorbed by the house of the text as the narrator is, we move through it by studying our absorption and reflecting on "how
it was," on the operation of its signs. The "black and lurid tarn" is plainly an
emblem of the mirror of art — in this case an especially lucid emblem because
a black surface would reflect clearer images. And if the narrator were a more
capable character — a person more like Dupin or the maelstrom fisherman —
he might have thought to make a slightly different arrangement of the particulars of that word "lurid." For in another arrangement the tarn is indeed "lucid" rather than "lurid." Casting the text in pictorial terms ("the details of the
picture"), the black tarn may even be a little piece of amusing code, referencing what artists call a "black mirror" which artists use to enhance the view of
the details of a painting.

Poe argued that in any composition "there should be no word written of
which the tendency, direct or indirect, is not to the one established design" of
the work. Though I've been looking closely at only a small part of Poe's tale,
its operation is entirely characteristic of the whole, and a similar analysis
might be brought to any passage whatsoever. Poe's works *are* that brainy and
self-conscious, which is what makes them not only brilliant and demanding,
but exceedingly amusing. Certain moments stand out as particularly outrageous, as in this sentence when the narrator finally meets Roderick Usher:
"The valet now threw open a door and ushered me into the presence of his
master." *Ushered* me! Here we are meeting the real master of this house,
Edgar Allan Poe, who flits quickly past like Hitchcock in one of his films, or
like Leporello listening to Mozart's music in the opera and remarking that he
recognizes it — as a tune from another opera by Mozart.

V

Let me close by way of a return through Wittgenstein. "But what is the meaning of the word 'five'?" he asked himself, and he answered: "No such thing was in question here, only how the word 'five' was used." Now consider Poe's notorious remark about the alliance of death, poetry, and beauty: "the death . . . of a beautiful woman is . . . the most poetical topic in the world — and equally it is beyond doubt that the lips best suited for such a topic are those of a bereaved lover." "But," I want to ask: "What is the meaning of that passage?" And now I want to reply: "No such thing was in question here, only how the passage was used."

The passage was used precisely to indicate that the forms of Beauty inherited by Romanticism were dying. Poe saw that Beauty was being kept alive in the art of his epoch largely by symbol and by sentiment — known not even, as Rossetti put the matter in his Botticellian terms, "by flying hair and fluttering hem," but less directly still, by what Wordsworth called "feeling." That feeling is a special type, however — what Wordsworth accurately named "the feeling of . . . loss." When Poe declares in "The Philosophy of Composition" that "Melancholy" is the emotional index of art, the judgment is exact because it is historically accurate, a true representation of the state of art at the inner standing-point of his time.

Poe's stories and poems are about that kind of art. Given his historical situation, this means they are about the death of Beauty. Or rather — to speak more accurately — about *the feeling of* Beauty's death. And of course they are all told from the point of view of Beauty's bereaved lover, the poet in the age of mechanical reproduction, which maintains a widespread practice of art in popular forms. These practices have been an embarrassment for persons aspiring to more pretentious positions in the industries of culture. But Poe published with pleasure and a will in venues like *Snowden's Lady's Companion, Graham's Magazine, The Southern Literary Messenger,* and *The Gift,* just as Emily Dickinson and the Brontës went to those same places for their literary models.

Poe is under no illusions about what kind of material one finds in these gift books and periodicals, as we see so clearly in his marvelous parody "How to Write a Blackwood's Article." By a "different arrangement of [its] particulars," this tale will become "The Philosophy of Composition," just as different arrangements of literary and linguistic conventions distinguish different types of *poiesis,* including those polarized abstractions good poems and stories v. bad, and vice versa. Poe inveighed against moral and intellectual pretentiousness in art, and he chose Wordsworth — perhaps somewhat unfairly — as his touchstone for a fastidious aesthetic standing-point — the poet as *spectator ab extra.* In various essays, perhaps most notably the 1842 review of Hawthorne's *Twice-Told Tales,* he states his commitment to popular forms of Intellectual Beauty — a serious art unashamed of its vulgarities. The move is significant and crucial. Frederick Turner has shown the functional relation between "the decay of Beauty" over the past two hundred years and a pervasive sense and fear of shame in the practice of art. Wordsworth was ashamed to write for the gift books, and when he did he was further mortified. Alas, unlike the narrator of Rossetti's poem "Jenny," he never came to be "shamed by his own shame," that brink of a new and better life. Shame is written all over the fearfully powerful but unbeautiful music of Alban Berg and the pictures of Lucien Freud, just as it is entirely absent from the music of Richard Strauss or the paintings of Balthus, those modern masters of Beauty. Beauty like Love cannot survive in an atmosphere of shame because shame is the sign that we imagine ourselves better, more beautiful, than we are. The Greeks were right, however. We know nothing more beautiful than the human form — that form in all its possibilities of form. As Blake shrewdly observed, "Attempting to be more than Man we become less." An ancient, touching human fault, this infatuated desire for what Poe called "the distant Aidenn."

What is important about Poe is that he uses his vulgar Gothic materials in a new way, at a second order. He does not represent his *poiesis* as an eolian harp, wisely passive to the wiser passing wind of "Nature" or God or, worse still, to Byron's "unspiritual god" of circumstance, Coleridge's famous "persons from Porlock." The difference between Coleridge's explanation of how "Kubla Khan" was written, and Poe's explanation of "The Raven," measures the distance Poe put between himself and his Lake school precursors. Both are imaginative explanations of two different theories of imagination.

Remember that we have no reason to believe Coleridge's realist account of how "Kubla Khan" came to be only a fragment. Norman Fruman has shown that the historical "facts" Coleridge sets out in his *Biographia Literaria* can never be relied on as actually having happened. And he chides Coleridge's editors for glossing over this important matter, leaving readers to assume that details offered by Coleridge as fact are true, when in *truth* they remain to this day without any independent corroboration whatsoever. I mention this here not to damage the archangelic Coleridge but because it demonstrates the resolutely imaginative status of some key Coleridge texts. In the case of "Kubla Khan" particularly, it also demonstrates Coleridge's adherence to an eolian harp view of poetic expression. Poe's explanation of how he wrote "The Raven" is very different, very self-conscious. Interestingly, it doesn't matter one way or the other whether his account is true to fact or not. Whether written in earnest or in jest, the account represents *poiesis* as a textual performance, a *geste* in language.

In an eolian Romanticism, Beauty will be known only like Wordsworth's Lucy, in forms of an absent presence, which for her lover, the artist, means — as Wordsworth fears in Lucy's case — as dead. Poe is closer — always — to Byron, who learned Manfred's magic of deliberately "turn[ing] what was once romantic to burlesque." Or to the commanding spirit Shelley prays to be in the "Ode to the West Wind." Poe becomes that spirit — a lucid lutenist, like Blake's devil, "a harper [singing] to the harp" in a netherworld he chooses to inhabit in order to transform. Becoming the artist of the death of Beauty, Poe makes all things possible.

The maelstrom fisherman is once again a touchstone. His power over certain death comes when he abandons all hope. At that point everything shifts into the clarity of the present tense. No more "little barks of hope," for even if one were found or built, where would one "steer? / There woos no home nor hope nor life, save what is here." That is Byron talking, Poe's chief influence, the very model of the utterly lost soul whose abandonment of hope involves an aesthetic of willfully suspended belief, as he repeatedly tells us in *Don Juan*. When faith and hope, those two great theological virtues, slip away from the artist's needs, only the third remains, "the greatest of these": Love, the damned Corsair's one last virtue, and the single devotion of the bereaved lover of that "rare and radiant maiden whom the angels name Lenore."

And for Byron, at any rate, the loss of those theological virtues installed a set of human ones, a faith and a hope that led him to western Greece where he gave his life away. The liberation of Greece rarely registers on the scale of world historical events. Set beside the American, the French, the Russian, or that much celebrated "Glorious" English revolution, it seems a small event. But it is warmly recalled to this day in that small country with the famous ancient history. Dying for liberty on that scale brings the right sort of *human* measure to issues of moral virtue and social commitment.

Do those comments seem out of place here? Not to my mind. The act of art, a human act after all, seems especially called to take the measure of our grand devotions and purify them of their *unearthly* dross. *Don Giovanni* is, we often think, a great masterpiece. But its greatness is a function of its sheer inconsequence — its swift, intense ephemera. This is what we may read "The Raven" to discover as well, what it was written to reveal. The poem's ostensive subject is wholly Romantic: Wordsworth's Lucy, here called — referencing Gottfried Burger's foundational Romantic ballad — "this lost Lenore." Poe's poem exposes the lover's desire to have her return, or failing that, to join her in another world. The poem precisely — emphatically — rules out the fulfillment of those desires. Think of the difference with, for instance, "Lucy Gray," where an apparition of the lost Lucy returns at the end, "sing[ing] a solitary song, / And whistl[ing] in the wind." There is the romantic "Comfort of Resurrection," as Hopkins called it, in a poem asking us to suspend any inclination we might have to disbelieve in it.

Instead of the lost Lenore, or an image of her, Poe gives us instead a raven — "*The* Raven": as the poem says, "Only this and nothing more." "The Raven" is Poe's version of Stevens's Snowman, unfolding "Nothing that is not there and the nothing that is." Flaunting its artifactuality, the poem continually calls attention to itself as an unfolding textual event:

> Back into the chamber turning, all my soul within me burning,
> Soon again I heard a tapping somewhat louder than before.
> "Surely," said I, "surely that is something at my window lattice;
> Let me see, then, what thereat is, and this mystery explore —
> Let my heart be still a moment and this mystery explore. . . .

"That is / lattice / thereat is": these are Poe's textual tappings calling us to explore the apparent mysteries of the poem. But the mysteries are not hidden away, they are all in perfect view if we would simply pay attention: for instance, the mysterious and amusing charm of those arbitrary multiple rhymings. One recalls not only "The Purloined Letter," but Poe's comment in his early theoretical "Letter to B ——": "As regards the greater truths, men oftener err by seeking them at the bottom than at the top; . . . in the palpable."

Artifice, the "mystery" of human creativity, is therefore to be exposed, not confused with surplus mysteriousness and its unhelpful unapparencies. Perhaps no passage in the poem makes a more startling display of that view than the following:

> Then this ebony bird beguiling my sad fancy into smiling,
> By the grave and stern decorum of the countenance it wore,
> "Though thy crest be shorn and shaven, thou," I said, "art sure no craven,
> Ghastly grim and ancient Raven wandering from the Nightly shore —
> Tell me what thy lordly name is on the Night's Plutonian shore!"
>   Quoth the Raven, "Nevermore."

If we had not noticed it before, this text throws in our face — by way of our ears, if I may so put the matter — certain dazzling verbal transformations. As we know from contemporary rhyming dictionaries plus the example of many poets, "decorum" held that the "g" terminating an "ing" ending is an unvoiced letter in poetry. This rule brings Shelley, for example, to the following rhyme: "And we shrank back: for dreams of ruin / To frozen caves our flight pursuing" (*Prometheus Unbound* 1.1.103 – 4). Knowing this rule, as Poe's readers did, they were being beguiled into smiling at the double transformation flirting in the phrase "Raven wandering." For that would be (also) to say: "Raven wanderin'." But juxtaposing precisely *those* two words licenses further transformational actions. Words terminating in a short *e* or *i* followed by an *n* become seeable as having undergone a literal, orthographic elision, so that the phrase also transforms to mean "Raving wandering." The transformations metastasize, affecting nearby texts ("craven" transforms nicely into "craving"). In fact, the whole system of the poem is undergoing a transformational invasion. Did we think we understood the title of Poe's poem? Did we know when we first read it that it also meant "The Raving"?

Or, most beguiling of all such transformations: when do we realize that "raven" is virtually "never" spelled backward?

From the lover's unforgotten and unforgettable "lost Lenore" comes the rare and radiant maiden that is Poe's poem, exactly like the LADY LIGEIA extruding herself by an outrageous act of will out of the body of the Lady Rowena. These are transformations that come about if we, Poe's readers, cooperate in them. The process can appear shameful, even shocking, if we follow it only along its sublimated levels, the haunted realms of the text's signifieds and its illusory, "realist" references. At the level of the signifiers an ultimate, absolute transformation is taking place, language turning into *poesie pure*.

At that level Poe becomes the valet of the Lady Beauty in the house of her new life, ushering ourselves, comedians as the letter U, past the apparitions of horror and into her real presence. And suddenly there she always is — Berenice, Madeline Usher, Ligeia, the Lenore "whom the angels name" — like Kit Robinson's "goddess," "really feeling great" in her marvelous crepuscular outfits. As if she never left at all.

Stevens wrote a wonderful little poem about how this act of secular transubstantiation takes place. Parodying the Shakespearean hymns we know, "The Worms at Heaven's Gate" brings the goddess back again in these wormy words. She is dressed up like an *Arabian Nights'* princess and looking very smart too. But we know who she is: Beauty herself, immortal in the flesh of the text that fills her out.

> Out of the tomb, we bring Badroulbadour,
> Within our bellies, we her chariot,
> Here is an eye. And here are, one by one,
> The lashes of that eye, and its white lid.
> Here is the cheek on which that lid declined,
> And, finger after finger, here, the hand,

The genius of that cheek. Here are the lips,
The bundle of the body and the feet.
. . . .
Out of the tomb we bring Badroulbadour.

Let be be the finale of this seeming — which is to say, if you want to know what the poem *means*, recite it. And after that?

What do then? how meet beauty? Merely meet it; own,
Home at heart, heaven's sweet gift; then leave, let that alone.

The rest is silence.

CODA

The Scholar's Art

Whether he knew about Grecian urns from pictures in books or had actually seen one, Keats only knew about them. The Grecian urn named in his famous poem had long ago, once upon a time, "fled away" into time's obscuring storm, like the lovers in "The Eve of St. Agnes." The urn is an impossible object, defined as such by the ode itself.

Defined as such so that Keats might demonstrate how one can possess impossible things:

> Heard melodies are sweet, but those unheard
> Are sweeter; therefore, ye soft pipes, play on;
> Not to the sensual ear, but, more endear'd,
> Pipe to the spirit ditties of no tone. . . .

Charmed by his desire for an unknown urn and the music of its images, Keats has only one resource, to reinvent them in another desirable form. "Therefore" he does, by the fiat the Greeks called *poiesis,* the primal command to *be:*

> As a new heaven is begun, and it is now thirty-three years since its advent: the Eternal Hell revives. And lo! Swedenberg is the Angel sitting at the tomb . . . Now is the dominion of Edom, & the return of Adam into Paradise. (Blake, *The Marriage of Heaven and Hell,* plate 3)

"Lo! . . . Now": in a poetic order of things, "the cherub with his flaming sword *is hereby commanded*" to run his transformational programs (my italics). For in

211

this way of thinking (this way of acting), "everything would appear to man as it is, infinite" were his doors of perception cleansed (plate 14). Nor can the event be postponed or simply promised, for the rule here is "Let be be finale of seem." The syntax always calls on certain magic words: in these two exemplary passages from Blake, "therefore," "lo!," "Now," "is," "hereby." Revelatory words written by angels "with corroding fires" are "now perceived by the minds of men, & read by them on earth" (plates 6–7).

All of this is composition performing an explanation of itself, as Gertrude Stein would say. Keats re-creates the terra-cotta object by reaching after an unrealized idea in the object, the music that the material object has made it impossible to hear. The unheard melodies that Keats wants get replayed in his verse, as we *see* (and miraculously now can also hear) the musical performance he mounts for us in a bibliographical display of words. Unheard, ear, endeared; on, no, tone. Keats isolates these two linguistic motifs so that their ravishing internal variations, their plaintive anthems, spread in echoes upon echoes: melodies, sweeter, soft, not, *spirit*. The sensual ear ends in the tones of a music being played in an unscaled key.

This is what a contemporary poet has called, playing on *his* words, "sound as thought." Meaning to say — perhaps rather to show — that this kind of thinking is more sound and reliable than the vehicular expositions we learn to live with. The difference lies in the performative status of the ideas and the consequent "awareness of all the room that exists within a single beat, and just exactly which point in that space you want to occupy, though the room itself may be moving at a very high rate of speed." This is thinking *in medias res,* at a Rossettian inner standing-point, occupied in the rooms the thinking creates to unbuild: "And Jean-Luc Godard last night on television spoke of his movies as 'the train, not the station, because I am no longer waiting'" (Coolidge, *Now It's Jazz* 93, 94).

Artists know that when you take the measure of something — for instance, the urn at the end of Keats's mind — your act of measurement is incorporate with the measure you take. A poetic investigation makes you an accomplice in the work you are studying. Quantum scientists gesture at the same situation when they say that their measurements alter the objects they experiment on. In humane studies, we pledge our allegiance to the hermeneutic circle and accept (in theory) the dialectic of Paul de Man's "blindness and insight." The presence of "textual indeterminacy" is a given in professionally sanctioned literary and cultural interpretive practice.

But all of these research and interpretive procedures emerge from a profession viewed with suspicion and often hostility in our extramural world. To think or imagine that texts and documents do not possess determinate meanings, to suggest — worse still — that they are not self-identical, seems ludicrous to many outside the academy and even to some inside.

We need an angel like Robert Burns to look us homeward, "to see ourselves as others see us." How seriously do we ourselves actually take these ideas and positions, these critical self-destroyings? Our schools of criticism are, paradoxically, proud and articulate, confident with Enlightenment. But what do we know and when did we know it? A famous historical question that all scholars should post on the wall above their desks.

This *is* a comical situation: to appear enlightened, the ones presumed to know, and at the same time to profess ourselves complicit agents of indeterminate practices? More pertinently, since academic work is only validated when it promotes imaginative rigor, how much do these interpretive procedures clarify the cultural work that we half perceive and half create? Scholarship that doesn't take its folly seriously can't be trusted. Starting from Paumonok and (or) Manhattan, we live in a house divided against itself.

The relevance of those matters appears when we encounter work that clearly does take its ideas and positions seriously: say, Plato, Montaigne, Thoreau, Wilde, Wittgenstein. These are great names, probably too great in the far more limited horizon of this book. Better to reflect on Susan Howe's exemplary *My Emily Dickinson,* a work of scholarship that labels itself a captivity narrative from the start, a meticulous report by someone who found herself lost in the wilderness of a great poet and a great poem.

"A house divided against itself cannot stand." That is a priestly, not a poetical, idea. And priests are hired to organize and administer, not to create, destroy, and explore. "These two classes of men are always upon earth and they should be enemies; whoever seeks to reconcile them seeks to destroy existence." *That* is a poetical idea. The question for the scholar is, "Which side are you on, boys?" And the answer is known: "both," which immediately (as in our catechisms) leads to the next question: "in the weeks of our lives, which ones are priestly days?" When ancient wisdom commands us to set the Sabbath aside for priestlike tasks, do we forget its assumption of a precursive, reciprocal command, that we live in fire and contradiction for the other six?

Deviance presides and preserves from Lucretian subatomics to the complexities of persons and societies. This is the great subject taken up in *My Emily Dickinson,* where the poet emerges not as spider artist but as demon lover. The explanation of how this is so comes as the demonic composition of Howe's own book, which — negatively capable throughout — assays (in both senses) the bittersweet of its Dickinsonian fruit. So Howe's Dickinson (*her* Emily Dickinson) tracks "paths of the Self that begin and end in contradiction" (11). "Like Victory, Justice, Words, my Mind must be ready to change

sides" (129). Howe's tensile prose does not shift from this perpetually changing key, which emerges in her initial *non serviam* written to William Carlos
Williams, Sandra Gilbert, and Susan Gubar. Loved or admired though they
are, all three get resisted. To Williams, Emily Dickinson is no poet but a starv-
ing Keatsian dreamer; to Gilbert and Gubar, she is the spider-artist, patching
and mending what is torn and cloven, "seam to seam, by the magical stitch-
ery of art." Neither way with Dickinson will do, but precisely because they
are invested with a feminist commitment, Gilbert and Gubar are Howe's greatest spiritual enemies: "Who is this Spider-Artist? Not *my* Emily Dickinson.
This is poetry, not life, and certainly not sewing" (14).

Howe seizes that pair of differences—Williams v. Gilbert/Gubar—and
returns them as an extended demonstration of how the *poiesis* of contradiction works.

> Orders suggest hierarchy and category. Categories and hierarchies
> suggest property. My voice formed from my life belongs to no one
> else. What I put into words is no longer my possession. Possibility
> has opened. The future will forget, erase, or recollect and deconstruct
> every poem. There is a mystic separation between poetic vision and
> ordinary living. (13)

An extractable prose of this passage may be taken to mean that "poetic vision"
is one thing and scholarship another. But the *actual* prose — the writing here,
Howe's book itself— argues something very different: "Wallace Stevens said
that 'Poetry is a scholar's art.' It is for some. It was for Dickinson" (15). And
Howe's book is a scholar's art as well, a model, it seems to me, of what we
want to be practicing in our secular weekday scholarly labors.

"Connections between unconnected things are the unreal reality of poetry" (97). This is Howe's version of Harold Bloom's quest for "the hidden
roads that go from poem to poem" (*The Anxiety of Influence* 96). In each case
the scholarly event is pursued as an archaeology of knowing. A tangle of hidden roads run through a scattering of unknown places: this is the landscape of
every scholar, poet or otherwise. And so Howe lays down her great scholar's
theme: "Contradiction is the book of this place" (*My Emily Dickinson* 45).

Poetry, it's true, is a mapmaking specially suited to the exposure of con-
tradicted connections. But we workday scholars must not be intimidated by
this scholar-poet's fierce critical exactitudes. Howe's is a critical model for our
schooling, a procedure and an ethos well worth study, opposition, imitation,
revision. "I am heading toward certain discoveries" (7). Not knowledge, or
what Howe in her book so brilliantly explores under the name "Sovereignty,"

but exploration. Every scholar's art ceases with the presumption of knowledge, when method itself has become an archaeology of *knowledge*. For the scholar there is only the knowing search and the knowledge, if such it is, that the game is endless and unwinnable, redeemed only by the scholar's commitment to thoroughness, precision, and candor.

This book's poor patchwork has tried to keep in view the immortal diamond of that kind of scholar's art.

NOTES

Page 47: lost on all sides: D. G. Rossetti, "Lost on Both Sides"

Page 48: compassed . . . danger: Milton, *Paradise Lost,* book 7

Page 49: moaning . . . voices: Tennyson, "Ulysses"

Chapter 3

Page 55: blank and pitiless as the sun: Yeats, "The Second Coming"

Page 55: all men . . . said "What": Emily Dickinson, letter to Thomas Higginson, August 1862

Page 58: a primer of modern heresies: T. S. Eliot, *After Strange Gods: A Primer of Modern Heresy* (1934)

Page 58: imagination of disaster: Susan Sontag, *Against Interpretation* (1966)

Page 61: dark songs before the sunrise: Swinburne, *Songs before Sunrise* (1871)

Page 63: poetry as the dream of Adam: John Keats, letter to Benjamin Bailey, November 22, 1817

Chapter 4

Page 73: "the Author of Waverley": the signature Scott chose for his novels, to preserve his anonymity

Page 73: "the shadow of futurity": in Shelley's "Defense of Poetry"

Page 74: this will never do: Francis Jeffrey's dismissive remark that opens his review of Wordsworth's *Excursion* (1814)

Page 87: to look upon and live: Exodus 33:20

Chapter 5

Page 91: borrow those words: Wordworth, *The Prelude* book 6; Tennyson, "Ulysses"

Page 91: the effort . . . as we move: Wordsworth, *The Prelude* book 6; Tennyson, "Ulysses"

Page 91: mirrors of the heart: Byron, "To the Po"

Page 91: cherished madness of the heart: Byron, *The Giaour*

Page 91: some divine despair: Tennyson, "Tears, Idle Tears"; grey-haired Saturn: Keats, *Hyperion*

Page 92: For a discussion of Baudelaire's theory, see my "Byron and the Anonymous Lyric," in *Byron and Romanticism* (Cambridge: Cambridge University Press, 2002), chap. 5. Brooks's discussion of poetic anonymity comes in his classic study *The Well-Wrought Urn* (1947).

Page 96: world's slow stain: Shelley, "Adonais"; too-much-with-us world . . . light of sense goes out: Wordsworth, "The World Is Too Much with Us"; "Tintern Abbey"

Page 99: O sensible lecteur, mon semblable, mon frère: Baudelaire, "Au lecteur"

Page 102: J. G. Ballard, *The Atrocity Exhibition* (1969)

Page 103: whole vocation is endless imitation: Wordsworth, "Intimations Ode"

Chapter 6

Page 108: a symbol standing for itself: Wagner, *Symbols That Stand for Themselves*
Page 111: A Poetic Abstract: See Blake's "A Human Abstract"
Page 117: Thy soul . . . from God: D. G. Rossetti, "Heart's Hope"
Page 117: fade . . . common day: Wordsworth, "Ode: Intimations of Immortality"
Page 119: now no more a singer but a song: Swinburne, "Thalassius"

Chapter 7

Page 126: seems . . . land of dreams: Matthew Arnold, "Dover Beach"

Chapter 8

Page 135: that is not me in any sense: D. H. Lawrence, "Manifesto"
Page 140: of the earth, earthy: 1 Corinthians 15:47 (King James Version)
Page 146: a game that must be lost: Ford Madox Ford, *Rossetti*
Pages 146, 147: Hejinian . . . virtues: "The Rejection of Closure"

Chapter 9

Page 165: make nothing happen: W. H. Auden, "In Memory of W. B. Yeats"
Page 154: Artifice of Absorption: the title of Bernstein's poem (1987)
Page 155: all text is marked text: http://jefferson.village.virginia.edu/%7Ejjm2f/blackwell.htm
Page 156: the knowledge of what is known: August Boeckh's *Erkenntnis der Erkannten*
Page 158: Interpretation in a New Key: http://www.rc.umd.edu/pedagogies/commons/innovations/mcgann3.html
Page 162: veil . . . glass: Shelley, "A Defense of Poetry" and "Adonais"
Page 166: a science of exceptions: Alfred Jarry, *Exploits & Opinions of Dr. Faustroll, Pataphysician*
Page 168: all interpretation is misinterpretation: Harold Bloom, *Anxiety of Influence*

Chapter 10

Page 179: all the sweetsickly . . . generations: *A Glastonbury Romance* (1932), 108
Page 181: brings all beings to their level: *Don Juan,* canto 4 stanza 2
Page 187: Lost on Both Sides: D. G. Rossetti, *The House of Life,* sonnet 91
Page 187: a hell . . . for other people: T. S. Eliot, *After Strange Gods: A Primer of Modern Heresy*

Chapter 11

Page 205: by flying hair and fluttering hem: *The House of Life,* sonnet 77
Page 206: attempting . . . become less: *The Four Zoas,* Night the Ninth
Page 206: unspiritual god: *Childe Harold's Pilgrimage,* canto 4 stanza 125

Page 207: turn . . . to burlesque: *Don Juan,* canto 4 stanza 3

Page 207: a harper . . . the harp: *The Marriage of Heaven and Hell,* plate 19

Page 207: little barks . . . what is here: *Childe Harold's Pilgrimage,* canto 4 stanza 105

Coda

Page 212: let be be finale of seem: Wallace Stevens, "The Emperor of Ice Cream"

Page 212: the urn at the end of Keats's mind: See Wallace Stevens, "Of Mere Being"

Page 213: to look us homeward: John Milton, "Lycidas"

Page 213: to see ourselves as others see us: Robert Burns, "To a Louse"

Page 213: what do we know and when did we know it: Recalling Howard Baker's question to President Nixon during the Senate impeachment hearings.

Page 213: half perceive and half create: William Wordsworth, "Tintern Abbey"

Page 213: Starting from Paumonok: Walt Whitman

Page 213: a house divided against itself cannot stand: Matthew 12:25

Page 213: these two classes . . . destroy existence: William Blake, *The Marriage of Heaven and Hell,* plates 16–17

Page 213: which side are you on, boys?: Natalie Merchant, 1947 Harlan County song

Page 213: bittersweet of its Dickinsonian fruit: John Keats, "On Sitting Down to Read 'King Lear' Once Again"

Page 215: poor patchwork . . . diamond: Gerard Manley Hopkins, "That Nature Is a Heraclitean Fire and of the Comfort of the Resurrection"

WORKS CITED

Adorno, Theodor. *Aesthetic Theory,* trans. C. Lenhardt. London: Verso Books, 1984.

Allen, Donald, ed. *The New American Poetry.* New York: Grove Press, 1960.

Allen, Michael. *Poe and the British Magazine Tradition.* Oxford: Oxford University Press, 1969.

Arnold, Matthew. *Essays in Criticism.* 1st series. London: Macmillan, 1865.

———. *The Poems,* ed. Kenneth Allott. 2nd ed. London: Longmans, 1979.

Ashbery, John. "The Impossible," *Poetry* 88 (July 1957).

Ashton, Rosemary. *The German Idea: Four English Writers and the Reception of German Thought, 1800–1860.* Ann Arbor: University of Michigan Press, 1980.

Ballin, Michael. "'A Certain Combination of Realism and Magic': Notes on the Publishing History of *Porius,"* *Powys Notes* (Fall and Winter 1992): 11–37.

Barber, Stephen L., and David L. Clark, eds. *Regarding Sedgwick: Essays on Queer Culture and Critical Theory.* New York: Routledge, 2002.

Barthes, Roland. *Critical Essays,* trans. Richard Howard. Evanston, IL: Northwestern University Press, 1972.

———. *S/Z,* trans. Richard Howard. New York: Hill and Wang, 1975.

Bennett, Tony. *Formalism and Marxism.* London: Methuen, 1979.

Bernstein, Charles. *Islets/Irritations.* New York: J. Davies, 1983.

———. *My Way: Speeches and Poems.* Chicago: University of Chicago Press, 1999.

Blake, William. *The Complete Poetry and Prose,* ed. David V. Erdman, commentary by Harold Bloom. Rev. ed. New York: Random House, 1988.

Bloom, Harold. *The Anxiety of Influence.* New York: Oxford University Press, 1973.

———. *Wallace Stevens: The Poems of Our Climate.* Ithaca, NY: Cornell University Press, 1977.

———— et al. *Deconstruction and Criticism*. London: Routledge and Kegan Paul, 1979.

Boeckh, August. *Encyklopädie und Methodologie der philologischen Wissenschaften*. Leipzig: Teubner, 1877.

Bostetter, Edward E. *The Romantic Ventriloquists*. Seattle: University of Washington Press, 1963.

Bradley, A. C. *The Oxford Lectures on Poetry*. Bloomington: Indiana University Press, 1961.

Brand, Peg Zeglin, ed. *Beauty Matters*. Bloomington: Indiana University Press, 2000.

Brooks, Cleanth. *The Well-Wrought Urn: Studies in the Structure of Poetry*. New York: Harcourt Brace, 1947.

————, and Robert Penn Warren, eds. *Understanding Poetry*. New York: Henry Holt, 1938.

Brown, G. Spencer. *Laws of Form*. New York: Julian Press, 1972.

Bruns, Gerald. *Hermeneutics Ancient and Modern*. New Haven, CT: Yale University Press, 1992.

Burnshaw, Stanley. *The Poem Itself*. New York: Holt Rinehart and Winston, 1960.

Byron, Lord. *The Complete Poetical Works*, ed. Jerome McGann. 7 vols. Oxford: Clarendon Press, 1981–93.

Cassirer, H. W. *A Commentary on Kant's "Critique of Judgement."* Methuen: London, 1938.

Cavell, Stanley. *In Quest of the Ordinary: Lines of Skepticism and Romanticism*. Chicago: University of Chicago Press, 1988.

Cohen, Philip, ed. *Texts and Textuality: Textual Instability, Theory, and Interpretation*. New York: Garland, 1997.

Coleridge, Samuel Taylor. *Biographia Literaria*, ed. James Engell and W. Jackson Bate. 2 vols. Bollingen Series 75. Princeton, NJ: Princeton University Press, 1983.

Coolidge, Clark. *Now It's Jazz: Writings on Kerouac and The Sounds*. Albuquerque, NM: Living Batch Press, 1999.

————. *Sound as Thought: Poems 1982–1984*. Los Angeles: Sun and Moon Press, 1990.

Crawford, Donald W. *Kant's Aesthetic Theory*. Madison: University of Wisconsin Press, 1974.

Crews, Frederick. *The Pooh Perplex: A Freshman Casebook*. New York: Dutton, 1963.

————. *Postmodern Pooh*. New York: North Point Press, 2001.

Crozier, Andrew, and Tim Longville, eds. *A Various Art*. Manchester: Carcanet, 1987.

Danto, Arthur C. "A Future for Aesthetics," *Journal of Aesthetics and Art Criticism* 51 (1993): 271–77.

Dargan, Joan. *Simone Weil: Thinking Poetically*. Albany: State University of New York Press, 1999.

Davies, Alan. *Signage*. New York: Roof Books, 1987.

Della Volpe, Galvano. *Critique of Taste*. 1960. Trans. Michael Caesar. London: New Left Books, 1978.

De Man, Paul. *Blindness and Insight*. New York: Oxford University Press, 1971.

Dickie, George. *Introduction to Aesthetics: An Analytical Approach*. Rev. ed. Oxford: Oxford University Press, 1997.

Drucker, Johanna. "Graphical Readings and Visual Aesthetics of Textuality," *TEXT* (2003).

———. *Sweet Dreams: Contemporary Art and Complicity*. Chicago: University of Chicago Press, 2005.

Eagleton, Terry. *The Ideology of the Aesthetic*. Oxford: Oxford University Press, 1990.

Eco, Umberto. *The Limits of Interpretation*. Bloomington: Indiana University Press, 1990.

Eliot, T. S. *Selected Essays*. New ed. New York: Harcourt Brace, 1950.

———. "Sweeney among the Nightingales," *The Little Review* 5 (September 1918): 10–11.

———. *The Waste Land and Other Poems*. New York: Harcourt Brace, 1934.

Elmer, Jonathan. *Reading at the Social Limit: Affect, Mass Culture, and Edgar Allan Poe*. Stanford, CA: Stanford University Press, 1995.

Fish, Stanley. *Professional Correctness: Literary Studies and Political Change*. Cambridge, MA: Harvard University Press, 1995.

Fitzgerald, F. Scott. *The Crack-Up*. New York: New Directions, 1945.

Fletcher, Ian. *Rediscovering Herbert Horne*. Greensboro: ELT Press, 1990.

Ford, Ford Madox [Ford Hermann Hueffer]. *Rossetti: A Critical Essay on His Art*. Chicago: Rand McNally, 1915.

Forrest-Thomson, Veronica. *Poetic Artifice: A Theory of Twentieth-Century Poetry*. Manchester: Manchester University Press, 1978.

Frankel, Nicholas. *Oscar Wilde's Decorated Books*. Ann Arbor: University of Michigan Press, 2000.

Fruman, Norman. *Coleridge, the Damaged Archangel*. New York: Braziller, 1971.

Genet, Jean. *Our Lady of the Flowers*, trans. Bernard Frechtman. New York: Grove Press, 1963.

Genette, Gerard. *Paratexts: Thresholds of Interpretation*, trans. Jane Lewin, foreword by Richard Macksey. Cambridge: Cambridge University Press, 1997.

Golding, Alan. *From Outlaw to Classic: Canons in American Poetry*. Madison: University of Wisconsin Press, 1995.

Graff, Gerald. *Literature against Itself: Literary Ideas in Modern Society*. Chicago: University of Chicago Press, 1979.

Harari, Josue, ed. *Textual Strategies: Perspectives in Post-Structuralist Criticism*. Ithaca, NY: Cornell University Press, 1979.

Hartman, Geoffrey. *Wordsworth's Poetry, 1787–1814*. New Haven, CT: Yale University Press, 1971.

Hejinian, Lyn. "The Rejection of Closure," in *Writing/Talks*, 270–91. Carbondale: Southern Illinois University Press, 1985.

Hickey, David. *The Invisible Dragon: Four Essays on Beauty*. Los Angeles: Art Issues Press, 1993.

Hirsch, E. D. *The Aims of Interpretation*. Chicago: University of Chicago Press, 1976.

Hoffman, Daniel. *Poe Poe Poe Poe Poe Poe Poe*. Garden City, NY: Doubleday, 1972.

Hollander, John. *Reflections on Espionage*. New York: Athenaeum, 1976.

Homer. *The Iliad,* trans. Richmond Lattimore. Chicago: University of Chicago Press, 1951.

Hopkins, Gerard Manley. *The Poems,* ed. W. H. Gardner and N. H. Mackenzie. 4th ed. London: Oxford University Press, 1990.

Horne, Herbert. *Diversi Colores*. Published with Selwyn Image, *Poems and Carols,* ed. with an introduction by R. K. R. Thornton and Ian Small. Oxford: Woodstock Books, 1995.

Howe, Susan. *My Emily Dickinson*. Berkeley, CA: North Atlantic Books, 1985.

———. "These Flames and Generosities of the Heart: Emily Dickinson and the Illogic of Sumptuary Values," repr. in *The Birth-Mark: Unsettling the Wilderness in American Literary History*. Hanover, NH: Wesleyan University Press, 1993.

Irwin, John T. *The Mystery to a Solution: Poe, Borges, and the Analytic Detective Story*. Baltimore: Johns Hopkins University Press, 1994.

Iser, Wolfgang. *The Range of Interpretation*. New York: Columbia University Press, 2000.

James, Henry. "The Art of Fiction," in *Henry James: Literary Criticism*. New York: Library of America, 1984.

Jarry, Alfred. *Exploits & Opinions of Dr. Faustroll, Pataphysician,* trans. Simon Watson Taylor. Boston: Exact Change, 1996.

Johnson, Galen A., ed. *The Merleau-Ponty Aesthetics Reader: Philosophy and Painting,* trans. Michael B. Smith. Evanston, IL: Northwestern University Press, 1993.

Kant, Immanuel. *The Critique of Judgement,* trans. James Creed Meredith. Clarendon Press: Oxford, 1952.

Keats, John. *The Poems,* ed. Miriam Allott. London: Longmans, 1977.

Kirwan, James. *Beauty*. Manchester: Manchester University Press, 1999.

Lang, Cecil Y. *The Pre-Raphaelites and Their Circle*. Chicago: University of Chicago Press, 1975.

———, ed. *Swinburne: Letters*. 6 vols. New Haven, CT: Yale University Press, 1959–62.

Lukács, Georg. *The Historical Novel*. 1937. Boston: Beacon Press, 1962.

Lyotard, Jean-François. "After the Sublime: The State of Aesthetics," in David Carroll, ed., *The States of "Theory": History, Art, and Critical Discourse*, 297–304. New York: Columbia University Press, 1990.

Mailloux, Steven. *Interpretive Conventions: The Reader in the Study of American Fiction*. Ithaca, NY: Cornell University Press, 1982.

Maturana, Humberto, and Francesco Varela. *Autopoiesis and Cognition*. Dordrecht, Holland: D. Reidel, 1980.

McGann, Jerome. *The Beauty of Inflections: Literary Investigations in Historical Method and Theory.* Oxford: Clarendon Press, 1985.

———. *The Textual Condition.* Princeton, NJ: Princeton University Press, 1991.

———, and Lisa Samuels. "Deformance and Interpretation," in *Radiant Textuality: Literature after the World Wide Web,* 105–36. New York: Palgrave/St. Martin's, 2002.

McKenzie, D. F. *"Making Meaning": Printers of the Mind and Other Essays.* Amherst: University of Massachusetts Press, 2002.

———. *Bibliography and the Sociology of Texts.* London: British Library, 1986.

McLeod, Randall. "Where Angels Fear to Read," in *Ma(r)king the Text: The Presentation of Meaning on the Literary Page,* ed. Joe Bray, Miriam Handley, and Anne C. Henry. Burlington, VT: Aldershot, 2000.

Merleau-Ponty, Maurice. "Eye and Mind," in *The Primacy of Perception.* Evanston, IL: Northwestern University Press, 1964.

Myers, Frederick W. H. "Rossetti and the Religion of Beauty," *Cornhill Magazine* 47 (February 1883): 213–24.

Nagy, Gregory. *Poetry as Performance.* Cambridge: Cambridge University Press, 1996.

Nelson, Cary. *Repression and Recovery: Modern American Poetry and the Politics of Cultural Memory, 1910–1945.* Madison: University of Wisconsin Press, 1989.

Nicholson, Marjorie Hope. *Mountain Gloom and Mountain Glory: The Development of the Aesthetics of the Infinite.* Ithaca, NY: Cornell University Press, 1959.

Paglia, Camille. *Sexual Personae: Art and Decadence from Nefertiti to Emily Dickinson.* New Haven, CT: Yale University Press, 1990.

Perloff, Marjorie. *The Dance of the Intellect: Studies in the Poetry of the Pound Tradition.* Evanston, IL: Northwestern University Press, 1996.

Pichois, Claude, ed. *Baudelaire: Oeuvres complètes.* Paris: Gallimard, 1976.

Poe, Edgar Allan. *Essays and Reviews,* selected and with notes by G. R. Thompson. Library of America. New York: Literary Classics of the United States, 1984.

———. *Poetry and Tales,* selected and with notes by Patrick Quinn. Library of America. New York: Literary Classics of the United States, 1984.

Pope, Rob. *Textual Intervention: Critical and Creative Strategies for Literary Studies.* London and New York: Routledge, 1995.

Pound, Ezra. *The Cantos of Ezra Pound.* 4th ed. London: Faber, 1986.

Powys, John Cowper. *A Glastonbury Romance.* New York: Simon and Schuster, 1932.

———. *Porius: A Romance of the Dark Ages,* ed. Wilbur T. Albrecht. Hamilton, NY: Colgate University Press, 1994.

Quartermain, Peter. *Disjunctive Poetics: From Gertrude Stein and Louis Zukofsky to Susan Howe.* New York: Cambridge University Press, 1992.

Richards, I. A. *Principles of Literary Criticism.* New York: Harcourt Brace, 1928.

Riding, Laura. *Anarchism Is Not Enough,* ed. Lisa Samuels. Berkeley: University of California Press, 2001.

———. *Contemporaries and Snobs.* Garden City, NY: Doubleday Doran, 1928.

———. *The Life of the Dead*. London: Arthur Barker, 1933.

———. *Progress of Stories,* with new material and a new preface. New York: Persea Books, 1994.

———. *The Telling*. New York: Harper and Row, 1973.

Riede, David. "Tennyson's Poetics of Melancholy and the Imperial Imagination," *SEL* 40 (Autumn 2000): 659–78.

Robbins, Ruth. *Literary Feminisms*. New York: St. Martin's Press, 2000.

Robinson, Kit. *Down and Back*. Berkeley, CA: The Figures, 1978.

Rossetti, Dante Gabriel. *The Complete Writings and Pictures of Dante Gabriel Rossetti: A Hypermedia Research Archive,* http://jefferson.village.virginia.edu/rossetti.

———. *Dante Gabriel Rossetti: Collected Poetry and Prose,* ed. Jerome McGann. New Haven, CT: Yale University Press, 2003.

Rossetti, William Michael, ed. *Ruskin Rossetti Pre-Raphaelitism: Papers 1854 to 1862*. London: George Allen, 1899.

Sahlins, Marshall. *Islands of History*. Chicago: University of Chicago Press, 1985.

Said, Edward. *The World, the Text, and the Critic*. London: Faber, 1983.

Saintsbury, George. *A History of English Prosody*. Vol. 3. London: Macmillan, 1910.

Scarry, Elaine. *On Beauty and Being Just*. Princeton, NJ: Princeton University Press, 1999.

Segal, Lynn. *The Dream of Reality: Heinz von Foerster's Constructivism*. New York: W. W. Norton, 1986.

Shatto, Susan, ed. *Tennyson's Maud*. London: Athlone Press, 1986.

Showalter, Elaine. *The New Feminist Criticism: Essays on Women, Literature, and Theory*. London: Virago, 1986.

Silliman, Ron, ed. *In the American Tree*. Orono, ME: National Poetry Foundation, 1986.

Soderholm, James, ed. *Beauty and the Critic: Aesthetics in an Age of Cultural Studies*. Tuscaloosa: University of Alabama Press, 1997.

Sokal, Alan D. "What the Social Text Affair Does and Does Not Prove," in *A House Built on Sand: Exposing Postmodernist Myths about Science,* ed. Noretta Koertge. London: Oxford University Press, 1998.

Steiner, Wendy. *The Trouble with Beauty*. London: Heinemann, 2001.

Stevens, Wallace. *The Collected Poems*. New York: Alfred A. Knopf, 1967.

———. *The Palm at the End of the Mind: Selected Poems and a Play,* ed. Holly Stevens. New York: Alfred Knopf, 1972.

Suleiman, Susan R., and Inge Crossman, eds. *The Reader in the Text: Essays on Audience and Interpretation*. Princeton, NJ: Princeton University Press, 1980.

Swinburne, Algernon Charles. *Swinburne: Major Poems and Selected Prose,* ed. Jerome McGann and Charles Sligh. New Haven, CT: Yale University Press, 2004.

Tennyson, Alfred Lord. *Tennyson: The Poems,* ed. Christopher Ricks. Harlow: Longmans, 1969.

Thackeray, William Makepeace. *The English Humourists of the Eighteenth Century.* London: Smith, Elder, 1853.

Thom, René. *Structural Stability and Morphogenesis,* trans. D. H. Fowler, with a foreword by C. H. Waddington. Reading, MA: W. A. Benjamin, 1975.

Todd, Mabel Loomis, and Thomas Higginson, eds. *The Poems of Emily Dickinson.* 3 vols. New York: Little, Brown, 1891, 1892, 1896.

Tucker, Herbert F., ed. *Critical Essays on Alfred Lord Tennyson.* New York: G. K. Hall, 1993.

———. *Tennyson and the Doom of Romanticism.* Cambridge, MA: Harvard University Press, 1988.

Turner, Frederick. *Beauty: The Value of Values.* Charlottesville: University Press of Virginia, 1991.

Veeser, H. Aram, ed. *The New Historicism.* London: Routledge, 1989.

Vendler, Helen. *On Extended Wing: Wallace Stevens' Longer Poems.* Cambridge, MA: Harvard University Press, 1969.

Von Foerster, Heinz. *Observing Systems.* Seaside, CA: Intersystems Publications, 1981.

Wagner, Roy. *Symbols That Stand for Themselves.* Chicago: University of Chicago Press, 1986.

Weil, Simone. *The Need for Roots: Prelude to a Declaration of Duties toward Mankind,* trans. Arthur Wills with a preface by T. S. Eliot. New York: Putnam, 1952.

Weiskel, Thomas. *The Romantic Sublime: Studies in the Structure and Psychology of Transcendence.* Baltimore: Johns Hopkins University Press, 1976.

Wellek, René. *A History of Modern Criticism, 1750–1955.* 4 vols. New Haven, CT: Yale University Press, 1955.

———, and Austin Warren. *Theory of Literature.* New York: Harcourt Brace, 1949; rev. 1956, 1970.

Wittgenstein, Ludwig. *Philosophical Investigations.* 3rd ed. Trans. G. E. M. Anscombe. New York: Macmillan, 1958.

Wordsworth, William. *The Poems,* ed. John O. Hayden. 2 vols. Harmondsworth: Penguin, 1977.

———. *Selections,* ed. Stephen Gill. Oxford: Oxford University Press, 1984.

Yeats, William Butler, ed., *The Oxford Book of Modern Verse, 1892–1935.* London and New York: Oxford University Press, 1936.

Zangwill, Nick. *The Metaphysics of Beauty.* Ithaca, NY: Cornell University Press, 2001.

Zukofsky, Louis, ed. *An Objectivists' Anthology.* New York: Objectivist Press, 1932.

INDEX